IMPLAUSIBLE DREAM

Implausible Dream

THE WORLD-CLASS
UNIVERSITY AND
REPURPOSING
HIGHER EDUCATION

James H. Mittelman

PRINCETON UNIVERSITY PRESS
PRINCETON & OXFORD

Copyright © 2018 by Princeton University Press

Published by Princeton University Press,
41 William Street, Princeton, New Jersey 08540

In the United Kingdom: Princeton University Press,
6 Oxford Street, Woodstock, Oxfordshire OX20 1TR

press.princeton.edu

Jacket design by Chris Ferrante

All Rights Reserved

ISBN 978-0-691-16518-9

British Library Cataloging-in-Publication Data is available

This book has been composed in Miller

Printed on acid-free paper. ∞

Printed in the United States of America

10 9 8 7 6 5 4 3 2 1

For Linda

CONTENTS

Illustrations

Tables

THE TITLE OF THIS BOOK takes a cue from "The Impossible Dream," a signature song in the acclaimed 1964 musical *Man of La Mancha*. The script
recalls Miguel de Cervantes's seventeenth-century masterwork, *Don Quixote*.
The story is a metaphor for unattainable ideals or, as the lyrics put it, an attempt "to reach the unreachable star . . . [n]o matter how hopeless, [n]o matter
how far." It is also about fierce competition among combatants: "to fight the
unbeatable foe" in order to make "the world better for this."

As in the musical production, universities' present-day ambitions are a
grandiose dream, "an unreachable star," though more businesslike than high-
minded. A top rank is unrealizable for all, especially those "covered with
scars": the less-heralded ones lacking economic means, let alone political can-
niness and sharp focus on the bedrock purposes of higher education. Not every
university can become a superstar. Their world is unlike author and humorist
Garrison Keillor's fictional town of Lake Wobegon, "where all the children are
above average."

In fact, knowledge institutions are increasingly stratified. While navigating global tides in myriad ways, universities are adopting a largely American
dream for achieving "world-class" standing. I will argue that this imaginary
is implausible, that universities are on a misguided path, and that plausible
alternatives are available. For the vast majority of institutions of higher learning, imagining preeminent stature parallels the plot in Cervantes's novel: however inspiring, trying to arrive at this exalted destination is romantic fiction.
And with contemporary globalization, the stakes in chasing their dream are
amplified.

The parallel between Quixote's quest to ennoble the world and university
strivings for admission to the upper class in a global hierarchy shows that in
pursuit of worthy goals, whatever the obstacles, it behooves students, faculty,
and staff to redouble efforts to live more meaningful lives. The analogy, however, is imperfect. Quixote, an individual tilting at windmills, unwaveringly
followed his own ideals. For him, the goal was internally generated. In a globalized age, universities, by comparison, are complex organizations that must
reckon with externally driven quality assurance standards and a host of other
structural challenges ranging from public disinvestment in higher education
to monumental technological shifts. Although important lessons can be drawn
from both stories, the one is made up; the other, a lived and evolving endeavor.
Allowing for this distinction, I believe that contemporary universities are in a
race that has gone off track in that it seeks quixotic ends—a proposition to be
fleshed out in this book.

My work on how and why universities' dreams have come to be misplaced grew out of the momentous changes in the academy since I first embarked on the path of higher education. As a seventeen-year-old freshman knowing little about the larger world around me, I gained access through the classroom and literature to great minds. This awakening aroused my interest and motivated me in ways that I had not expected. It was the beginning of a foray into higher learning, a universe that has taken several turns over the past half century.

I have seen them from multiple angles while studying, working, and living in Finland, Malaysia, Tanzania, Uganda, and the United States. So, too, I have benefited from holding visiting teaching and research positions in Japan, Mozambique, and South Africa, plus short-term appointments as a resident scholar elsewhere. Strikingly, in each case, the higher education system has undergone extensive reforms since the 1970s, shaking the foundational purposes of the academy. Common elements, traced in this volume, connect these diverse experiences.

From one decade to the next, and the more I moved from one country to another, the whys and wherefores of regulatory reform baffled me. These issues piqued my curiosity about what is happening to the marrow of universities—the staying power of their core values—and what is eating at it. I revel in the university but worry about its future.

The writings of philosophers, sociologists, scholars in schools of education, and (generally former) university presidents and provosts offer helpful insights into shifts in higher learning. The discipline in which I was trained, political science, often looks at the American case and treats it as sui generis. And with rare exceptions, International Relations pays scant attention to universities as actors in the global arena. Although the emergent fields of globalization and global studies fill gaps, they only begin to tackle the specific questions about the transformation of the academy posed in the introduction to this book. The nexus of education and globalization is crucial for world order, but major facets of this relationship remain unexplored and unknown.

More than anything else, the opportunity to teach interdisciplinary courses on global political economy and social theory led me to critical readings of classical and contemporary texts on the ways in which knowledge and power are interwoven. Much of this conceptualization informs my approach, which seeks to encapsulate a personal journey of discovery and scholarly research in a single framework. The analysis presented here entailed a lot of self-reflection, forcing me to confront my own position, hopes, and dreams for university life. I will try to honestly disclose them and identify my standpoint as we proceed.

The students who traveled on this voyage with me brought enthusiasm and passion to engaging the material and deserve heartfelt thanks. They challenged my initial arguments and prompted reformulations. Special mention goes to my research assistants, whose energy and initiative contributed vitally

PREFACE AND ACKNOWLEDGMENTS [xiii]

to this project: Daniel Dye, Yoonbin Ha, Patrick Litanga, Manuel Reinert, Nicholas T. Smith, and Jan Westö.

I want to express deep appreciation to the institutions that supported this research: the provost's office and the School of International Service at American University. Dean Jim Goldgeier and Associate Dean Nanette Levinson facilitated this undertaking in countless ways. Fortunately, our school values pluralism and has heretofore withstood the wave of monism, the insistence on a single dominant paradigm of knowledge. Funded by the Academy of Finland, the collaborative project "Policy Instruments and Global Governance: Concepts and Numbers" also assisted this study. The Helsinki Collegium for Advanced Studies and the Makerere Institute of Social Research (MISR) hosted me and were crucial for carrying out fieldwork.

Giving lectures and seminars on the research presented here elicited valuable feedback, especially at the following venues: the American University Program at the University of Nairobi, the Global Governance Roundtable at the University of Helsinki, the Helsinki Collegium for Advanced Studies, the Institute for African Development at Cornell University, the International Studies Association's annual conventions, MISR, the National Planning Authority of Uganda, the Political Science Department at the City University of New York Graduate Center, and the School of International Service at American University Faculty Research Colloquium.

I also owe a debt of gratitude to colleagues with whom I have long enjoyed many stimulating discussions about the power of ideas and knowledge: especially Robert W. Cox, Locksley G. Edmondson, James N. Rosenau, and J. Ann Tickner. Joel Barkin, Tero Erkkilä, Frank Holmquist, Nelson Kasfir, Mahmood Mamdani, Heikki Patomäki, and Hunter Rawlings kindly put me on to important sources of information. Once preliminary versions of chapters were drafted, Adam Branch, Ken Conca, Tero Erkkilä, Daniel E. Esser, Charles Husband, Patrick Thaddeus Jackson, Manfred Steger, Teivo Teivainen, Turo Virtanen, Paul Wapner, and Linda Yarr offered critical comments on them and wise counsel.

In grappling with the practicalities of key issues treated in this book, I have benefited enormously from serving on the American Civil Liberties Union's Academic Freedom Committee and the International Studies Association's Academic Freedom Committee.

I must pay tribute as well to my publisher and the three external readers commissioned to review a draft of this manuscript and offer suggestions for honing it. My editor and Princeton University Press director, Peter J. Dougherty, along with assistant editor Jessica Yao, kept me on track and helped bolster my arguments. Eric Crahan, senior editor (political science and American history), also provided sage advice. Terri O'Prey, associate managing editor, and Jennifer Backer, copyeditor, repaired and improved my manuscript. They set high standards for producing this work, and I hope that I have met their expectations. My experience with Princeton University Press has been satisfying in every respect. I could not have asked for better.

Finally, and above all, my wife, Linda, and our children, Alexandra, Jordan, and Alicia, provided steadfast encouragement, patience, and love that sustained writing this book. They have enabled me to carry out this project. Together, we have navigated personal and professional life in a joyful way. Linda, my life partner, shared the journey of researching, revising, and converting my draft manuscripts into a book. Her acumen and creativity and the felicity of our marriage have been sources of strength. Any errors in this work are, however, solely mine.

ABBREVIATIONS

AAU   Association of American Universities

AAUP   American Association of University Professors

ARWU   Academic Ranking of World Universities

CEO   chief executive officer

CHEA   Council for Higher Education Accreditation

EEA   European Economic Area

EGM   emerging global model

EHEA   European Higher Education Area

ENQA   European Association for Quality Assurance in Higher Education

EU   European Union

FIIA   Finnish Institute of International Affairs

FINHEEC   Finnish Higher Education Evaluation Council

GATS   General Agreement on Trade in Services

GDP   gross domestic product

IFC   International Finance Corporation

IIE   Institute of International Education

ILO   International Labour Organization

INQAAHE   International Network for Quality Assurance Agencies in Higher Education

MEC   Ministry of Education and Culture

MISR   Makerere Institute of Social Research

MIT   Massachusetts Institute of Technology

MOES   Ministry of Education and Sports

MOOC   massive open online course

MSU   Michigan State University

NCHE   National Council for Higher Education

NORAD   Norwegian Agency for Development Cooperation

NPM   new public management

NUS   National University of Singapore

NYU   New York University

OECD   Organisation for Economic Co-operation and Development

PHEA   Partnership for Higher Education in Africa

QS   Quacquarelli Symonds

R&D   research and development

SAP   structural adjustment program

THES   *Times Higher Education Supplement*

TNC   transnational corporation

UNDP   United Nations Development Programme

UNESCO   United Nations Educational, Scientific and Cultural Organization

USAID   United States Agency for International Development

WISE   World Innovation Summit for Education

WTO   World Trade Organization

A NOTE ON TERMINOLOGY

AS USED IN THIS TEXT, the term "university" (in the singular) refers to common patterns that characterize institutions of higher education. It highlights systemic features, the key structural elements that form a distinctive matrix, without positing that general tendencies are universal or sweeping particularities under the rug.

In fact, the university is a mosaic, contingent on time and place. The word "universities" (plural) picks up on nuances in the evolution of varied educational cultures. The former calls attention to collective traits; the latter, divergent forms. It is important to look through both prisms.

I employ the designations "tertiary education," "higher education," and "colleges" interchangeably to refer to accredited postsecondary, degree-granting programs of study. From one country to another, there are discrepancies in what is counted in and excluded from official statistics on the university in both the singular and plural sense: community and technical colleges, theological seminaries, virtual institutions, and paper mills granting fake academic degrees accredited by fictitious accreditation bodies, some with marketing operations abroad. In the chapters that follow, I note the major differences.

The language adopted here *partly* emanates from the American case because of its vast scale, enormous material resources, and great influence throughout the world. Granted, universities in some countries and regions (for example, China, much of the Middle East, and parts of Europe) do not aspire to the ideals for which U.S. universities strive. To steer clear of U.S.- and West-centric predilections, historical specificity, multiple research sites, diverse standpoints, and myriad voices from above and below appear throughout this book. The objective is to decenter this study.

University missions in democratic versus undemocratic societies are demarcated. It would however be a mistake to draw too fine a line between the purposes of universities in authoritarian, semi-authoritarian, and non-authoritarian settings. Even when leaders do not espouse or only pay lip service to values such as freedom of expression prized in certain Western environments, they, like their counterparts at universities in democratic countries, aim to maintain the prevailing order, manage change, and provide social deliverables. The functions of social control and change coexist and play out in sundry ways. Above all, university missions are contested, mutable, and sometimes protean. Although the teaching of absolute truths, passive thinking, and rote memorization are the norms in parts of the postcolonial world, there are examples, such as in Tunisia under President Habib Bourguiba, of a different ethos and democratic reforms in learning. This reflects impulses for alterations in higher education institutions' moral principles, evident under both autocratic and democratic rule, as considered in the case-study chapters ahead.[1]

1. For additional evidence on how these alternative values are gaining momentum or eroding on different terrains, see Philip G. Altbach, *Global Perspectives on Higher Education* (Baltimore: Johns Hopkins University Press, 2016), especially 238–53; Paul Tiyambe Zeleza, *The Transformation of Global Higher Education* (New York: Palgrave Macmillan, 2016), 337, 355n15, and passim.

IMPLAUSIBLE DREAM

Questions and Arguments

WITH THE RISE OF CROSS-BORDER COMPETITION and market-friendly globalization, universities are in remarkable flux. They are transitioning to a contested future. This book is about what is transposing the old and what constitutes the new. It delimits a global shift in higher education, why this transformation is happening, and what can be done to meet adaptation challenges.

Engaging those questions, my unifying argument is threefold. First, over the last half century, the scale, reach, and impact of higher education institutions have expanded exponentially. Universities have become major actors on the global stage, generating market power. A vexing issue is how to exercise this power in a wise and responsible way, a concern addressed in succeeding chapters.

Second, my message is that the central academic purposes of the university are imperiled. While not universally adopted, they began to take root in the nineteenth century, developed gradually in the nineteenth and twentieth, and encounter novel tensions in the twenty-first. In this century, the triad of core educational missions in nonauthoritarian societies—cultivating democratic citizenship, fostering critical thinking, and protecting academic freedom—is losing footing. A new form of utilitarianism is gaining ground. It prioritizes useful knowledge and problem-solving skills at the expense of basic inquiry. It elevates market values over educational values. It stresses rationalist thinking rather than other modes of reasoning, as in the arts, classical languages, history, and philosophy. And it features a form of globalization that favors an educational-services-export model in lieu of an emphasis on forging organic curricular links across borders. In short, universities are *repurposing*.

Third, given simultaneous pressures for improved performance and public disinvestment in most countries, the dominant paradigm of higher education is unsustainable for all but a small group of marquee universities. The luxury brand offered by a clutch of research-intensive, elite institutions caters to fewer than one-half percent of the world's students, mainly in the prosperous countries. Rising university tuition and fees discourages many less affluent students from incurring heavy debt before entering a dubious job market; enrolling in large classes, many of them taught by a temporary workforce replacing full-time, tenure-track faculty; and compensating a growing number of administrators at an exorbitant level that diminishes trust in them.

When purposiveness is crucially needed, universities are under the illusion that they should strive to compete in the premier league. Institutions in far different contexts increasingly harbor the same dream of becoming world class. Lofty aspirations are commendable, but today's vogue aims have become impossible to fulfill. They are dreamlike because in a multitiered system, not all players can qualify for the top echelon. Some are advantaged, and others marginalized without requisite financial means and at a competitive disadvantage. Yet, in their dream world, legions of educators view Harvard and its cohort, primarily a handful of affluent private institutions in the upper stratum of research universities, as the gold standard. But Harvard has the largest university endowment in the world—$35.7 billion, tax-exempt, according to mid-2016 figures—and charges an annual tuition fee of $63,025. Its knowledge and economic environment in Cambridge, Massachusetts, serves as a hub for a cluster of research-intensive universities, including the Massachusetts Institute of Technology (MIT), cutting-edge biotech and pharmaceutical companies such as Pfizer and Novartis, and offices of Amazon and Google, businesses that offer well-paying jobs to mainly wealthy students, many of whom graduate from Harvard and a smattering of other very selective institutions with robust endowments and reputations.

As this book's title, *Implausible Dream*, suggests, the world-class university is a figurative expression for what proves counterfactual and deceptive. It conjures up ideas and practices constituting a win-win scenario when in fact globalization is marked by hierarchies and inequalities among winners and losers.[1] The winning institutions in global excellence initiatives command an average annual budget estimated at $2 billion as a result of national priorities for rewarding performance, effectively channeling resources away from less resourced universities, attended by the majority of students in the United States and several other countries.[2]

1. For evidence, see Dani Rodrik, *The Globalization Paradox: Democracy and the Future of the World Economy* (New York: Norton, 2011); Saskia Sassen, *Expulsions: Brutality and Complexity in the Global Economy* (Cambridge, MA: Harvard University Press, 2014); Jan Aart Scholte, *Globalization: A Critical Introduction*, 2nd ed. (New York: Palgrave Macmillan, 2005); Joseph E. Stiglitz, *Globalization and Its Discontents* (New York: Norton, 2002).

2. Ellen Hazelkorn, "Could Higher Education Rankings Be Socially Transformative?" *University World News* 432 (October 14, 2016).

Furthermore, "world class" is a trope that obscures specific policies in higher education, practices, and statements. It also serves as an omnibus category encompassing subnarratives. These discourses of the predominant form of globalization include strategic planning, best practices, branding, benchmarking, performance-based productivity measures, and the like, a grammar to be discussed more fully. They fuel one another, forming an amalgam—the world-class university. And more than a manner of speech, it is way of thinking and seeing higher education from above. Its pervasiveness reaches the subconscious, usually escaping critical scrutiny.

Today, the consequences of the global imaginary of attaining world-class status are both normative and material.[3] As I will detail, this narrative is curated by a network of global governance agencies such as the World Bank to legitimize certain courses of action and used by educational policymakers. Universities use this beguiling, shared narrative as a justification for hiring more and more administrators to prepare numeric scores for exercises like global rankings. Students and their families use it to help decide where to apply for admission. Accreditors use it as a destination for evaluating where universities are and should be headed. Governments use it as a gauge for allocating funds and determining where their scholarships for study abroad are tenable. And other governments use it in immigration laws that privilege applicants for citizenship with degrees from the world's top-ranked universities.

Although the world-class rubric is widely adopted, several questions about its deployment linger.[4] How is "world class" defined, what level of resources must be mobilized to meet its criteria, and which strategies are appropriate for climbing to the rarified rank of flagship institutions? Should universities mimic the elite, and what is their relationship to other institutions in the national system in which they are infixed? Globally, is this path leading the academic community to stray from its foundational purposes?

I'm not saying that universities should refrain from pursuing their dreams. Like great symphonies or murals, dreams can inspire. Used as motivational tools, dreams often spur improvement. But if the bar is set too high and if the aspirations are altogether out of reach, dreaming creates false expectations, resulting in disappointment, frustration, and sometimes resistance to new initiatives. When the disparities between the dream and the barriers to living it are too great, participants are apt to be cynical or demoralized. If expected to

3. The concept of social, national, and global imaginary is explored in Benedict Anderson, *Imagined Communities: Reflections on the Origin and Spread of Nationalism*, rev. ed. (London: Verso, 1991); Manfred B. Steger, *The Rise of the Global Imaginary: Political Ideologies from the French Revolution to the Global War on Terror* (Oxford: Oxford University Press, 2008).

4. Philip G. Altbach, "The Costs and Benefits of World-Class Universities," *International Higher Education* 33 (Fall 2003): 5–8, touches on these concerns.

run a four-minute mile, bench-press 500 pounds, or reach for Michael Phelps's world records in swimming, many competitors would find the whole exercise pointless. It would seem implausible and cause generalized confusion about the purpose of this endeavor. This gap is key to explaining why public confidence in institutions charged with developing the minds of the next generations has plummeted.[5]

In the chapters ahead, I will examine whether the objectives and practices of world-class universities are implausible because of structural obstacles confronted when they strive for similar goals and whether this kind of quality and excellence is even appropriate for contexts apart from where the model is derived: namely, affluent, mainly private, big-league institutions, primarily in the global North. This is not to suggest that other higher education institutions should embrace a lower level of ideals and procedures. Rather, the point is that they ought to be different ones, informed by comparative experiences, befitting their own educational landscapes and reflecting multiple approaches to changing conditions. The challenge then is how to overcome deep-rooted barriers to an enhanced environment for education and research.

The world-class designation is therefore important for analysis of restructuring higher education because it provides a window on the thinking that lies behind the prevailing sense of the mission of universities and how it influences educational policies. In a climate wherein higher education is increasingly deemed a private investment and financial interests take on major importance, questions about how to meet public needs are rife. Given these patterns, the soul of the university is at risk. With metrics pervading the agenda of the academy, the question of what is the university really for is displaced. The everyday fare of performance measures deflects attention from the clarity of mission. The problem is not merely which measures and how to improve them but rather a matter of what is measured.

While supposed to subscribe to high purposes, educational institutions have to cope with the jaggedness of the global marketplace and the ideas integral to it: namely, productivity, competition, and efficiency. These practices and norms alter the collegial and democratic basis of shared governance at universities, leading to unintended consequences.

Part 2 of this book presents stark evidence of unanticipated results. Specific examples, discussed there, include the observations of the heads of universities in the United States who approved sources of external funding but came to rue certain consultancies, royalty and patent arrangements, and contracts with large corporations like pharmaceuticals because these university-industry partnerships generated explosive clashes between proprietary knowledge and

5. For documentation of this point about changing perceptions of universities' performance, see part 2.

profit-making, on the one hand, and the allegiance of faculty and the principle of academic freedom, on the other. In another case, Finland, universities adopted policy frameworks that apply regional and global standards so as to reap benefits from globalization yet proved to undermine homegrown educational values of mutual trust, cooperation, and egalitarianism. And in Uganda, agreements with overseas universities afforded access to the domestic market but unexpectedly threatened to transgress national laws and were deemed an affront to local culture, exemplified by the dicey experience of a British university that operated a campus in Uganda. When the Ugandans flatly refused its counterpart's demands, this overseas university promptly terminated the affiliation.

Taken together, these stories show the interplay of differing clusters of university missions, the historic and newer ones, in unexpected and contradictory ways. They also demonstrate that the financial and educational objectives of higher education institutions may conflict but need not be at odds if, going forward, they are properly aligned. There is not a sharp dichotomy between them.

The problem then is not that universities are changing but the ways in which they are changing. A major task in this work is to etch options for improving higher learning in more purposeful ways and indicate what alternative transformations would entail. I will contend that there is no pat formula or single kit of policy "solutions" for fixing the problems besetting higher education. Rather, five modest suggestions are elaborated in the final chapter of this book. They beacon structural reforms for transformations in higher education.

To leverage my multisited account of university restructuring, I advance concrete proposals on how to deflate the implausible dream shared by most universities around the globe. In its stead, I offer a more sustainable vision of pluralism in the service of nurturing local-global, critical thinking. Unlike a lot of gloomy prognostication about higher education circulating in our times, my forward-oriented analysis favors a sober, upbeat view.

Implementing the structural reforms that I advocate is not a utopian exercise. The practicalities of institutional adaptation require resolute leadership from above and below. While university administrators can provide vision and experience, so too leadership is a combination of trustees' acumen, central administrators' perspicacity, faculty initiatives, the staff's ideas, student vitality, and social movements' impetus. Multiple actors can serve as catalysts, leading universities beyond ad hockery and palliative reforms. A coalition of these thought agents has the potential to shine new light on old purposes and create scenarios that have eluded policymakers.

Scenarios

Despite the inherent difficulty of calculating what comes next, it is possible to project scenarios that are not fanciful but anchored in historical evidence.

The main tendencies are integration *and* fragmentation.[6] These counter-vailing trends are embodied in higher education reforms. A preview of these scenarios for remaking the purposes and structures of the university frames what follows.

The first trajectory is greater convergence in university programming. Regardless of whether their effects are intended, standard-setting agencies and processes—among others, academic accreditation, an internationally traded service, and global university rankings, a lucrative industry—are promoting isomorphism in learning objectives and outcomes.[7] University programs veer toward resemblance in degree requirements, credit-transfer systems, literature assigned, the definition of faculty positions, and even course titles. Universities within the European Union (EU) countries, for instance, are harmonizing their educational systems, as in the formation of the European Higher Education Area (EHEA) (chapter 3).[8] Yet sameness is not the only tendency.

The second direction is toward vast divergence in university programming. Global scripts blend with local and national histories, cultures, legal frameworks, and economies of scale, thereby augmenting differences. In addition, ample research shows that educational globalization heightens stratification between rich and poor institutions, accentuates inequalities in access to higher learning, and can feed into decreasing social mobility.[9] In much of the world,

6. James N. Rosenau is among the researchers who approached globalization as a hybrid of integration and fragmentation. See his *Along the Domestic-Foreign Frontier: Exploring Governance in a Turbulent World* (Cambridge: Cambridge University Press, 1997); James N. Rosenau, *Distant Proximities: Dynamics beyond Globalization* (Princeton: Princeton University Press, 2003), 11–16ff.

7. On the longstanding trend toward convergence of norms, especially in primary and secondary education, see John Meyer and other "world polity" sociologists: G. Kruecken and G. Drori, eds., *World Society: The Writings of John W. Meyer* (Oxford: Oxford University Press, 2009). Ronald J. Daniels and Phillip Spector, "Converging Paths: Public and Private Universities in the 21st Century" (New York: TIAA Institute, 2016), trace the convergence of public and private universities in the United States.

8. More and more, students on distant continents are assigned the same books and articles to read. As a visiting professor in China and Japan, I found that participants in my seminars were more familiar with the work of leading American scholars than were many of their counterparts in the United States. In substantial ways, universities increasingly look alike.

9. While universities are supposed to be a gateway for social mobility, they may in fact contribute to or ease different forms of inequality. Consult "Has Higher Education Become an Engine of Inequality?" (a forum), *Chronicle of Higher Education Review*, July 2, 2012, http://chronicle.com/article/Has-Higher-Education-Become-an/132619/ (accessed January 25, 2016). Suzanne Mettler, *Degrees of Inequality: How the Politics of Higher Education Sabotaged the American Dream* (New York: Basic Books, 2014), claims that universities in the United States have generated inequality. See reactions to her book in the review symposium "Higher Education and the American Dream," *Perspectives on Politics* 14, no. 2 (June 2016): 486–97.

universities are situated in environments that are becoming more unequal. These socioeconomic landscapes impinge on higher education institutions, making them more varied, less standardized. A proliferation of public and private, for-profit and nonprofit, secular and faith-based, virtual and physical, rich and poor, urban and rural, large and small, and conventional and "popular" institutions differentiates the universe of higher learning.[10] Notably, the range between the publics and privates is narrowing. The former are taking on major features of the latter. In fact, nominally public, supposedly nonprofit institutions are mounting for-profit programs.[11]

Paradoxically, globalizing processes are forging both greater *convergence* and *divergence* in higher education. In this incongruous dynamic, a third trajectory is emerging. It is nascent and does not yet have a name. For wont of an established narrative, this trend may be called *polymorphism*. As used in the natural sciences, the term means passing through many different stages. I will deploy it as a descriptor that allows for a multifaceted constellation of higher education institutions.[12] It consolidates contradictory and variegated phenomena. The polymorph combines homogeneity and heterogeneity, takes on multiple shapes and appearances, and grants contingency. In short, polymorphism is a liminal force between the present and future of educational globalization.

Reclaiming the cardinal educational purposes of promoting democratic citizenship, critical reasoning, and academic freedom, polymorphism can

10. The term "popular university" is used to depict the working-class universities that emerged in Europe and Latin America during the early twentieth century and initiatives for educating activists and leaders in social movements in our times. See Boaventura de Sousa Santos, *The Rise of the Global Left: The World Social Forum and Beyond* (London: Zed Books, 2006), 148; Boaventura de Sousa Santos, *Epistemologies of the South* (Boulder, CO: Paradigm Publishers, 2014). In his *Long Walk to Freedom: The Autobiography of Nelson Mandela* (Boston: Little, Brown, 1994), Mandela discusses the "prison university" with reference to the curriculum and specific courses designed by inmates on Robben Island.

11. Among these activities are the business of big-time athletic teams, privatized consulting services, the commercialization of intellectual property rights, and the work of research faculty and physicians paid large sums by pharmaceutical and medical-device firms. Moreover, some universities seek to compensate for budget shortfalls by market-pricing courses of study: charging elevated fees for high-demand offerings, including requirements for graduation.

12. In biology and chemistry, the term "polymorphism" signifies the multiform character of a phenomenon. Less known in the social sciences, it has been used to study political regimes in Eastern Europe, the Algerian War, and urban politics in France: Thomas Lowit, "Le parti polymorhe en Europe de l'Est," *Revue française de science politique* 29, no. 4–5 (August–October 1979): 812–46; Jean-Pierre Rioux, "En Algérie, une guerre polymorphe (1954–1962)," *Vingtième Siècle: Revue d'histoire* 68, no. 1 (October–December 2000): 122–24; Crispian Fuller, "Urban Politics and the Social Practices of Critique and Justification: Conceptual Insights from French Pragmatism," *Progress in Human Geography* 37, no. 3 (October 2013): 639–57.

embrace the spirit of modern universities' time-tested, humanistic values. The agenda would encompass reembedding higher institutions in their distinctive settings. The mission reflects contextual nuances, for there is not a universal form of democracy, critical inquiry, and free expression within and across the Western and non-Western worlds. And given limitations on our ability to know the future of higher learning, this move is still more a potential than an actuality. The outcome remains open-ended, not predetermined.

In this study, I will stress the stakes in university repurposing, the value of analyzing them comparatively, and the need to recognize globalization drivers without treating them as totalizing phenomena. To foreshadow my own position, I believe that polymorphism is the avenue to the most promising opportunities for refocusing universities' missions and resuscitating higher education. Whether this road will be taken is a matter of not only powerful structures but also agency, strategy, and fortuity.

Plan

This project fleshes out my arguments by grounding them in three case studies: pronounced forms of private-sector-led globalization, characteristic of the United States; the strong public sphere, evident in Finland; and a developing country with a historically public but now increasingly private university structure, found in Uganda.[13] I have selected these cases as a heuristic for examining diverse encounters with educational repurposing. They illustrate neoliberal, social democratic, and postcolonial variations, explicated in chapters to come. Each prototype is marked by a range that distinguishes regional and national experiences. To be exact, both inter- and intraregional similarities and differences, for example, among U.S. and Canadian, Finnish and Swedish, and Ugandan and Kenyan universities, matter.

The adaptation to globalization scrutinized here offers a wide-angle view and demonstrates multiple ways to address knowledge governance. The United States and its variant of the English language have of course had contagious influence on universities around the world. Finland's approach, while encountering growing stress on the country's academic programs, maintains

---

13. I employ the term "public sphere" advisedly in that it suggests open debates and active deliberation. In the public realm, discursive limitations on the state of universities, demarcated later in this book, spell out how my case studies correspond in varying degrees to the model developed by Jürgen Habermas, *The Structural Transformation of the Public Sphere: An Inquiry into a Category of Bourgeois Society*, trans. Thomas Burger (Cambridge, MA: MIT Press, 1989). While there are different public sphere theories, Habermas's work is widely regarded as the foundation. For elaboration of this point and discussion of the need to extend Habermas's conceptualization to encompass not just one but many publics, see chapter 8.

high ratings as a spearhead education system yet is subject to extensive alterations under its new Universities Act, the reforms introduced in 2009. And Uganda's flagship university, Makerere, exemplifies a mix of state and burgeoning market reforms as well as the hopes and difficulties of seeking to set an agenda for decolonizing knowledge. Makerere is not just an instance but in many respects also a harbinger of contested shifts in higher education institutions in the postcolonial world.

This choice of case studies admittedly leaves out other important instances. Readers of preliminary drafts of this text suggested incorporating additional cases. One said China, another Malaysia, and still others a country in Latin America. Frankly, I do not have the resources and energy to undertake more fieldwork. Nor do I want to delay completion of this book, already several years in the making. True, each country and university system has its own story, with vast differences among them. Yet all are undergoing widespread reform in higher education. Some things are noticeably similar about the directions in which universities are moving—in respect to the role of knowledge institutions in a globalizing world, the rise of a competitive ethic, and the use of technology in the knowledge market.

While diverse university systems have bought into the implausible dream of world-class standing as the model for educational policy, I aim to enrich and modulate analysis of this construct without shoehorning it into a singular master interpretation. My preference is to adopt an evidence-based methodology that picks up on vernacular knowledge and historically specific conditions. Better to listen to the local accent and indigenous voices by offering a small number of in-depth cases rather than a large number lacking historical and cultural texture. Charles Tilly justified this strategy by emphasizing that big data sets are valuable for looking across several systems, but attentiveness to a small number of case-study countries allows for contextual comparisons and has more staying power.[14]

My approach to three historical cases then centers on sets of knowledge institutions and the distinctive social structures undergirding them. In each case, I render the variability of history not as a detailed chronology that primarily identifies milestones but rather in periods churning irregularly with connections to underlying social forces and powerful global structures. A point of departure then is that an analysis of universities that focuses on institutional shifts without linking them to social stratification is incomplete. This is palpable in our volatile times, with rising economic inequality and social divisions. To pinpoint the many ways that university systems are bolted to class, race, ethnicity, and gender, I highlight their intersections. The emphasis in this work

14. Charles Tilly, *Big Structures, Large Processes, Huge Comparisons* (New York: Russell Sage Foundation, 1984), 76–78.

is in sharp contrast to much of the literature on higher education institutions, which gives insufficient scope to, or stonily silences, these interactions. The empirical investigation consists of close analysis of primary documents ranging from government papers, international organizations' reports, and published statistics to histories and other literature. I also draw on targeted discussions with educational leaders at universities, international institutions, state offices, and philanthropies and other nonprofits, as well as with scores of professors, students, and support staff. I canvassed people intimately familiar with shifts in higher education, including university presidents, provosts, deans, governmental ministers, accreditors, and rankers, about their roles, plans, and hopes. I wanted to know how these educational change agents narrate universities. In active dialogue with them, I probed their stories. The semi-structured discussions for this project took place in Helsinki, Kampala, Nairobi, New York, Pretoria, Shanghai, and Washington, D.C. They may not constitute a scientific sample of any larger population. But the on-site visits and the information elicited instead offer firsthand accounts of knowledge governance.

In addition, I have had a front-row seat at bellwether moments in bold, sweeping reforms repurposing higher education. This book shares observations from my own experience as a student in the United States and Uganda, a faculty member on four continents (Africa, Asia, Europe, and North America), a department chair, a dean at public and private universities, a director of a foundation, and a consultant for global governance agencies. I feel as though I have been in the thick of the repurposing of higher education for much of my career.

My involvement with universities and encounters with pressures on them is a source of down-to-earth illustrations of the interplay of institutions of higher learning, the state, and the market. I draw, too, on other observers' memories and oral history projects as a mode of recovery. As a method, this storytelling is not just a matter of recalling anecdotes. Narratives are a way of knowing that can illuminate larger issues. The vignettes refract large structural forces through personal experience. Memories are an important source of information especially because they can serve as an inspiration for both excavating history and exploring prospects. Memories from different countries and regions are potentially generative of theoretical and critical thinking. They are a form of voicing, reclaiming tales of social cohesion and discord and stimulating interest in listening. They also afford an opportunity to home in on particular moments in history and elucidate the complexity of what appears as chaos in our lives. In this research, they provide a tool for examining dynamic forces, a means of making sense of the raisons d'être of universities, and a vehicle for connecting the past to the present and the future.

Distinct from linear accounts of history, memories can be used as a way to reckon with not a dead but rather a living past. To this point, William Faulkner commented, "The past is never dead. It is not even past."[15] This relationship may be construed as dialogue about how the past presses into the present.[16] Speaking to this point at a 2017 conference on the ties between universities and slavery, Drew Gilpin Faust, Harvard's president, indicated how an institution's genealogy is baked into present-minded expressions of purpose: "Only by coming to terms with history . . . can we free ourselves to create a more just world."[17]

Other concrete examples of recent efforts, many of them in response to campus activism, to address the soiled legacies of racial, ethnic, and international conflict abound in the text ahead.[18] The objectives of these initiatives are to retrieve a past for informing reconciliation in our times and to open an equitable future. Although we cannot return directly to bygone days, whether halcyon or shameful, recalling them may serve as a reminder about the need for transcendence and recompense.

Memory research as an approach to thinking about the past therefore suggests possibilities for meliorating the present and steering universities to a better future. For higher education, the future is now in that it is being shaped by contemporary forces.

But beware that archives of old can be fallible and countermemories must be assessed. Memorists are obliged to do their due diligence to avoid misremembering and embellishing phenomena. To establish veracity, I felt obliged to cross-check information by consulting colleagues who shared the same historical instances and by working with multiple sources: diaries, correspondence, and other documents. With the aid of digital and other forms of information technology, many of these items are stored and accessible. In some jurisdictions, laws such as the Freedom of Information Act in the United States compel disclosure of records and data when requested, though with exceptions, for example, under safeguards for intellectual property and national security.

Before proceeding, I want to make known my orientation.[19] My stance is conservative in that it reaffirms the orthodox purposes of modern universities, provided that they are adapted to meet the formidable challenges of our day. It is critical in my effort to betray a stock representation of their mission as entering a global competition and moving toward the upper tier of performance among institutions of higher education. The costs and benefits of educational globalization are borne unevenly, adding to rising socioeconomic inequalities.

15. William Faulkner, *Requiem for a Nun* (New York: Random House, 1951), 92.
16. Jacques Lacan, *Past and Present: A Dialogue*, trans. Jason E. Smith (New York: Columbia University Press, 2014).
17. Quoted in Jennifer Schuessler, "Confronting Academia's Slavery Ties," *New York Times*, March 6, 2017.
18. Especially chapters 4 and 8.
19. An issue developed in chapter 8. The roles of an author's standpoint and of subjectivity in analysis are explored more fully throughout what follows.

Were it otherwise—if another dream for higher education could come true—is the theme in the concluding chapter.

The rest of this book is organized in three interrelated parts. Next, in part 1, chapters 1, 2, and 3 provide a framework for exploring the changing purposes of universities and the resultant reforms in higher education. Part 2 contains the historical case studies. And the capstone chapters comprising part 3 look at responses to educational restructuring and venture plausible alternatives.

PART I

Global Knowledge
Governance

CHAPTER ONE

A Crisis of Purpose

THE PURPOSES OF HIGHER EDUCATION—the very reasons for undertaking activities—are literal and symbolic. Official mission statements express an institution's moral values, claims about its accomplishments, and aspirations. Mission proclamations may thus be read as philosophical documents: transcripts subject to myriad interpretations and tacit understandings reached through consensus and conflict. They may also be used as rhetorical strategies, public relations devices, and tools for recruitment and fund-raising.[1] To grasp their intended and unintended consequences, one must look at and beyond public pronouncements in which higher education institutions tout themselves. It is important to search for subtexts and their contexts. Normative values and deep philosophical ideas are educational policy issues. The challenge is to come to grips with the workings of multipurpose universities and how they are evolving.

The language used in their public statements is emblematic of changes in the purposes of higher education institutions. They have become preoccupied with strategic planning, benchmarking, branding, visibility, rankings, productivity indices, quality assurance systems, students as customers, and measurable outcomes. Before the 1980s, members of the higher education community rarely expressed themselves in these terms. Just as this parlance is commonplace in the business world, it is customary in the academy.

Yet the purposes of the university have long distinguished it from those of other endeavors. By purposes, I mean the premises and values on which the university rests. Understood as steering mechanisms, purposes provide a basis for making decisions, galvanizing stakeholders, and legitimating policy. They can be used to transform thinking and action.

---

1. See Barrett J. Taylor and Christopher C. Morphew, "An Analysis of Baccalaureate College Mission Statements," *Research in Higher Education* 51, no. 5 (August 2010): 483–501.

Universities, however, are not solely mission-driven; they are mission- and market-driven, with varying degrees of state intervention in their development.

Transformation

Scrutinizing the business of the university in 1852, John Henry Newman, a Roman Catholic priest and later a cardinal, presented a series of lectures on "the idea of a university."[2] He laid the groundwork for enduring debates about reforms in higher education. Schooled at Trinity College, Oxford, Newman emphasized the teaching mission of the university and contemplated the "real worth in the market of the article called 'a Liberal Education.'"[3] Newman held that "to set forth the right standard, and to train according to it, and to help forward all students towards it according to their various capacities, this I conceive to be the business of the University."[4] In this respect, the university is for cultivating the intellect. Newman deemed this pursuit as a sufficient good.

Newman compares his belief in the transmission of knowledge as the university's principal objective to the familiar view that the end of higher education is professional knowledge. While granting that practical courses in law or medicine, for example, should be taught, he responds to the contention that an education must be useful to university graduates—in today's terminology, "relevant." After all, "a cultivated intellect, because it is a good in itself brings with it a power and a grace to every work and occupation which it undertakes, and enables us to be more useful, and to a greater number."[5] In other words, Newman's riposte to the claim that higher education ought to be useful is that the business of a university is to stimulate minds and build character.

For the sake of brevity, I want to fast-forward to the first half of the next century when Abraham Flexner, the founding director of the Princeton-based Institute for Advanced Study, extended Newman's position. Flexner argued that utility means that universities are supposed to do useless things. In an essay titled "The Usefulness of Useless Knowledge," he maintained that researchers should strive for knowledge without an anticipated outcome.[6]

2. These lectures are combined with his other discourses in John Henry Newman, *The Idea of a University*, ed. Frank M. Turner (1852; New Haven: Yale University Press, 1996).

3. Ibid., 110.

4. Ibid., 109–10.

5. Ibid., 119.

6. Abraham Flexner, "The Usefulness of Useless Knowledge," *Harpers* 119 (June/November 1939): 544–52. Expounding on Flexner's distinction between "useful" and "useless" knowledge, Robbert Dijkgraaf, the current director of the Institute for Advanced Study in Princeton, points out that this demarcation is not hard-and-fast. He references Nobel laureate George Porter's term "not-yet-applied" for the zone from fundamental research to practical applications. The route between them is often irregular. Befitting times

He claimed that useless knowledge is the source of unmatched utility. Citing Guglielmo Marconi, the inventor of the wireless radio, Flexner submitted that this innovation resulted from technical detail added to a lot of useless work by major theorists in the field of magnetism and electricity. In this case and others, the scientists who offered useless ideas had no practical payoff in mind. What then motivated them? The driver was their intellectual curiosity, which eventually provided immensely useful rewards for humankind. Crucially, training students in the scientific spirit in seemingly useless but vital investigative areas can yield unforeseeable ways to address concrete problems. According to Flexner, enabling free inquiry untrammeled by demands for usefulness promises illumination.

To wit, the famous British scholar G. H. Hardy took pleasure in pure mathematics and expressed disdain for applied research, leaving it to other minds. In his cogent formulation: "they [branches of applied mathematics] are indeed repulsively ugly and intolerably dull."[7] He made a landmark contribution to what became known as the Hardy-Weinberg law, a theorem that addresses controversies over what proportions of dominant and recessive traits spread in a sizable mixed population. Several years after his formulation first appeared, Hardy's work had tangible spinoffs in genetics that he had not intended and would not have imagined. This experience suggests that the ivory-tower stereotype of universities misses the point: the programs of scholars with their own agendas for basic research can have relevance to the "real world." Seen from this angle, the knowers and the doers may be one and the same.

These modes of reasoning about the value of useless and useful knowledge resonate in times like our own when the value of higher education is widely debated. By all means, some present-day educational leaders share Newman and Flexner's vision of the role of the university. In the words of Daniel Zajfman, president of Israel's Weizmann Institute:

When we look at the values of knowledge for the sake of knowledge, we realise 100 years later what we can do with this. If you look at the history of science, you will find that most of the discoveries were never made by trying to solve a problem, rather by trying to understand how nature works, so our focus is on understanding.[8]

---

of slashing public and considerable private expenditure on basic inquiry without immediate payoff, Dijkgraaf's foreword, "The World of Tomorrow," to a new release of Abraham Flexner, *The Usefulness of Useless Knowledge* (Princeton: Princeton University Press, 2017), 3–47, provides a salutary message.

7. G. H. Hardy, *A Mathematician's Apology*, Canto ed. (New York: Cambridge University Press, 1993), 140.

8. As quoted in Karen MacGregor, "Looking beyond the Shanghai University Rankings," *University World News* 285, August 31, 2013, http://www.universityworldnews.com /article.php?story=20130830153013382 (accessed September 6, 2013).

But today's public skepticism about this thinking, when used to defend the performance of universities, is palpable.[9] A concern is that given their high costs, universities are providing insufficient returns, variously understood in light of the informational needs of prospective students and their parents, learning outcomes, student loan debt, qualifications for jobs, salaries earned by alumni, and the employment rate among graduates.[10]

These sorts of expectations of the university were brought home to me in a conversation with the parents of a student admitted to our MA program in International Relations. Her father got right down to business and asked me how much his daughter would earn upon graduation. I deferred, explaining that my school offers an interdisciplinary degree and that the salary range varies depending on which career track a student takes. I mapped five of them: government, nongovernmental agencies, intergovernmental organizations, transnational corporations, and research and teaching. The father would hear none of it. He wanted a single figure for a pay grade. When I reinforced my message and also mentioned the long-term benefits of higher learning, he hammered his point: parents seek a yield on their investment. What would it be worth in two years? I tried to provide helpful information and recognize that for a family, university education is a big expense and commitment of time. While the expected economic dividends can be quantified, the social and intellectual bounty is hard, if not impossible, to denominate. The conversion of building character into a currency would be a hazardous exercise.

Another illustration from personal experience helps elucidate the university's business. Toward the end of my stay as a visiting professor in Japan in 2000, I was pleased to receive an invitation to join four professors from the University of Tokyo for lunch. After graciously welcoming me, they inquired about my assessment of Japanese universities. I shared favorable impressions and added that I thought I had been well prepared for my teaching post in Japan. After all, I had visited Japan on previous occasions. Nevertheless, I was in store for surprises. For example, students enrolled in about twenty courses each term. At the last class session, reserved for the final exam, a student could decide whether to complete the course. I recounted other unanticipated aspects of this system of higher learning as well. My colleagues replied: "Your observations are correct. But you do not understand one thing. Japanese

9. The degree of confidence in and doubt about universities, of course, varies by country. In this regard, the Finnish and U.S. cases differ markedly. (See chapters 4 and 5.)

10. On this concern, see Richard Arum and Josipa Roksa, *Academically Adrift: Limited Learning on College Campuses* (Chicago: University of Chicago Press, 2011); William J. Bennett and David Wilezol, *Is College Worth It?* (Nashville: Thomas Nelson, 2013); Jeffrey J. Selingo, *College (Un)Bound: The Future of Higher Education and What It Means for Students* (Boston: Houghton Mifflin, 2013).

universities are not about education. The role of the university is to credential and rank students for jobs in corporations and government."

My Tokyo colleagues were being earnest rather than ironic or cynical. They had a point about pragmatic aims in higher education. Under the banner of institutional reforms, credentialing is often understood as a principal purpose of universities.[11] The Japanese case, of course, has its distinctive features. But which case is not special in certain respects? My hosts' remarks bring to light a move, in general, toward career preparation as the business of the academy. Many proponents of professional degree programs subscribe to the notion that university curricula should have closer ties to the employment market in the contemporary "knowledge society" and "knowledge economy." As my student's father asserted, the idea is that a degree is a return on financial investment. But there are other perspectives on the purposes of universities.

Drawn from nineteenth-century England, twentieth-century America, and twenty-first-century America and Japan, the foregoing perspectives epitomize the university's conundrum. From Newman's era to our own, the purposes of the university are being redefined. Notably, his notion that the university should attend to the moral and religious supervision of students is set aside. And arguably, higher education's missions have always been evolving.

Relative to other institutions in the corporate sector and the health care industry, the university has been sluggish in adapting to shifts in society and economy. Concurrently, the state is in the throes of restructuring. It acts less as a shield that protects the domestic economy against the international economy, as it did during the 1960s and 1970s, and more of a facilitator of domestic interests and an agent that promotes globalization.[12]

In this dynamic, the university is instrumental for a people's aspirations. "Knowledge," C. Wright Mills wrote, "is no longer widely felt as an ideal; it is seen as an instrument. In a society of power and wealth, knowledge is valued as an instrument of power and wealth, and also, of course, as an ornament in conversation."[13] An emphasis on the production of useful knowledge spiraled after World War II. But it became instrumental to precisely which groups and whose interests? A particular religious order? Certain social strata rather than others? A political persuasion? A business-model bottom line? Is higher learning an end, as Newman believed, as well as a means? If the answer to the latter question is yes, then the mix is rapidly changing.

True, the *specific aims* of the modern university reflect variations in the history of individual locales and institutions. Yet from the early 1800s, the *core*

11. Jane Jacobs, *Dark Age Ahead* (New York: Random House, 2004), 44–63, provides an intriguing discussion of the origins of credentialing in higher learning.

12. Robert W. Cox, "A Perspective on Globalization," in *Globalization: Critical Reflections*, ed. James H. Mittelman (Boulder, CO: Lynne Rienner, 1996), 21–30.

13. C. Wright Mills, *The Power Elite* (New York: Oxford University Press, 2000), 352.

purposes developed gradually and, at a broad level, remain similar, at least in nonauthoritarian contexts. But the settings cannot be neatly classified on the basis of democratic and undemocratic systems, and the implicit goal at universities in a democratic country like France, unlike in instances such as Britain or the United States, is preparation for republican citizenship with emphasis on *laïcité* (secularism).[14] While such differences are salient, the key point is that the primary missions are training for democratic citizenship, nurturing critical thinking, and defending academic freedom. In our era, however, historical transformations are supplanting these established principles.

To trace this path, just imagine in Newman's day, a major university in England, Germany, or the United States defining its mission as serving as an engine of economic growth and increasingly orienting its academic programs to the job market. Furthermore, try to conceive of them as preparing graduating students for national security and building a country's "soft power," even while the academy still professed its devotion to promoting a love of learning.[15] These images of the makeover of universities are hard to conjure because the precepts that Newman and like-minded educators denoted have had a lasting impact, even if, bit by bit, they are fading.

Strikingly, it was only a generation ago that universities were not enamored with the keywords—strategic planning, benchmarking, branding, visibility, rankings, productivity, and quality assurance—that have been translated into metrics.[16] In this move, more is at stake than modish ways of burnishing an institution's reputation. Rather, as we shall see, numbers have power and are insinuated as policy. The new shoptalk portends changing priorities, with costs and benefits. The current narratives spring from a political and economic context far different from, say, the landscape of Newman's Oxford University and of the Catholic University of Ireland (now University College, Dublin), where he was the first rector, in the 1800s or Flexner's Princeton almost a century later.

Allowing that in our day, conditions differ from those of bygone eras, Derek Bok, Harvard University president emeritus, plants his analysis of

14. On these points, I am grateful for comments on a preliminary draft of this work by Patrick Thaddeus Jackson, professor of International Relations in the School of International Service, American University, email message to author, January 28, 2016, and by Louis Goodman, professor of sociology in the School of International Service, American University, email message to author, January 29, 2016.

15. In Joseph S. Nye's usage, "soft power" is the ability to attract or persuade rather than force. See his *Soft Power: The Means to Success in World Politics* (New York: Public Affairs, 2004).

16. These terms have multiple sources: in the military and other branches of the public sector, business schools, and private companies. A management tool, strategic planning seeks to bring together mission, values, and capabilities. Michael E. Porter's work *Competitive Strategy* (New York: Free Press, 1980) has been particularly influential.

higher education on the terrain of academe's deeply rooted educational values.[17] He certainly knows the importance of money for running a complex institution. Yet Bok points out that seeking revenue can be a never-ending proposition, luring institutions into more and more activities for pecuniary rather than intellectual reasons.[18] To underline his point, he asks his audience to suppose that Coca-Cola offered Princeton University $25 million for the right to chisel the words "Things Go Better with Coke" at the entrance to Nassau Hall. Princeton would no doubt scotch a bid to advertise this product on a historic building. Bok asks why, since universities often bestow the names of corporate donors on endowed professorships and scholarships. The problem with this hypothetical deal is that posting the message in a location that symbolizes the university itself would suggest that "money can buy almost anything at Princeton."[19] The Coca-Cola icon would imply that "no place is too sacred if the price is right."[20] Bok adds: "By communicating its materialism so brazenly, the university would threaten to undermine any other efforts it makes to keep commercial pressures from eroding academic values."[21]

I witnessed a real-life situation in Malaysia in 1997–98 just like Bok's made-up scenario. Administrators at the University of Malaya, the country's oldest and generally considered leading university, gave permission to McDonald's to open a franchise at its main gate. This entrance is next to the university mosque. Faculty, staff, and students vehemently protested this initiative on the grounds that the golden arches are a Western commercial artifact out of keeping with a repository of higher learning in Asia and an affront to Islamic values. Confronted by angry demonstrations, the university's senior administrators backed down and found another location for this fast-food franchise.

Academic Globalization

While McDonald's originated in the United States, this transnational chain signifies the spread of market-oriented globalization. As in Malaysia, institutions of higher education throughout the world are in the throes of academic globalization: a transformation in the domain of knowledge. That is to say, educational transformation is not a self-contained phenomenon; it takes place in a globalized environment marked by expansionary tendencies.

17. Derek Bok, *Universities in the Marketplace: The Commercialization of Higher Education* (Princeton: Princeton University Press, 2003).
18. Ibid., 166.
19. Ibid., 173.
20. Ibid.
21. Ibid.

In a prescient analysis, published in 1944, the social economist Karl Polanyi evoked powerful insights about transformation in general that extend beyond the particular object of his study, namely, the growth of the market economy in the nineteenth century.[22] The title of his celebrated book, *The Great Transformation*, encapsulates the relationship between the market and the other central institutions of society. In the first phase of a double movement, Polanyi showed, market reforms wrought large-scale disruption in society. Hurt by the jagged effects of this massive transformation, some of the most vulnerable groups, especially workers, pushed back and engaged in collective action. Their response to economic liberalism constituted a countermovement that sought to assert greater control over market forces. Polanyi maintained that by the 1800s, a "planetary" surge of market economy supplanted Europe's old order: a system wherein political and social imperatives had maintained precedence over the market.[23] The double movement, a thrust and counterthrust, soon transcended national territories. Polanyi's study revealed the way that these gears can advance a global transformation.

Although Polanyi did not examine universities as a social institution, his thinking helps grasp how they are being transformed. Yes, they are subject to a historical metamorphosis and, at the same time, serve as actors in educational globalization. The academy is both lodged in and propels the current phase of globalization.

That said, our era may be understood as a syndrome of transformative processes that compresses time and space.[24] In other words, globalization shrinks horizons and distance. It is a multidimensional complex of political, economic, and cultural structures. It slices across national borders and touches down differently in various contexts. Its structures are not all external to a given country or region. They are entwined with the domestic sphere. All locales and sundry institutions, including universities, must respond to an unprecedented set of globalizing pressures.

Whereas Polanyi neatly spelled out the dynamics of transformation, a difference between the arena he examined and the educational realm lies in pushback: it is less conspicuous in today's mode of knowledge production. But

22. Karl Polanyi, *The Great Transformation: The Political and Economic Origins of Our Time* (1944; Boston: Beacon Press, 1957).

23. Ibid., 89.

24. Anthony Giddens, *The Consequences of Modernity* (Cambridge: Cambridge University Press, 1990); David Harvey, *The Condition of Postmodernity* (Oxford: Basil Blackwell, 1990); Roland Robertson, *Globalization: Social Theory and Global Culture* (Newbury Park, CA: Sage, 1992); James H. Mittelman, *The Globalization Syndrome: Transformation and Resistance* (Princeton: Princeton University Press, 2000); James H. Mittelman, *Whither Globalization? The Vortex of Knowledge and Ideology* (New York: Routledge, 2004).

if one digs empirically, the evidence presented ahead corroborates that the glimmerings are apparent.

Global Pressures

Our era is marked by a combination of four transformative forces buffeting universities. In most countries, higher education systems are grappling with a congeries of similar pressures.[25] One is the extension of the market in the business of the university. Outsourcing means that services on a given campus, such as dining, security, cleaning, grounds and maintenance, and security, are contracted to private companies. Universities and corporations often enter joint ventures, particularly in the natural sciences and medicine to patent products. Offshoring entails working across borders to recruit international students, open franchise campuses, negotiate management fees, and undertake related initiatives. As noted, the distinctions between public and private, and for-profit and nonprofit institutions become blurred. For example, the scholarly community takes advantage of the Khan Academy's vast library of outstanding educational videos and other platforms, visited by millions of users each year. Similarly dedicated to disseminating new ideas, the nonprofit TED draws intellectuals to its conferences and produces well-researched videos.[26] Overall, these groups not only complement but also compete with the university. They are part of the intense market competition now characteristic of higher education. The rivalry is among institutions in a single country and among countries, between faculties on the same campus and throughout the world, as well as within individual academic units. The competition is also to capture the attention of students who devote less time to the content of academic activities and more to entertainment, the social media, and technological vehicles: computer games, smartphones, Facebook, Twitter, and the like.[27]

Second, state disinvestment in the public sphere cuts deeply into university budgets. In the American case, state sources of funding higher education reached a twenty-five-year low in 2012.[28] According to Hunter Rawlings, a

---

25. See James J. Duderstadt, Jerry Taggart, and Luc Weber, "The Globalization of Higher Education," in *The Globalization of Higher Education*, ed. Luc E. Weber and James J. Duderstadt (London: Economica, Glion Colloquium, 2008), 273–90, http://www .glion.org/pdf_livres/g08_the_globalization_of_hied.pdf (accessed September 19, 2013).

26. Tobias Denskus and Daniel E. Esser, "TED Talks on International Development: Trans-Hegemonic Promise and Ritualistic Constraints," *Communication Theory* 25, no. 2 (May 2015): 166–87.

27. For data on the amount of time that undergraduates spend on their studies, entertainment, social life, and recreation, see Derek Bok, *Higher Education in America* (Princeton: Princeton University Press, 2013), 184–85.

28. Eric Kelderman, "States Push Even Further to Cut Spending on Colleges," *Chronicle of Higher Education* 58, no. 21 (January 27, 2012): A1–3.

former president of Cornell and the University of Iowa, later president of the Association of American Universities (AAU), by the beginning of 2012, 41 states had slashed their spending on public universities, from 1 percent in Indiana to 41 percent in New Hampshire, atop prior reductions.[29] These constraints have been accompanied by contractions in federal grants and other aid, which affect research output, opportunities for low-income students, and thus social mobility and levels of social inequality. As of 2013, the legislature in Sacramento downsized its share of the University of California's higher education budget from 27 percent in 2000 to slightly more than 10 percent. Its flagship campus, Berkeley, suffered a cut of half of its state funding from 2004 and now receives 12 percent of its budget from the state. For most Big Ten universities, the portion provided by the state capital is in the single digits. The University of Virginia receives just 6 percent and, like many public universities, must comply with government restrictions on the amount of tuition that it can charge state residents. The University of Colorado's state revenue is 4 percent of its budget.

Citizens of Virginia, Colorado, and other states allege that admissions officers favor higher-paying, out-of-state (including international) applicants, at the expense of their own students. Some universities have been stripped of substantial parts of their infrastructure: budget for maintenance of facilities, supplies and equipment in labs and departments, and support personnel. Proportionally, state defunding at public universities in many countries in the global South is even greater than in the United States. The former is often down from nearly 100 percent at the time of decolonization to the 20 to 25 percent range today.

To keep their institutions afloat, university managers are obliged to hunt for revenue in new ways. Hence, to address budget shortages at Canada's Dalhousie University, its medical school is selling ten vacant seats to full-pay students from Saudi Arabia for CA$75,000 (US$75,797) annually, considerably above the rate for their domestic counterparts, whose tuition and government funding come to under CA$40,000 (US$40,425).[30] The dean of medicine, Tom Marrie, explained that cuts in provincial funding necessitated making money from empty seats and increasing international student enrollment. Surely, the pressures on deans are mounting. Their tenure is becoming shorter—at the top twenty-five schools with MBA programs, less than five

29. Hunter R. Rawlings III, "The Biggest Problem Confronting Universities Is Not What You Think It Is" (paper presented at the conference "The Future of the Research University in a Global Age," Rice University, Houston, TX, February 27–28, 2012). Rawlings cites data compiled by the Illinois State University Center for the Study of Higher Education (1).

30. James Bradshaw, "Dalhousie Medical School to Sell Saudis 10 Seats," *Globe and Mail* (Toronto), March 18, 2011.

years, a figure buoyed by a few long-serving officeholders.[31] For U.S.-based business schools, the average deanship is 5.73 years; the median, four years.[32] Now, "serial deans" are moving between positions at rival institutions.[33]

Deans are subject to stiff demands from upper executives, many of whom set enrollment targets and quotas for external funding. As middle managers, deans often delegate portions of their administrative burden to department chairs. Typically, the deans must generate numbers: more students, faculty publications, and sums of money. And pressure frequently emanates, too, from their academic units. It is not unusual for a dean to encounter anti-leadership sentiment from professors who want resources, are disposed to resist institutional change, and are bent on protecting their own interests. Yet the deans' directive from senior management is to produce more and more innovation. In many instances, they are told to shake up the status quo: what Joseph Schumpeter called "creative destruction"—disrupt the old structure and create a new one.[34] Deans and their supervisors engage in creative destruction through activities such as continually changing the rules in faculty manuals, replacing staff, and hiring new professors, albeit in reduced numbers. Faculty turnover can be a net gain in revenue but expensive in terms of recruitment and start-up costs for the new professors. From the 1900s to the contemporary knowledge environment, the emphasis in the decanal job has shifted from providing intellectual leadership toward managing efficiently and networking effectively.

To amass tuition and fees, deans may feel compelled to lower admissions standards. Besides privatizing more operations, they place a share of responsibility on professors who will be rewarded for their entrepreneurial activities. So, too, new recruits in academia are socialized into valuing these practices, often through criteria used in considerations for tenure and promotion.

Only a handful of countries have so far not experienced deep cuts in state support. At present, China and some Southeast Asian nations are major exceptions to the general pattern, though this may change. And they, too, encounter demands for adopting market practices, such as mobilizing money from donors, meeting managers' standards of productivity, and time-consuming reporting in lieu of boosting their research and conferring with students.

Third, demographic swings present immediate challenges for admissions, staffing, and physical capacity (classrooms, accommodations, office space,

31. Della Bradshaw, "From the Editor: The Dean Hunters," *FT Business Education* (London), October 23, 2013.

32. Ibid.

33. Della Bradshaw, "Short Tenure of Deans Signals Leadership Gap," *Financial Times*, April 27, 2015.

34. Joseph A. Schumpeter, *Capitalism, Socialism and Democracy* (1942; New York: Harper, 1975), 82–85. Popularized by Schumpeter, the idea of "creative destruction" preceded him and has been developed by other authors.

library, labs, and other facilities). Aging populations in the global North and growing numbers of the young in the global South have direct effects on university recruitment, finances, and physical plant. This trend dovetails with a move in recent decades away from elite education toward what Europeans call massification: increases in the proportion of the population enrolled in tertiary education. Enrollments have grown substantially in the last twenty or more years. For example, the number of students at Senegal's Cheikh Anta Diop University now tops 60,000; Arizona State University has 73,000; and the University of Vienna, 92,000. Online, distance learners add to the total. The Open University in the United Kingdom enlists 250,000 students. The figure is even higher at for-profit providers. The University of Phoenix registered 600,000 students in 2010; however, its intake subsequently declined due to fierce competition from other online suppliers, negative publicity surrounding questionable recruitment practices, low graduation rates, heavy debt burdens incurred by students, and a poor record of job placement.[35] The largest for-profit U.S. company by higher education enrollment, Laureate Education, owns 75 schools in 30 countries and has 800,000 students.

Ironically, massification promised social mobility and appeared to enhance the role of the university in society, but it has actually diminished it. In bygone days when universities focused more on educating the progeny of elites, they were premier knowledge providers. Yet with massification, large numbers of graduating students with higher degrees sought jobs at universities, which could not absorb the bulk of them. Many graduates then found employment as knowledge producers and knowledge brokers outside academe. Having earned PhDs and master's degrees, the younger cohorts looked for niches elsewhere in the epistemic community.[36] The new recruits brought their energy and intellectual skills to think tanks, research departments of national and global governance agencies or corporations, and policy analysis divisions of nongovernmental organizations, all of which invest in research and development (R&D). The nouveau knowledge producers and distributors participate in global knowledge networks. Globalized knowledge is multifaceted and the nets have spread.

Massification thereby renders the university as but one among multiple sources of innovatory knowledge and centers of training.[37] It is hard to

35. Valerie Strauss, "Largest For-Profit U.S. University Expects to Be Put on Probation by Accreditor," *Washington Post*, February 26, 2013, http://www.washingtonpost.com/blogs/answer-sheet/wp/2013/02/26/largest-for-profit-u-s-university-expects-to-be-put-on-probation-by-accreditor/ (accessed January 20, 2013).

36. An epistemic community is a network of professionals with expertise on particular areas and issues. Peter M. Haas, "Epistemic Communities and International Policy Coordination," *International Organization* 46, no. 1 (Winter 1992): 1–35.

37. See Michael Gibbons, "Higher Education Relevance in the 21st Century" (paper presented at the UNESCO World Conference on Higher Education, Paris, October 5–9, 1998), http://www-wds.worldbank.org/servlet/WDSContentServer/WDSP/IB/2000

determine whether higher education institutions remain the principal venue for knowledge production and dissemination. Certainly, nontraditional providers are now playing larger roles in higher education. Nontraditional education encompasses options outside the classroom and increasingly away from the learning cultures of full on-campus universities in the form of online, distance, experiential, and competency-based training offered on the job and by private firms. Higher education is becoming more of a hybrid of traditional-institutional and extra-institutional components.

Compared to other knowledge producers, universities are ill-suited to change rapidly. In countries such as Ireland, the United Kingdom, and the United States, shared governance, a collegial culture of deliberation, and the regulatory environment limit the pace of their responses to global pressures. In the teeth of increased competition for grants, contracts, and standing among social institutions, university senior executives fret that their organizations are laggards saddled by outdated values, antique managerial practices, and aged technology. Policy analysts differ about the extent to which these concerns have prodded institutions of higher education to adapt in an auspicious manner.

Fourth, and closely related, universities have of course placed renewed emphasis on new technologies. Virtual learning and online courses can lessen the demand for space on campus. Although they are expensive and require more support staff, technologies also serve as a way to make money and subsidize the high-end model of tertiary education, that is, at least for certain universities like Stanford that pilot and negotiate contracts for technological innovations. At the same time, the disruption in educational life is enormous. Consider, for example, massive open online courses (MOOCs). First offered in 2008, now available worldwide and thus far at low cost, they unbundle the university's student learning experiences, assessment, enrollment services, and other management functions. Experience with MOOCs portends that the university is in the throes of a transformation from serving as a consolidator of academic programs and of educational services to an agent in the reaggregation of the knowledge business.

Platforms like MOOCs dislodge institutions of higher learning from their home locales. MOOCs outsource instruction to remote sites where star professors at prestigious universities offer lectures. The potential of these courses lies in the promise to democratize higher education and make it continuously available for young and adult learners, including students unable to attend an on-site institution. Nevertheless, a backlash against MOOCs is happening because of concern that they will lead to dismantling academic units, cutting jobs, and crowding

---

/07/19/000094946_9912220532351/Rendered/PDF/multi_page.pdf (accessed October 29, 2013).

out homegrown educational innovations, not least in the global South. On such grounds, the faculty on some U.S. campuses—Amherst College, Duke University, and Middlebury College—voted against participating in these ventures.

Similarly, in 2013, Darrell Steinberg, president pro tem of the California State Senate, presented a bill requiring colleges and universities to award credit for MOOCs in overly subscribed introductory courses, and faculty reacted strongly to his bid to transform higher education. They deemed the pending legislation as political interference, a dilution of academic standards, and another step toward privatizing higher learning at public institutions. Opposition from faculty in the California State University system, community college professors, and faculty unions softened Steinberg's measure into incentives for designing MOOCs.[38]

Resistance by academics to change is not unusual. Arguably, the professoriate tends to be institutionally conservative. Most of us enjoy our work and the privileges that come with it. Not surprisingly, there are efforts to maintain them. Yet we also bear responsibility for the good of our students and the virtues for which universities stand. Consequently, responding to the pressures on institutions of higher education is taken with a matter of utmost purpose.

All told, the demands of the educational marketplace are increasingly weighty. The ascendant notion that education is a private benefit for which individuals and their parents must pay correlates with the idea that the public sphere should shrink. In many countries, taxes are not covering the high-cost model of public universities, which turn more to the private sector for revenue. The changing agenda stems not only from financial capacity but also from evolving value systems. The state is shedding much of its fiscal responsibility for safeguarding the educational needs of society, transferring the onus to universities. In contemporary policy frameworks, higher education institutions are expected to address the economic exigencies of government.[39] Key stresses of government are increasingly displaced onto universities. With diminished state allocations, they are supposed to develop a scientific-technical infrastructure to strengthen national defense as well as the economy. In this respect, the relationship between the state and the university is revamped. The old triangle of government-higher education-industry is breaking apart. This aspect of the social contract is in tatters. What is replacing it?

38. David L. Kirp, "Tech Mania Goes to College," *The Nation* 297, no. 12 (September 23, 2013): 12–17.

39. James J. Duderstadt, "Higher Education in the 21st Century: Global Imperatives, Regional Challenges, National Responsibilities and Emerging Opportunities," in *The Globalization of Higher Education*, ed. Weber and Duderstadt, 195–206, http://www.glion .org/pdf_livres/g08_the_globalization_of_hied.pdf (accessed September 19, 2013); author telephone discussion with Duderstadt, president emeritus and University Professor of Sciences and Engineering, University of Michigan, February, 15, 2013.

Ben Wildavsky, director of higher education studies at the State University of New York's Rockefeller Institute of Government, posits that the new arrangement appears more in tune with the logic of the market.[40] He finds that boundary-straddling competition is the motor of transformation in higher education. Globalization brings a revolution in the academic marketplace—one that, in his view, is generated by its material wherewithal and potential. He describes how universities in several countries are striving to reach standards like those of Harvard and Cambridge and seek to become world-class institutions. In Wildavsky's judgment, globalization is promoting excellence in academe. His engaging and richly detailed book makes the case that the university is changing directions and that money business is becoming preeminent in the academy. To his credit, Wildavsky adduces valuable data from interviews and peppers his oeuvre with an assortment of pertinent examples. His stories help punctuate points. But an abundance of illustrations, however apt they may be, cannot substitute for a methodical approach with conceptual rigor and historical depth. While tales have a role in analysis (and I tell them too), a principal task in making sense of large shifts in universities' roles in the global arena is to link systematic findings to historical trajectories.

Much of the research on the globalization of higher education advances nuanced agendas that differ from Wildavsky's straightforward, congenial recognition of the global marketplace. Global modelers know the pressures, understand that productivity has become a watchword, and note the overall context of performance-based systems. Inasmuch as this genre of research is quite repetitive, I shall spare the reader the time and myself the labor of surveying the scholarly literature. However, a few highlights, as succinctly as possible, are important to my analysis. Three exemplar works merit attention.

Drawing on his experience as president of MIT from 1990 to 2004, followed by six years as president of the U.S. National Academy of Engineering, Charles Vest postulates that a "global meta-university" is on the horizon.[41] It is evolving because information technology is a transformative force in higher education. It is happening because of economies of scale realized by the collective use of high-quality equipment and systems that individual institutions cannot afford to purchase. The advantages of sharing digital information and materials include novel opportunities for excellence and access.[42] Entering the debate about whether the virtual university will replace

40. Ben Wildavsky, *The Great Brain Race: How Global Universities Are Reshaping the World* (Princeton: Princeton University Press, 2010).

41. Charles M. Vest, *The American Research University from World War II to World Wide Web: Governments, the Private Sector, and the Emerging Meta-University* (Berkeley: University of California Press, 2007); author discussion with Vest, Washington, DC, March 11, 2013.

42. Vest, *The American Research University*.

brick-and-mortar campuses, Vest believes that the buildings, grounds, and face-to-face interactions will remain centerpieces of higher education. Even so, universities are gradually edging toward a global template, traced in Vest's 2007 book.[43]

Developing a similar theme, Kathryn Mohrman and her coauthors map an "emerging global model" (EGM) of research universities based on intensified globalization and delimit its several characteristics.[44] In the EGM, the research university assigns utmost importance to searching for new knowledge, especially in science and technology, and producing advanced research workers. Inasmuch as key alliances and programs are global, the competitive recruitment of faculty, students, and administrators crosses national borders. Imparting global perspectives, EGM universities shift from lone scholars' independent inquiry to interdisciplinary teamwork aimed at innovating applied knowledge. Increasingly costly and relying on more technological infrastructure, these initiatives rest on new complexes composed of parts of universities, the state, and corporations. In addition, universities join forces with intergovernmental and nongovernmental organizations in encouraging collaborative research, mobility, and validation of status. Normatively, the EGM prizes entrepreneurial activities. While this model primarily emanates from the United States, it permeates other parts of the world. In brief, the implication is that nation-states have less control of universities in what has been regarded as their domestic jurisdiction.

In a complementary piece, Roger King's book about the global governance of universities details a symbiotic relationship between academe and globalization.[45] Acknowledging that universities have mainly been anchored in national systems of finance and regulation, King depicts the manner in which the playing field is becoming global. The players are imbued with market norms of competition, as well as of performance evaluation and other managerial devices, all of which traverse territorial borders.

Normally, this soft regulation elicits voluntary compliance. Building consensus on standards of quality and excellence is mediated by a host of public and private agencies such as big philanthropies. Also important to forming consensus, the use of discursive power manifests in businesslike narratives of strategic planning. But if consensus fails to hold, markets penalize noncompliance by actors that refuse to adopt economic reforms. Hence, in the face of ballooning costs, their funding dwindles. And if governmental or

43. Ibid.

44. Kathryn Mohrman, Wanhua Ma, and David Baker, "The Research University in Transition: The Emerging Global Model," *Higher Education Policy* 21, no. 1 (March 2008): 5–27.

45. Roger King, *Governing Universities Globally: Organizations, Regulation and Rankings* (Northampton, MA: Edward Elgar, 2009).

nongovernmental regulators such as accreditors and rankers give notice of inadequacies, student and faculty recruitment suffers, compounding shortages in institutional finances and leading to programmatic cuts.

In global modelers' accounts of these phenomena, subtle research discerns a range of institutions and contexts. On this basis, analysts can detect systemic patterns while giving scope to regional, national, and subnational differences. But to my mind, the general framework is foundational yet underspecified and in want of refinement. The story is more complicated than encapsulating educational developments in a universal image and acknowledging some variation. It is a matter of pinpointing how the global and local merge and interpenetrate. Let me be specific about the grounds for honing analysis of these interactions.

The Stakes

On the one hand, educational globalization brings enormous opportunities. It spurs strivings to improve teaching and research. One may, of course, dispute the means—incentive systems intended to drive achievement—in a professional community that esteems learning and wherein the most important motivations are intrinsic. However, a great benefit of globalization is the mobility of scholars and students who are able to come to know their counterparts elsewhere and gain entrée to other cultures.

While more information, exchange of knowledge, material, and experience are laudable, grave risks in university reforms linked to educational globalization are apparent. One of them is a danger long ago identified by the philosopher Friedrich Nietzsche. In his writings on politics and society, he perceived a demand in education for sameness.[46] Nietzsche detected the tendency of social institutions to gravitate toward uniformity. He was wary that schooling can produce an unhealthy conformism.

Although in our times, many educational cultures value free inquiry, concerns about its decline and fears of the threat of groupthink on campuses are frequently expressed.[47] Seeking to counter intellectual orthodoxy, political officials, university trustees, and others sometimes adopt measures to assure "balance" in academic programming. However, balance is ultimately in the eye

---

46. Friedrich Nietzsche, *Beyond Good and Evil: Prelude to the Philosophy of the Future*, trans. Helen Zimmern (New York: Russell and Russell, 1964), 20–21; Friedrich Nietzsche, *The Will to Power*, trans. and ed. Walter Kaufmann and R. J. Hollingdale (New York: Vintage Books, 1968), 156–63.

47. See Jonathan R. Cole, *The Great American University: Its Rise to Preeminence, Its Indispensable Role, and Why It Must Be Protected* (New York: Public Affairs, 2009), 494; author discussion with Jonathan R. Cole, John Mason Professor of the University and a former provost and dean of faculties, Columbia University, New York, March 8, 2013.

of the beholder. Contra efforts to balance knowledge and ideas, the antidote to a perceived herd mentality and restrained discourse is to throw more free speech at them so as to protect academic freedom.

Yet as universities become more receptive to transnational models of higher education, the notion of autonomy is being redefined. Its historical roots in their varied contexts are weakening. Educational globalization is bleaching universities' distinctive histories. True, the origins of institutions and their founders are memorialized. Tribute to old norms is typically paid at commencement, rehearsed in mission statements, monumentalized in statues, and celebrated at photo exhibits. These adornments are nods to the past and can serve to legitimate new ways. Besides, they are mostly something to get done before moving on to what is deemed more compelling business.

Even though they are enshrined, by and large, universities' distinguishing traditions are being eclipsed. Other priorities are gaining global traction. Programmatic activities and values are more enmeshed in the world at large. As a result of systemic and global processes, some universities are disengaging from their own backyards on the ground that retrenchment strips resources for community outreach. Meanwhile, they are cutting and pasting best practices from external templates. They are downloading language and initiatives, often at the expense of local sources of knowledge such as stories told by elders. This problem is particularly acute in the global South. There, as well as in developed countries with first nations, projects for reviving indigenous knowledge are underway, though such endeavors often lack support or may not be well executed.

Reflecting on her experience at universities in Nigeria, Oyeronke Oyewumi, author of the award-winning book *The Invention of Women: Making an African Sense of Western Gender Discourses*, pointedly asks: "Are they African universities or universities located on the African continent?"[48] Her provocative question can be transposed into: Who owns the university when it is in the throes of a parametric transformation? Whose business is it? And whose knowledge and values are predominant? Such avenues of inquiry verge on the proposition that autonomous discourses have been effaced, devoicing local peoples. Indeed, the corruption of knowledge structures can impair worthy initiatives to regenerate them.[49]

Educational value systems and key constituencies—administrators, faculty, and students alike—are susceptible to this corruption. With hypercompetition,

48. Oyeronke Oyewumi, "The Coloniality of Power and the Production of Knowledge on Africa" (keynote address at 4th European Conference on African Studies, Uppsala, Sweden, June 16, 2011).

49. In Susan Strange's sense, a knowledge structure is a system of power relations: who and what discovers, stores, and communicates knowledge. *States and Markets: An Introduction to International Political Economy* (New York: Basil Blackwell, 1988), 117–19.

financial reductions, and a push for high-performance standards, the drive to excel or profit comes with growing temptations to cheat. In some cases, academic misconduct has reached epidemic proportions. According to research recorded in the U.S. *Proceedings of the National Academy of Sciences* in 2012, the percentage of retractions of scientific articles owing to fraud or suspected fraud has increased tenfold since 1975.[50] Why are there more attempts to beat the system? Digital technology makes it easier to both short-circuit established processes and detect violations. Diminished grant funds, the value attached to publishing in the most prestigious journals, and competition in a tightening job market are also factors.[51] Unethical behavior is manifested in a research environment that has become a huge business. Johns Hopkins University, for instance, usually wins more than $600 million per year from a single funder, the National Institutes of Health.[52] The cumulative effects of these developments cut to the central purposes of a university.

Consequences

Reactions to the impact of budget trimming include students' complaints that hikes in tuition fees accompanied by plummeting government spending are unfair: enrollees pay more and receive less. On many campuses, students are unable to take courses in certain foundational subjects in the humanities. For wont of public money, some universities are winnowing degrees in foreign languages. In the United States, European languages (save Spanish), in particular, are being phased out of many instructional programs. At the same time, there is rising demand for languages like Arabic and Chinese. Critics point out the irony of eliminating language offerings just when universities are affirming the value of an international mission and aiming to develop as world-class institutions.

According to 2013 reports, Harvard experienced a 20 percent drop in humanities majors in the past decade. At 7 percent in the United States, humanities majors are down from 14 percent in 1970. Perhaps part of this decline is attributable to faculty members' proclivity for a relativizing postmodernism, which certain critics regard as an intellectual playground. It has led some career-minded students to switch from the humanistic sciences to applied fields more genial toward traditional forms of reasoning.[53] Meanwhile, the administration on many campuses is according primacy to science and

50. As cited in Peter Whoriskey, "Behind Acclaimed Research, Doubts," *Washington Post*, March 12, 2013.
51. An issue detailed in chapter 7.
52. Ibid.
53. For additional reasons for this decline, see chapter 4.

technology.[54] Also, an up-and-coming priority in some countries is cyber-education. Funded by the National Security Agency and the Pentagon in the United States, the discipline of cybersecurity is becoming a national brand in the online market. The University of Maryland University College, the largest U.S. public online program in this field, enrolls about 93,000 students and is one among many providers.[55] Funding is available from the U.S. Department of Homeland Security, which envisages that "the academic community will play a key role in securing America."[56] It supports "centers of academic excellence" in the cognate subject of information assurance.[57] Along with other government agencies, Homeland Security offers incentives for establishing courses, certificates, and degrees in homeland security, including funding for a consortium to coordinate these efforts.[58]

In the hierarchies of curriculum and research support, rationality is outcompeting other forms of reasoning. Rationalists believe that a large share of human affairs is manageable by scientific knowledge and that higher education is a way to escape society's doldrums. In the face of this strong conviction, moral reasoning and moral imagination have taken disproportionate reductions. Defenders of the humanistic sciences cry out that different kinds of reasoning merit backing. Reasoning, they say, should not be restricted to a predominant form. By their thinking, rationalism, with its belief in objectivity and, for some, numeric logic, denies the intuitive mind and the inner self as sources of insight. Art, philosophy, music, dance, and theater also provide learning from valuable ways of knowing and relating to the world. If the space for developing this capacity shrinks, is higher education downgraded? Do all fields of study then suffer?[59]

University of Chicago legal scholar and philosopher Martha Nussbaum affirms that the humanities are being sidelined in the university's efforts to compete in the global marketplace.[60] Scope for teaching the classics is whittled

54. Tamar Lewin, "Interest Fading in Humanities, Colleges Worry," *New York Times*, October 31, 2013.

55. Established in 1947 as a branch of the University of Maryland, the University of Maryland University College has been an independent institution since 1970.

56. U.S. Department of Homeland Security, www.dhs.gov (accessed May 29, 2007).

57. James H. Mittelman, *Hyperconflict: Globalization and Insecurity* (Stanford: Stanford University Press, 2010), 146–47; Nick Anderson, "Cybersecurity," *Washington Post*, Education Issue, November 3, 2013.

58. For instance, the National Consortium for the Study of Terrorism and Responses to Terrorism is based at the University of Maryland; the National Academic Consortium for Homeland Security, Ohio State University; and the Institute for National Security and Counterterrorism, Syracuse University. See Mittelman, *Hyperconflict*, 146–47.

59. I am grateful to Sara Heinämaa for her insights, Helsinki, July 1, 2010.

60. Martha C. Nussbaum, *Not for Profit: Why Democracy Needs the Humanities* (Princeton: Princeton University Press, 2010).

down and applied skills are the order of the day. Policymakers and corporate executives are giving precedence to generating short-term profit rather than equipping cosmopolitan citizens with long-range abilities for a globalized world. To buttress her contentions, Nussbaum pores over numerous studies, reports, and indices of human development. Her work prompts readers to think about whether higher education is going astray.[61]

Like Nussbaum, the American Academy's Commission on the Humanities and Social Sciences 2013 report observes that economic insecurities are inducing the public to favor a narrow orientation to education that values quick payoffs.[62] The academy underscores the need to recognize that investment in broad-based learning brings surprising dividends:

> The ability to adapt and thrive in a world certain to keep changing is based not on instruction in the specific jobs of today but in the developing of long-term qualities of mind: inquisitiveness, perceptiveness, the ability to put a received idea to a new purpose, and the ability to share and build ideas with a diverse world of others.[63]

It refers to surveys showing that employers share the view that if practical problems are to be solved, the humanistic underpinnings of scientific and technological skills require support. Corporate and government recruiters are not calling for job training at universities. They know very well that their own institutions provide instructional programs for on-site operations. By virtue of their educational background, experience, and skills, do professors really have a comparative advantage in teaching hands-on work, much of which is rapidly changing and specific to a particular concern such as an individual firm or state agency?

Curiously, universities are contradicting the preferences of employers by favoring more vocationally oriented programs when students seek entry-level positions. Higher education institutions are evidently acting against the short- and long-term interests of their constituents whose welfare is a prime obligation. More pragmatically, they are also a major source of revenue, especially at tuition-driven institutions. Strikingly, too, a number of universities, or their boards, are led by chief executive officers (CEOs) who are not professional educators. In many cases, they came from the business world or have held political office and are reputed to know about fiscal matters. These non-educators are supposed to be adept at raising money from the private sector,

61. Ibid.
62. American Academy of Arts & Sciences, Commission on the Humanities and Social Sciences, *The Heart of the Matter* (Cambridge, MA: Academy of Arts & Sciences, 2013), http://www.humanitiescommission.org/_pdf/hss_report.pdf (accessed September 27, 2013).
63. Ibid., 32.

legislatures, and government agencies. Few of them teach or do research or ever have. Imagine other institutions such as banks calling on individuals without training and experience in a respective subject like finance to serve as their top leaders.[64] Even though health-care facilities and investment houses also champion neoliberal values, they rarely recruit their foremost officials without expertise in their field.

While governance procedures vary by country and university, heads of universities are usually elected or selected and recommended by search committees or university councils, subject to approval. Those named must be endorsed—actually appointed or confirmed—by a political authority or a statutory board: trustees, variously known as regents, visitors, and other titles in different contexts. Leaving aside situations under illiberal regimes, board members are generally drawn from an array of sectors ranging from investment banking, insurance, real estate, information technology, law, politics, media, and the arts to academia. Hardly a recent phenomenon, many trustees lack knowledge and understanding of the complex world of universities and its traditions of shared governance.[65] Their actions can contribute to diminishing the institution of the university presidency.[66] Typically, they adopt business-style management, emphasizing efficiency, performance, and high-quality products.

To cite one instance: University of Minnesota president Eric Kaller faced an annual loss of nearly $140 million in state aid between 2008 and 2012 and responded in pithy terms: "Institutions must standardize operations to a much greater degree and apply lessons learned from business."[67] Kaller and other senior managers want to apply market principles of the private sector to universities. They bring managerialism, which is a mind-set as well as a tool kit of methods and practices. From one country or region to another, the new management philosophy goes under various guises. This "techno-economic paradigm"[68] takes different forms. But everywhere, managerialism is a mentality, an approach that uses rational-choice techniques entrenched in neoclassical economics to optimize policy decisions.[69] It exists side by side with older ways of thinking and is reforming them.

Paradoxically, the new managers promise efficiency and university bureaucracies swell. A good deal of administrative bloat is attributable to more

64. Pasi Sahlberg, *Finnish Lessons: What Can the World Learn from Educational Change in Finland?* (New York: Teachers College Press, 2011), 92.

65. Cole, *The Great American University*; author discussion with Vest.

66. Further discussed in chapter 4.

67. Eric W. Kaller, "Cost-conscious at the University of Minnesota," *Washington Post*, January 5, 2013.

68. Gibbons, "Higher Education Relevance in the 21st Century," 22, 26, 56.

69. The neoclassical school posits that economic actors seek to maximize satisfaction in a rational manner and that competition leads to the efficient allocation of resources and market equilibrium.

elaborate auditing and assessment practices. Britain and Australia have adopted some of the most extensive research assessment exercises. More broadly, rules and procedures proliferate and become more complicated. The number of meetings multiplies. The managers have a penchant for empaneling committees and task forces. They typically establish positions for more deputies who hire a legion of assistants who in turn require secretaries, all of them needing office space, supplies, and equipment.[70] They also pay outside consultants to introduce techniques used in top business schools and the private sector. This reformation usually means that the administrative side of the budget increases relative to the instructional side.

With rising administrative costs, savings need to be found in academic programs. Managers have good financial reasons to be wary of overspecialization in a particular field, and are apt to merge departments, colleges, or even entire universities. The rationale behind consolidation is also that bigger units with more faculty will offer opportunities for new interdisciplinary programs and possibilities for collaboration, elevate a university's profile, and boost the institution in rankings. But these induced arrangements are frequently met with consternation or fierce opposition, even at universities with a culture of trust and a tradition of teamwork. And implementation of amalgamation can beget knotty problems. While cross-border mergers and acquisitions are common occurrences among corporations, the difficulties with them are different at the institutions of higher learning that hold dear the principles of shared governance and academic freedom. If consolidating academic units is mandated, the challenge is to get professors with competing philosophies of teaching and research to buy into a conjoint structure. For senior executives, educing consent among educators proves to be the path of least resistance, and with globalization, is not confined by territorial borders.

Also, it is worth laboring my point that in developing an outward orientation and reaping advantages from globalizing processes, universities have become global actors in their own right. They have foreign policies, serve as major sources of export earnings, and help propel economic growth.

Moreover, the mentoring that universities provide is ultimately realized in local, national, and global governance. South Africa's minister of trade and industry Rob Davies drove home this point. He attested that a root problem in his ministry is the education of staff, whose training is dominated by one standard paradigm—neoclassical economics.[71] Calling for position papers and briefs on myriad pressing matters, Minister Davies lamented the lack of rival frameworks to compete with the efficient-market hypothesis and inform

70. See Ben Ginsberg, *The Fall of the Faculty: The Rise of the All-Administrative University and Why It Matters* (Oxford: Oxford University Press, 2011).
71. Author discussion with Rob Davies, Pretoria, March 29, 2010.

debate. He emphasized the need to encourage heterodox views.[72] For good governance, be it in the state or corporate sphere, the task is to see complex problems from a variety of angles.

The connection to universities is patent. Higher learning is supposed to foster inquiring minds, some as staff expected to bring intellectual heft to governance units. Yet governors are handicapped if their aides are versed in a central way of thinking and without sufficient knowledge of different paradigms. Ultimately, the caliber of the next cadres of government officials will reflect their higher education.

While the geopolitics of higher education is an increasingly salient motif in international relations, the university's very purposes are being called into question anew.

72. Ibid.

CHAPTER TWO

Contending Purposes of
Modern Universities

IN A 1952 LETTER to the *New York Times*, Albert Einstein chided proponents of an education that gives priority to specialization over "an understanding of and a lively feeling for values." He maintained that the former can turn out "a well-trained dog [rather] than a harmoniously developed person."[1] A valuable education develops instead what Einstein deemed "precious" abilities: an appreciation of beauty and ethics.

Like the Spanish philosopher before him, José Ortega y Gasset, author of the famous treatise *Mission of the University*,[2] Einstein assigned top priority to a general education engaged in ideas and aesthetics. He regarded single branches of learning and professional specialization as worthy but of less importance. Most disciplines have nonetheless become more specialized and professionalized. The reasons include mounting pressure on the university for near-market returns, gauged by short-term performance measures; students' bona fide worries about finding gainful employment; and an incentive system

---

1. Albert Einstein, "Education for Independent Thought," *New York Times*, October 5, 1952, http://mczcm.wordpress.com/2006/12/19/albert-einstein-education-for-independent-thought/ (accessed October 4, 2013).

2. José Ortega y Gasset, *Mission of the University*, trans. Howard Lee Nostrad (London: Routledge and Kegan Paul, 1952). Reflecting on the British and German traditions in education, Ortega highlighted the crucial point that university reform and a higher education institution's overall purposes are intimately related. In his words: "The root of university reform is a complete formulation of its purpose. Any alteration, or touching up, or adjustment about this house of ours, unless it starts by reviewing the problem of its mission—clearly, decisively, truthfully—will be love's labour lost" (36). For Ortega, "this house" was only part of a national entity; the university, he believed, must be understood in a national context. It should be noted that he crafted this statement in 1930, a time of nationalism and during the run-up to the Spanish Civil War and World War II.

that rewards rapid publication—the number of articles and books in prestigious venues where judges tend to prize arcane and collectively self-referential articles. While the world needs good diplomats, doctors, dentists, lawyers, and other professionals, the university must incubate not only practical skills but also sensibility for ethics, history, and aestheticism.

My point is that higher education is a business unlike other businesses. The academic values integral to it matter because the university is in the public interest. Producing new knowledge and teaching future generations can benefit society at large. But this high ideal must be reconciled with down-to-earth challenges. As the university evolves, its purposes serve as guideposts for practice.

In this chapter, let us first peer into these issues by revisiting the historic purposes of modern universities. The initial task is to paint a broad-brush picture before detailing it. In the second section, the discussion turns to rival understandings of these purposes. Third, we will assess how the dominant views have been translated into reforms in higher education. The fourth section looks at tensions among value systems. Finally, we take stock of the unfolding principles that are reshaping higher education.

The Historic Missions of the University

Historically, universities have contributed to developing the interior mind and enabling humans to make sense of the outer world. The knowledge landscape is huge, and people need ways to make sense of their encounters with their social and natural environment. Higher learning leads to discovery of these interactions. Beginning in the nineteenth century, teaching and research at many (not all) universities have been for sowing curiosity about the mysteries of our universe. A main purpose of these institutions is to pose penetrating questions and search for meanings.

That said, universities make room for different kinds of knowledge, including big, beautiful theories without any apparent application, as well as other forms of inquiry that seek to remedy the imminent and intractable uncertainties of daily life. So, too, various types of knowledge can enrich a proud heritage and help cope with a difficult past. They transmit civilizational values from one generation to the next. They may also undermine those values. Scholars' métier is unsettling existent knowledge. It disturbs conventional ways of thinking. At the same time, academics must also reconstruct prevailing paradigms. They are obliged to offer alternatives—some of them, offbeat ideas. In this vein, universities are special arenas worth defending because uniformity of thought can crowd out dissent and limit possibilities for the future. But this freedom is not automatically conferred or upheld. The right for open debate about values and social justice cannot be taken for granted lest it be infringed. It must be won time and again.

For scholars, striving to cherish learning and to stimulate the imagination is a lifelong calling. The idea of the university is to make an appreciation of learning last forever. For Newman and like-minded thinkers, this kind of education would best serve students.

Is Newman's classical outlook antiquated? Have the time-tested priorities of the university shifted? How should they be updated? The need to refine them is evident partly because Newman's reflections on the relationship between the state and the university are undeveloped. Also, unprecedented challenges and subsequent debates about the role of higher education in relation to power and the market have arisen. This is certainly evident in contemporary Europe, where the evolution of universities has influenced the course of higher education in other parts of the world.

Newman's emphasis on teaching made a strong imprint on higher learning for generations to come. It stands in contrast to the model that Wilhelm von Humboldt, a late eighteenth- and early nineteenth-century philologist and political theorist, had already pioneered.[3] As head of the Section for Education, Religion, and Culture in the Prussian Ministry of the Interior, he piloted higher education reforms. Proceeding from his belief that the main purpose of the university is to advance science and then transmit knowledge to students, Humboldt organized state-funded research institutes and labs at the University of Berlin and supported general education suffused with research for students embarking on professions.[4] Dedicated to the spirit of scholarly discovery, the university offered the doctorate (the first and only degree at the time) to students, except in theology, though as candidates for advanced degrees, they could receive unofficial first degrees.[5] In addition, the Humboldtian model of research-based education placed a premium on academic freedom: individual scholars' right to research and teach as they please and the collective right of the faculty to manage its own affairs. During the nineteenth century, this ideal stemmed from the principles of freedom to teach (*Lehrfreiheit*) and freedom to learn (*Lernfreiheit*). This conception of higher education gradually spread across borders, including to France, with its Napoleonic, state-run, specialized *grandes écoles*, a structure unlike what the German reformers proposed.[6]

In the evolution of the university's purposes, widely used national terms of reference—the English, German, and French models—are noteworthy. Of

3. This paragraph draws on Daniel Dye, unpublished background paper, February 7, 2012.

4. Christophe Charle, "Patterns," in *A History of the University in Europe, Vol. 3: Universities in the Nineteenth and Early Twentieth Centuries (1800–1945)*, ed. Walter Rüegg (Cambridge: Cambridge Press, 2004), 47–48.

5. Daniel Fallon, *The German University: A Heroic Ideal in Conflict with the Modern World* (Boulder: Colorado Associated University Press, 1980), 33–34, 38–39.

6. Charle, "Patterns," 33–82.

course, there are subnational variations, too. Oxford and Cambridge, let alone other universities in Britain, are not replicas of one another. And no wonder that national archetypes of university missions proliferated in an age of nationalism. They are saturated with the larger socioeconomic environment around them.

In the late twentieth and early twenty-first centuries, educators gave expression to universities' global aspirations. More and more, distinctions between national and transnational education are withering. Exterior elements fuse with local dynamics, though not necessarily easily. The mission statements formulated in the 2000s have framed educational policies beyond national borders, sometimes igniting sharp opposition from those who favor bolstering nationalism or West-centrism as a mainstay of higher education.

Contentious Issues

At least four issues surrounding the upgrading of early models of purpose created by Newman and Humboldt have stirred controversy. Ultratraditionalists launched one line of attack against the directions of higher education, especially moves that derail teaching classical knowledge and embrace the study of non-Western civilizations and multiculturalism. A second in a series of interventions came from more historically minded academics. Third, emphasis is given to educators' failure to effectively deliver the university's rationale. Lastly, for other observers and participants, the material factor is front and center. The correlation of academic values and money has drawn extensive commentary from varied perspectives.

Scholars inspired by the philosophy of Leo Strauss of the University of Chicago mount an ultratraditional argument, stressing what they regard as enduring truths. These are deemed essentials in the Western legacy. Pride of place is given to great texts, such as the writings of Plato and Aristotle, and not context. In sharp contrast to cosmopolitans like Kwame Anthony Appiah, who picks up on the Kantian concept of humanity's linked fate,[7] Straussians regard history and culture as outside the compass of landmark contributions to Western civilization.

Adopting Strauss's precepts, Allan Bloom charts a paradox wherein openness taught in the schools eliminates the ability to make decisive moral and intellectual judgments and results in the closing of minds.[8] The culprit is fostering tolerance for different value systems and for a jumble of cultural

7. Kwame Anthony Appiah, *Cosmopolitanism: Ethics in a World of Strangers* (New York: Norton, 2006).

8. Allan Bloom, *Closing of the American Mind: How Higher Education Has Failed Democracy and Impoverished the Souls of Today's Students* (New York: Simon and Schuster, 1986); cf. James H. Mittelman, "Opening the American Mind: International Political Science," *PS: Political Science & Politics* 22, no. 1 (March 1989): 52–58.

standards. Bloom finds that the advent of new subjects of study and departments championing knowledge formerly excluded from the university are emblematic of political and economic decay, at least in the United States. According to Bloom, this tendency is an intellectual mistake rooted in universities' lack of purpose. Students are not gaining an appreciation of magisterial literature and ideas advanced by the great philosophers of the past.

Strauss's convictions have deeply influenced courses offered by esteemed professors like Harvard political philosopher Harvey Mansfield, and the thinking of other admirers such as *Commentary* magazine's longtime editor in chief Norman Podhoretz, the *Weekly Standard*'s founding editor Irving Kristol, and former U.S. deputy secretary of state and World Bank president Paul Wolfowitz, to name a few. Some of Strauss and Bloom's other intellectual heirs have parlayed their anti-relativist philosophy into curriculum at institutions where canonical works are mainstays of the academic program.

Second, it is argued that the problem that pervades higher education lies not in neglecting imputed verities but in failing to historicize the *longue durée*. One can pay homage to the classical texts produced by various civilizations and, at the same time, benefit from historical perspective. For example, Aristotle's many insights may be construed in the context of the Athenian polis with particular hierarchical relations among men and women, masters and slaves. On this view, a worrisome tendency in higher education is courting ahistorical readings of seminal works. Over the years, as the American Academy of Arts & Sciences reported, the balance has tipped toward narrow and fast payoffs and away from the grand flow of historical change.[9] The latter encompasses the ebbs and flows—the movements—undergirding here-and-now events. For academic programs, the challenge is to come to grips with the specific ways in which the world confronts both present-day issues and long-run shifts.

A third position is that the delivery system is at fault. Rawlings, a classicist who, as president of the University of Iowa and Cornell and the AAU, long lobbied on behalf of higher education, finds that a flaw in the efforts to secure public support for universities is the unconvincing ways in which academics have advocated for institutional needs and hopes.[10] Educators have not done enough to communicate a sense of the university's purposes and programs. Greater emphasis should be placed on how we explain to policymakers and the public what universities do and what we contribute to the well-being of societies.[11] Added to this, Rawlings and others who speak for universities call

9. American Academy of Arts & Sciences, Commission on the Humanities and Social Sciences, *The Heart of the Matter*, 32.

10. Rawlings, "The Biggest Problem Confronting Universities Is Not What You Think It Is," 6.

11. Ibid.; author telephone discussion with Hunter R. Rawlings III, September 20, 2012.

on the professoriate to provide education, especially at the undergraduate level, more effectively. This is a matter of the content of courses, how today's students learn, and the integration of knowledge across the curriculum.

Yes, universities should improve. But what would account for a failure to convince captains responsible for the fiscal health of the university and the general public to adequately support its operations? After all, many higher education institutions are home to schools or departments of communication. And most universities employ media and marketing experts skilled in messaging. These messengers are supposed to be torchbearers of university missions.

Thorstein Veblen, an economist and a sociologist, answered the question posed above in 1918. His response remains apt. Veblen pointed out that much of academic research and higher learning is, by its very nature, "obscure." He held that to the "laity," the university's work is "unseen, and it stays in the background."[12] I believe that he meant that major elements of higher education are inconspicuous because they are composed of numerous qualitative exchanges of ideas within the academic community and sometimes in informal settings such as corridors and coffee shops.[13] As indicated, these dialogues may materialize in the future and not immediately. But how then to react to demands for accountability and justify expenditure, particularly in hard times?

This query brings us to the fourth consideration: money. The correlation of academic values and pecuniary ends is a particularly vexing issue. Even before Veblen, the educational philosopher John Dewey had observed that intellectual energy is often directed to material rewards. He recognized that universities necessarily require revenue to maintain their operations—for libraries, equipment, staff, and so on—yet bear the risk of "academic materialism."[14] His admonition about how the pressure of finances can erode the ideals of the university gives pause:

> The great event in the history of an institution is now likely to be a big gift, rather than a new investigation or the development of a strong and vigorous teacher. Institutions are *ranked* by their obvious material prosperity. . . . The imagination is taken more or less by the thought of

12. Thorstein Veblen, *The Higher Learning in America: A Memorandum on the Conduct of Universities by Business Men* (New York: B. W. Huebsch, 1918), 139.

13. Veblen maintained that physical plant and material equipment are the visible elements that capture attention. Today, in the United States, these elements include lavish facilities, such as posh housing, fancy gymnasiums, retail outlets, and even spas, which help fetch exorbitant tuition and fees. But the Internet of course brings notice to both the tangible and less tangible aspects of higher education as well.

14. John Dewey, "Academic Freedom," in *The Middle Works, 1899–1924*, vol. 2, 1902–1903, ed. Jo Ann Boydson (1902; Carbondale: Southern Illinois University Press, 1976), 62.

this force, vague but potent; the emotions are enkindled by grandiose conceptions of the possibilities latent in money.[15]

The material factor not only occupies the intellectual imagination but is risky in terms of recalibrating the purposes of a university. Indeed, there is tension between two sets of values, the one based on market logic, the other on the intrinsic worth of learning. The former is an ethos of capital accumulation springing from pressure to expand monetary value. The latter is a spirit of knowledge accumulation, which pivots on developing the mind, and some such as Newman say for its own sake. Can the two be joined? On the one hand, both require forms of accountability. On the other, although the different values need not be pitted against one another, scarce resources and ascendant political ideas that favor market norms necessitate hard choices. So, yes, different kinds of purposes can be combined, but melding them is not a seamless matter. The rub is which and whose values are predominant in the mix.

If material thinking permeates the university, the peril lies in viewing the university as an "industry" that builds "intellectual capital" among "customers" and "managed" enrollments. In this idiom, both graduates and degrees are "products." Present-day discourse gives precedence to the notion that students are consumers and that the customer is always right. The risk lies in misvaluing the university's worth for invigorating the mind, bequeathing intellectual pleasure, and building character. Slipping into a monetized narrative at the expense of long-lasting intellectual values can hasten a transformation of the university's mission. The reward in adopting a critical perspective on this move lies in coming to grips with collective delusions in the form of shared dreams. The objective is not only to deconstruct normal knowledge but to reconstruct it and offer concrete alternatives.

In the pantheon of university purposes, critical reasoning thus involves unmasking established "truths."[16] An umbrella and often underspecified term, it entails recognizing and upsetting orthodoxies. Although this reflexive process may be discomforting, it involves more than skepticism and debunking. This cast of mind provides understanding of conventional wisdom and attempts to constitute a new common sense.

---

15. Ibid., 62–63, emphasis added. Also see Joan W. Scott, "Knowledge, Power, and Academic Freedom," *Social Research: An International Quarterly* 76, no. 2 (Summer 2009): 451–80.

16. On the centrality of questioning authority in higher education and advancing active learning, see Henry Giroux, *Critical Pedagogy in the New Dark Ages*, ed. Maria Nikolakaki (New York: Peter Lang, 1998); Paulo Freire, *The Politics of Education: Culture, Power and Liberation*, trans. Donaldo Macedo (South Hadley, MA: Bergin and Garvey Publishers, 1985); Paulo Freire, *Pedagogy of the Oppressed*, trans. Myra Bergman Ramos (New York: Continuum, 2002).

A critical thinker, Dewey posited that the goals of higher education institutions hinge on teaching about democracy and, more crucially, steeping students in a democratic milieu. He believed that a principal goal of higher education is to produce good citizens equipped with civic virtues: moral citizens who contribute to democratic life.[17] Dewey also emphasized that the university is a social experience comprised of qualitative human interactions. A constituent part of democracy, education requires "freedom of social inquiry and of distribution of its conclusions."[18] Dewey, the founding president of the American Association of University Professors (AAUP, launched in 1915), whose stated mission is to help organize the educational community to stand up for important principles and interests, insisted that the production and dissemination of knowledge at universities presupposes academic freedom, which he implored the professoriate to defend. To extend his reasoning, market values, unlike core educational values, promote quantities construed as capital and maintain restrictions that protect goods, including intellectual property, against competitors.

What Dewey called "academic materialism" is also a matter of governance. Good governance entails accountability. Hence, standards for private corporations are inscribed in law, monitored by professional associations, and engraved in codes of conduct. When business practices fail to correspond to legal and ethical norms, enforcement measures are sometimes available. For their part, universities, in principle, endeavor to live up to Dewey's belief in democratic governance, which was important particularly in the wake of the war against Hitler. They take pride in self-governance: peer review, rigorous tenure and promotion procedures, prerogatives among their internal stakeholders for making decisions on the directions of academic programs, and so on. But should the academy be exempt from ways in which other fields, such as engineering, medicine, and law, are subject to public scrutiny? The public pays taxes to governments, which in turn make direct and indirect allocations to public and private higher institutions. Why then treat universities as a special case?

The question of accountability is perforce a matter of regulation. As intimated, it has come to the fore in our times when some analysts and members of the public believe that the university is underperforming. One response to this concern is to stress that institutions of higher education are already accountable to bodies such as accrediting agencies and auditors that have recourse if they find that standards are lax. Another answer is that while university

17. The genesis of this view may be traced through Aristotle, *Politics*, trans. Ernest Barker (Oxford: Oxford University Press, 1995), 251–300, and Émile Durkheim, *Education and Sociology*, trans. Sherwood D. Fox (New York: Free Press, 1956), 61–90.

18. John Dewey, *The Public and Its Problems* (Athens: Ohio University Press, 1927), 168; Daniel Dye, unpublished background paper, February 14, 2012.

personnel sometimes err, the principles of autonomy and academic freedom mean that allowing them to do so and to seek to self-correct are better than the alternative, namely, external political control of intellectual inquiry and expression. Besides, insofar as universities no longer operate strictly or even primarily within a state's domestic jurisdiction, governments are unable to fully harness all their activities. Relying on new technologies, open universities have long-distance programs spanning national borders. Virtual universities do not require brick-and-mortar campuses in particular territories.

More and more, the university deploys corporate decision-making techniques and acts like a transnational corporation (TNC). True, TNCs seek profit and, in principle, universities pursue knowledge. Yet corporations also invest in R&D. They are knowledge producers, too. Globally, a growing number of universities are for-profit; and others are home to, or partners with, for-profit endeavors. Moreover, both public and private universities derive revenue from profitable ventures in the form of corporate contributions, government subsidies for grants and scholarships, and, in some instances, tax exemptions that partially offset the costs of MBA and other executive-training programs.

Just as universities differ from one another, TNCs are of course not all alike. But both sets of actors maneuver in a global environment characterized by incertitude and insecurity. In this arena, capitalists are ensconced in both the corporate and academic communities. Sparring for market share, they come into more intense competition with one another and have greater reach. For universities, the latter can take the form of franchise education with branch campuses or dual-degree programs; for TNCs, subsidiaries and joint business enterprises. Seeking economies of scale, these actors enter coalitions: university partnerships, interfirm alliances, and university-industry linkages. There is no mistaking another combination integral to academic life: the adage "publish or perish" is accompanied by the saying "partner or perish."[19]

So as not to invite easy accusations of reductionism, it cannot be overstated that the abovementioned patterns entail more than the global economy taking charge of universities. Necessarily, finances have long been a factor in higher education, notably when wars deeply affected its personnel, funding, and operations. Since the 1980s, the expansion of the market in university affairs, however, is patent. Increasingly effected by transnational networks, the spread and deepening of the market in the academy is variously called "commercialization," "commodification," and "corporatization." Although the

19. To signal the unevenness of some of these arrangements in the global South, the vice chancellor of a South African university turned this phrase into "partnerships of perish." As quoted in Gibbons, "Higher Education Relevance in the 21st Century," 55.

meanings assigned to these designations vary, their purveyors readily recognize the benefits and costs of engaging the world marketplace.[20]

In terms of gains, educational globalization can free people from provincialism and instill doubt against certitudes. A desire to reap the advantages of advanced technologies, troves of information, and access to new sources of knowledge is leading universities to reposition themselves. The propellant is not only the market, understood as an economic system. This would be too narrow a conception of how the market works. The material explanation needs to be stretched. The market is not all-determining. The ideology of the marketplace and ambition are in play.

Nowadays, some students readily embrace the market and want to prepare to enter it as knowledge workers. To cite an example from personal experience: in a PhD seminar called "Social Theory," a doctoral candidate wrote but one comment on the course evaluation form: "This course is not very marketable." At first, I was surprised at this seemingly enigmatic reaction to fourteen weeks of reading and discussing powerful concepts—those of Marx, Weber, Durkheim, Foucault, Said, Spivak, and others—about what binds societies and why some of them are torn apart. On second thought, the statement aroused my curiosity. What was the student really saying? I was sorry to disappoint and aware that an individual response may not reflect the sentiments of a peer group. Yet I took the criticism to heart and mulled the insight. What did this message signal about changing student needs and wants? Relevance construed as problem-solving in an applied form rather than basic, curiosity-driven learning? A preference for useful knowledge and contemporariness instead of historically grounded analysis? An ethic of value for money? Consumerist culture? The implicit standard for the caliber of higher learning increasingly betokens a new corps of knowledge workers oriented to entrepreneurial values, in keeping with faculty entrepreneurship.[21] More than career aspirations and pecuniary motives are integral to this standpoint. Likely, marketability

20. Sheila Slaughter and Larry L. Leslie, *Academic Capitalism: Politics, Policies, and the Entrepreneurial University* (Baltimore: Johns Hopkins University Press, 1997); Stanley Aronowitz, *The Knowledge Factory: Dismantling the Corporate University and Creating True Higher Learning* (Boston: Beacon Press, 2000); Bok, *Universities in the Marketplace*; Sheila Slaughter and Gary Rhoades, *Academic Capitalism and the New Economy: Markets, State, and Higher Education* (Baltimore: Johns Hopkins University Press, 2004); Robert A. Rhoads and Carlos Alberto Torres, *The University, State, and Market: The Political Economy of Globalization in the Americas* (Stanford: Stanford University Press, 2006); Harry Eyres, "Inspired by a True Amateur," *Financial Times*, January 12/13, 2013. For an effort to encircle the critical flank in a single framework, see Jeffrey J. Williams, "Deconstructing Academe: The Birth of Critical University Studies," *Chronicle Review* 58, no. 25 (February 24, 2012), B7–8.

21. See Matthew M. Mars, Sheila Slaughter, and Gary Rhoades, "The State-Sponsored Student Entrepreneur," *Journal of Higher Education* 79, no. 6 (November/December 2008): 638–70.

embodies a multifaceted and widely shared way of thinking about what universities should accomplish.

Universities state what they want to accomplish in formal goals articulated in their strategic plans. Strategic planning is shorthand for an institution's ambitions in the chase for status, prestige, and revenue. This exercise trumpets purposes, missions that intermingle the old and the new, continuities and discontinuities. The customary ones are not vanishing. Rather, they are receding relative to rising market values. This is an unsteady configuration inclining toward realignment.

Acknowledging this turn, Michigan State University (MSU) president Lou Anna Simon sent a message to alumni:

> We love our traditions and seasonal rhythms, but we are also energized by the *forces that are converging to reshape the higher education landscape*. MSU must boldly march to a different drummer as we become the university that defines the relevance of a land-grant mission for the 21st century.[22]

Noticeably, Simon composed her words soon after the demolition of Morrill Hall, one of the oldest buildings on campus. It was erected in 1899 as the Women's Building and named for the 1862 Morrill Land-Grant Colleges Act that established higher education in the United States.[23] Although the president of MSU, the country's first land-grant college, did not spell out "the forces that are converging" on higher education, she outlined her initiatives. Under the banner "Boldness by Design," they consist of aims to set the university at the forefront of innovation, a campaign to advance "high performance," and plans for transforming the educational experience through the use of leading-edge technology. Seemingly unremarkable in terms of the way in which people now talk about higher education, this discourse itself constitutes a major feature of a changing cognitive landscape.

For decision makers, reframing narratives about institutional missions and strategies is salient because it is a way to convince stakeholders to support policies. Echoing them periodically, say, at university events, is a way to build consensus. It legitimates moving modern universities from their avowed priorities of democratic citizenship, critical inquiry, and academic freedom toward other values.

Careful empirical research shows that in the last four decades, market logic has gained ground on academic-science logic.[24] Before the 1970s, and despite

22. Lou Anna K. Simon, "President's Message," *MSU Alumni Magazine* (Fall 2013): 3, emphasis added.

23. Further discussed in chapter 4.

24. Elizabeth Popp Berman, *Creating the Market University: How Economic Science Became an Economic Engine* (Princeton: Princeton University Press, 2012). The information in this paragraph is derived from her work, especially 8–9, 11, 39, 44.

the *Sputnik* space race during the Cold War, market logic played a small role in pure science. Back then, scientific knowledge was deemed useful primarily for its intrinsic value, not as a tool for private enterprise and as an engine for national economic growth. In the late 1970s and 1980s, new practices, such as faculty entrepreneurship, stemming from market logic, became more widespread. In her book on this shift, Elizabeth Berman traces the upswing of "the idea that science's value is realized through the marketplace."[25] The belief that science could solve growing practical problems came on stream. Visible signs became evident where people would pay for results produced by biotech, patenting, research centers, and technology parks. Among policymakers, innovation and public-private partnerships became watchwords.

Following upon industrial society, the advent of information capitalism provided a conducive context for orienting technological and scientific development to economic advances. Policymakers recognized that global flows of information and technology are key features of globalization, and have sought to ride these waves. In the final quarter of the 1900s, policy intellectuals framed the narratives "knowledge society" and "knowledge economy." And in 1996, World Bank president James Wolfensohn heralded his institution's role as a "Knowledge Bank." During Wolfensohn's tenure, the bank supported a vast amount of research and continues to do so. It has produced and circulated knowledge in the form of numerous papers and large data sets in keeping with its pro-market, globalizing projects. The emphasis is on lowering regulatory barriers and stoking cross-border trade, including imports and exports of science- and technology-intensive products subject to, and sometimes facilitated by, the strictures of intellectual property rights, albeit with backlashes against neoliberal globalization. The business of education has not gone untouched by such economic reforms. This domain is in fact central to them.

Reforms

At university after university, higher education reforms adapt to globalization. New knowledge and technology-driven industries are mainstays of globalizing economies. Universities tie into a web with other knowledge producers and technologists in corporations, national governments, and global governance agencies. In this cross-border epistemic network, some interplay is virtual and some of it touches down at research centers and training programs on university campuses. Striving for innovation, these endeavors converge in university globalization.

To make universities more innovative and globally competitive, higher education systems around the world have introduced reforms. The impetus

25. Ibid., 9.

stems from a desire to make educational policies work more efficiently, efficiency itself being linked to other shifts in the zeitgeist that knowledge is ever more important to economies and societies and that universities are vital for producing the skills and expertise requisite for the evolving global order. Universities are a pillar of this order. Reforms are meant to strengthen them.

Emphasizing the common elements of education reform throughout the world, some writers posit a "Global Educational Reform Movement."[26] An unofficial agenda, it borrows management models and methods from the corporate sector, such as data-driven assessment performance and numerical measures for accountability. It parallels the decentralization of public services in much of the world and homogenizes curriculum. This transnational movement lessens the scope of national policymaking. The alignment is toward the logic and operations of private firms. A push in this direction comes from the incentives offered by corporate philanthropy, bilateral funders, and global governance agencies.[27]

A Global Education Reform Movement scenario appears plausible because it looks like transformative processes now in train, subject of course to national and local variation. But there are other viewpoints. Tade Aina, executive director of the Partnership for African Social and Governance Research in Nairobi and a former program officer at the Carnegie Corporation of New York, calls for inflection in the reform thesis.[28] He holds that higher education restructuring in Africa has gone beyond reforms: "In spite of over a half century of interventions and waves of 'reforms,' higher education in Africa today consists of institutions, systems, and practices that lack distinct values and goals, or a mission and vision connecting them to the major challenges of their local and global contexts."[29] Aina is right about the reach of reforms. They constitute structural adjustment in the educational sphere.

One must come to grips, too, with different genres of reform in lieu of a single kind of global education reform. The social philosopher André Gorz marked reformist reforms and structural reforms.[30] Reformist reforms finetune the status quo. They rationalize it. These modifications emanate from above; they are top down. In comparison, structural reforms unsettle the prevailing system. According to Gorz, they fundamentally alter it and come from

26. Sahlberg, *Finnish Lessons*, especially 99–106. He credits, among others, Andy Hargreaves, *Teaching in the Knowledge Society: Education in the Age of Insecurity* (New York: Teachers College Press, 2003), and Andy Hargreaves and Dennis Shirley, *The Fourth Way: The Inspiring Future of Educational Change* (Thousand Oaks, CA: Corwin, 2009).

27. Sahlberg, *Finnish Lessons*.

28. Tade Akin Aina, "Beyond Reforms: The Politics of Higher Education Transformation in Africa," *African Studies Review* 53, no. 1 (April 2010): 21–40.

29. Ibid., 21.

30. André Gorz, "Reform and Revolution," *Socialist Register* 5 (1968): 114–43.

below. The one is partial; the other, more comprehensive. While piecemeal reformism does little to tug at the roots of problems, structural reforms promise to pull at them.

Gorz's formulation can be extended by reflecting on the experience of higher education since the 1970s. For one thing, regardless of whether reforms are minor or major in scope, they are not a totality. Reforms are introduced, then elaborated, and later amended, some of them inscribed in law. They are chain-like, with several links. Thus it may be possible to combine the types of reform that Gorz delineates without drawing too sharp a line between them.

Educators can initiate reforms that enable other reforms, reaching a new balance of power among actors. Impetus comes from above and below. It springs from within higher education institutions and outside them. In seeking to navigate this course, universities face the challenge of how to respond to the tensions that reforms generate.

Tensions

The predicament is that to some extent, universities need to be congruent with the knowledge environment, but prevalent reforms can entail a drift in their guiding purposes and mission. The scramble to benefit from globalizing forces and outperform competitors takes universities either in or out of line with their commitment to pursue wisdom.

The tension between wisdom and power is an age-old concern. When Plato distinguished between those with wisdom and those with power, he noted that the former rarely have power and the latter rarely have wisdom. The Platonic ideal was to keep them separate from one another.[31] In our era, friction in the pursuit of wisdom not only is over power but also concerns academic freedom, autonomy, governance, and culture. These conflicts in values, ideas, and social relations are connected to the contestation of power in different spheres of authority.

Operationally, political officials have used power to authorize transboundary activities, including global business deals. Yet porous borders invite problems. Surely this was a lesson of 9/11, leading to reassertions of state sovereignty in the interrelated ambits of national security and immigration. Certain policies in these realms, such as visa restrictions, deeply affect universities in their transnational efforts to recruit students, star faculty, and accomplished administrators.

Although discord in the quest for wisdom may be local, it is increasingly global, as universities expand their core missions to include international

31. *The Republic of Plato*, trans. Francis MacDonald Cornford (New York: Oxford University Press, 1965), 29, 262ff.

work. Efforts to link local and global engagement frequently take the form of joint ventures. Many of them are cross-continental programs. For example, the joint program run by the Kellogg School of Management neighboring Chicago and Hong Kong University of Science and Technology placed first in the *Financial Times* executive MBA ranking of the top one hundred programs. Its alumni have the highest average salary three years after graduation, are among the most international cohorts, and place in the leading ten for career progress, work experience, and goals attained.[32]

Cross-border MBA programs are prime instances of franchise education. Learners are located in one country and the degree-granting institutions in another. The collaboration may be between public and private universities. As mentioned, the line between them is indistinct. Permutations on the basic concept include twinning arrangements, joint or dual-degree programs, branch campuses, and regional hubs of education.

Few countries have remained idle or passive and allowed this trend to follow its own course. It has become too important to neglect. Many states' and higher education institutions' foreign policies are termed "internationalization" or "globalization strategies." Moving in this direction, certain actors such as the government of Singapore have thought more carefully and opportunistically than others about how to dial into educational globalization.[33]

To optimize its position in the knowledge business, Singapore launched its "Global Schoolhouse" initiative in 2002.[34] Following several reviews of its

32. Laurent Ortmans, "What Makes an Excellent MBA?" *FT Business Education*, October 21, 2013.

33. This process is spawning a burgeoning business for consultants who specialize in designing higher education globalization strategies. Drawing on a wide range of universities' encounters with globalization, they tailor plans for particular contexts. Most of their presentations display an array of data and feature technological sophistication. Yet the consultants often fail to include two crucial components of agreements with overseas universities. One is guidelines on academic integrity, especially important in cross-cultural arrangements that take place in different settings. Second, an exit scenario with a clause for ending a contract should be a key provision of a memorandum of understanding. These stipulations ought to allow for cause for early termination. Moreover, the drawback to many internationalization strategies is a lack of coherence. Typically, they consist of a list of sundry activities. The rubrics can be packaged as pat phrases—"enhancing the university's international presence," "creating new international partnerships," and "advancing global dimensions"—without serious reflection on organic connections to the home campus's history, academic priorities, and ongoing activities. In short, extant strategies mainly offer add-ons, partly driven by a desire to catch up with competing universities. For the most part, the success of these programs is then gauged by quantity, such as the sheer number of study-abroad centers. Lastly, forward thinking about reshoring, that is, twenty-five-year scenarios when overseas universities are no longer needed or desired, is also wanting.

34. Information in this paragraph is borrowed from Kristopher Olds, "Global Assemblage: Singapore, Foreign Universities, and the Construction of a 'Global Education Hub,'" *World Development* 35, no. 6 (June 2007): 959–75, and Ka Ho Mok and Kok Chung Ong,

higher education system, plus overseas trips to ascertain best practices, Singapore established a reform process. The objectives were to improve the quality of its human resources, tap into the lucrative market for education, and attract foreign knowing experts. Initially, the reforms comprised three phases: empaneling an International Academic Advisory Board of eminent scholars and high-level corporate officers to assist the government in developing world-class universities; building up a new private university, the Singapore Management University, in cooperation with the Wharton School of Business at the University of Pennsylvania and in competition with the local public universities; and granting them greater autonomy in return for more accountability.

Additional steps have been taken to advance Singapore as an international education hub. The arrangements increase the number of alliances between local Singaporean universities and prestigious overseas partners. Among others, innovative graduate degree programs and research endeavors in engineering, founded by the National University of Singapore (NUS), the Nanyang Technological University, and MIT, have drawn notice around the world. The Singaporean approach looks to partnerships to link with brand-name institutions abroad. These have included the Australian National University, Carnegie Mellon University, Centre National de la Recherche Scientifique, Cornell University, Shanghai Jiao Tong University, Stanford University, the University of Pennsylvania, and Waseda University. In short, the government of Singapore has been proactive in its attempt to craft a coherent globalization strategy and concert various actors.

While Singapore is more deliberate in the higher education field than most countries, its experience illustrates a shift in the role of the state and in the regulatory environment. While the state serves as a facilitator for market forces, we come to the crux of the issue. In principle, the university is dedicated to open-ended inquiry, and globalization is also devoted to openness. But the one is about free expression; the other, free markets. Growing tensions emerge in this relationship and are palpable.

Universities' pledge to uphold academic freedom is neither a given nor an abstraction.[35] While traditions, codification, and parameters vary from one context to another, the idea of academic freedom rests on a set of rights and responsibilities for members of the university community. These are respect for the dignity of others, critical inquiry, the importance of dissent, and the

---

"Asserting Brain Power and Expanding Education Services: Searching for New Governance and Regulatory Regimes in Singapore and Hong Kong," in *The Emergent Knowledge Society and the Future of Higher Education: Asian Perspectives*, ed. Deane E. Neubauer (London: Routledge, 2012), 139–60.

35. For an elaboration of points in this paragraph, see James H. Mittelman, "Who Governs Academic Freedom in International Studies?" *International Studies Perspectives* 8, no. 4 (November 2007): 358–68.

call for debate and intellectual integrity. And with academic freedom, some scholars advise the prince; others tilt against convention. We have the right to ratify or challenge received wisdom and engage controversy, including repugnant views. Yet as a matter of practice in some countries, including the United States, with its legacy of McCarthyism, academic freedom remains fragile. Public trust in the university declines if the academy is too insular. Undoubtedly, insularity within the university can become a danger. The antidote is continuing effort to ensure openness to criticism from outside groups so that academics engage the public.

The ideal of openness at universities is unlike that of profit-making enterprises. Global firms do not operate according to the ethical code to which universities pledge to subscribe. Granted, some companies endorse social responsibility compacts. Still, they want their employees to do what is commercially viable and eschew public controversy. Ultimately, corporations are hierarchical organizations that attempt to generate wealth and guard their innovations from competitors. Many businesses promote open borders and open information insofar as the arrangements heed the bottom line.

In fact, some university-industry partnerships have resulted in acute conflicts. In the 1970s, Harvard and Monsanto, a transnational agricultural and biotechnology corporation, negotiated a contract for research collaboration in the area of a substance believed to regulate tumor development. This business deal offered potential for fighting cancer as well as $23 million for the study. At the time, questions were raised. Would the project circumvent peer review? Would proprietary knowledge and profit-making contravene academic freedom? What would these market dynamics mean for other university contracts?[36]

More recently, universities seeking to secure their market share of global education have opened campuses abroad and then faced restrictions on political discussions. Chinese authorities stopped the Johns Hopkins University School of Advanced International Studies center in Nanjing from showing a documentary on the 1989 Tiananmen Square uprising. The government of China also prohibited the campus from distributing a student journal.[37]

China, Singapore, Malaysia, and the Gulf states, among others, have offered attractive deals to prestigious universities and museums to lend their imprimatur and start branches in host countries. The United Arab Emirates has offshoots of New York University (NYU), the Sorbonne, the Louvre, and Guggenheim. Qatar's Education City has Cornell, Georgetown, Northwestern, Texas A&M, and Carnegie Mellon. NYU and Yale University have been two of the more ambitious institutions going forward with these projects. Yet the

---

36. Berman, *Creating the Market University*, 8.

37. Jim Sleeper, "Liberal Education in Authoritarian Places," *New York Times*, September 1, 2013.

presidents of NYU and Yale, John Sexton and Carl Levin, respectively (and now emeriti), encountered resistance to their universities' global ventures in authoritarian settings. Yale's faculty passed a nonbinding resolution expressing reservations about these initiatives. The signatories cited concerns in respect to constraints on free speech, including self-censorship by participating professors at the Yale-NUS College, as it is known.[38] The climate for free expression is tempered and "out-of-bounds markers" remain.

In such ventures, safeguards for academic freedom are rarely formalized.[39] Questions crop up regarding the compatibility of overseas academic programs not only with outright political controls but also in respect to restraints on human rights in areas such as gender, sexual orientation, and disabilities. The problem is the fit between liberal arts values and illiberal regimes that rein in academic freedom.

The contention over branch campuses, degree programs overseas, training courses abroad, and advisory services, as well as the financial implications of these partnerships, are fundamentally about a university's purposes. The discomfort of some faculty with the agenda and procedures relates to academic prerogatives. Who decides on amending an institution's mission and its global ambitions? Although the word "consultation" is often used, the concern is basically one of ownership. In the case of the Yale-NUS College, some Yale faculty members frame the root issue as a matter of university governance.[40] Who has a say, and how are differences resolved?

For host countries, university reforms also create tensions over cultural protection. The increase in the number of students and faculty from abroad, use of the English language in academic programs, and alignment with international education frameworks may be seen as marginalization. In some settings, local intellectuals, parliamentarians, and members of civil society groups claim that deemphasizing a national language leads to domination of the mind. For instance, the adoption of English in university courses in France and Italy has fueled discontent and triggered protests. Language is part of the larger fabric of ways of life that come with overseas programs and that can be at odds with local customs and violate laws, as with homosexuality.[41] And in host and home countries, universities' policies on recruiting international

38. Ian Wilhelm, "As Higher Education Goes Global," *Chronicle of Higher Education Almanac* 59, no. 1 (August 31, 2012): 93; Jackson Diehl, "An F in Academic Freedom," *Washington Post*, January 24, 2013. Alleging that NYU's Tisch School of Arts in Singapore failed to provide high-quality education, its former students pressed the case in court and, as a result, the home university closed Tisch Asia in 2012.

39. See n33 above.

40. Karen Fischer, "What's in a Name? For Yale in Singapore, a Whole Lot," *Chronicle of Higher Education* 58, no. 36 (May 11, 2012): A1, A22–24. Also see Olds, "Global Assemblage."

41. Exemplified in chapter 6.

students have caused consternation. In the United States, "bounty hunters"—a burgeoning consultancy industry—receive a fee per tuition-paying student whom these recruitment agencies enlist from overseas.[42] This allegedly predatory practice has provoked indignation. Such unanticipated consequences of reforms provide occasion to revisit the basic purposes of universities.

Then and Now

That there is no single perspective on the university's purposes is in keeping with its spirit of encouraging free expression. Global pressures have not quelled this spirit. But the tides of reform endanger it.

In the 2000s, university reforms came amid deep transformations wrought by a global economic crisis. As pointed out, the consequences of neoliberal policies include expanding space for "relevant" areas of study and reducing it for foundational fields, especially the arts, classical languages, history, and philosophy. The risk is that today's relevance may become tomorrow's irrelevance. And after all, the space for higher learning differs from other spaces in economic and political life: universities are for forming minds, training the next generation, and developing new knowledge. On the one hand, they must share the burden of economic stagnation or downturns and adjust to changing times. On the other, the accommodations need not elevate the value of money culture and hypercompetition, undervalue the importance of local context, and diminish elemental principles.

To recapitulate, the modern university's raisons d'être are threefold: building democratic character, fostering critical understanding, and safeguarding academic freedom. Within this compass, the university allows for pluralism and has a variegated set of purposes. In a complex world, much can be said for adding to the university's illustrious missions. But an inclusive approach is one thing, and mission creep that entails confusion about a higher institution's objectives is another. Navigating these channels requires more careful consideration of steering the course.

While continuing to bring intellectual gratification, universities are striving to respect students' legitimate job needs and link more effectively to the labor market. Many institutions of higher education realize that they must strike a balance appropriate to their own context. Clearly, a love of learning

---

42. Tamar Lewin, "Schools Use Controversial Commissioned Agents to Recruit Foreign Students," *New York Times*, May 13, 2008; "NACAC Assembly Approves New Policy for Recruiting International Students," National Association for College Admission Counseling (Arlington, VA, 2013), http://www.nacacnet.org/media-center/PressRoom/2013/Pages/NACAC-Assembly-Approves-New-Policy-for-Recruiting-International-Students.aspx (accessed October 8, 2016); Stephanie Saul, "Recruiting Students Overseas to Fill Seats, Not to Meet Standards," *New York Times*, April 19, 2016.

and practical skills are not necessarily opposed to one another. Both require curiosity integral to the process of discovery.

The reason to nurture higher learning is the sheer joy of it. Intellectual pleasure becomes a habit of the mind. The journey is lifelong. Testimony to its rewards arrived in a 2011 email message that began: "I'm certain that you don't remember me after so much time has past [*sic*]. I attended a contemporary civilization section at Columbia University which you taught in the fall of 1979."[43] By way of introduction, this former student from decades ago also related that he had earned an advanced degree in biology and is enjoying a career at a research center, where he heads a lab. He then conveyed how our course together had made an impact on his perspective of the world. "I still remember the two quotes on the board the first day of class: The owl of Minerva spreads its wings only at the coming of the dusk. and [*sic*] The philosophers have interpreted history now we must change it."[44]

Drawn from Hegel's *Philosophy of Right*, the first allusion is to Minerva, the Roman goddess of wisdom and her companion the owl, which flies at dusk, suggesting that knowledge is retrospective and can provide understanding only after an event. The second reference is to Marx's *Theses on Feuerbach* (thesis 11), a critique of idealism. Marx contends that socioeconomic forces condition ideas and interpretation, and calls for action to alter unfolding events. The tension between these passages, argued in class by students, prompts questions about the correlation of ideas and material power, an issue later addressed by Weber in his treatise on religion and capitalism, as well as by postmodernists and poststructuralists.

By confronting historic debates, graduates are better prepared to develop their own perspectives on the world. The success of higher education is not just being versed in great literature; it also lies in knowing where one stands in relation to competing positions. In the case of the author of the email—by no means, an atypical graduate—his curiosity aroused by issues posed in a freshman seminar has informed pathways in his marvelous career. He has savored our texts for decades. And for me, that's what makes the university a splendid place to work.

Seen in this light, the university is an arena for intellectual engagement. How to forward students toward that end, as Newman put it, may now be by different means, such as with new technologies. But the university remains a distinctive space, whether physical or virtual, yet, given the magnitude of world problems, ever more "precious"—to recall Einstein's adjective describing the knowledge that the humanities convey to younger generations.[45]

43. A former student, email message to author, January 7, 2011.
44. Ibid.
45. As quoted in the opening paragraph of this chapter. Einstein, "Education for Independent Thought."

Intellectuals need their own space for debate and creativity. This space is a sanctuary for critical reflection, though not to be detached from societal conditions. These safe places harbor nonconformists and are homes for stewards of the future. They are a locus where faculty and students may choose to channel their energies in ways that produce an altered kind of education and society. But this is a question of what's transforming universities and who is spearheading university reforms.

CHAPTER THREE

Drivers of Reform

WHAT IS DRIVING UNIVERSITY REPURPOSING and who are the reformers? Insofar as these forces animate education policy, they are key to understanding global knowledge production and distribution.

In this chapter, my argument is that a loose meshwork of actors and processes is transforming higher education. By meshwork, I mean a complex in which networks form and may reconfigure universities. They participate in a global knowledge structure.[1] The university is one among many knowledge-producing actors in this structure.

In their own ways, multiple knowledge actors are fabricating the world-class dream. Differences among the purveyors of education reform are of course great. These groups compete for resources and influence and are rife with internal debate. Yet an approximate consensus on what constitutes "objective" excellence in higher education is emerging. Globalizers are shaping means of generating and propagating standards. This involves setting agendas and influencing opinion makers. It entails forging discourses and symbols and harmonizing programs. It includes rewarding certain practices and designing instruments for evaluating the results.

While one would not expect a grand design of repurposed higher learning, global standard-setting is brought about by building interelite consensus.[2] To explore this consensus formation, let us first investigate segments of the whole. We can thereby unravel knowledge governance. The trajectories will then come into focus.

1. On the concept of knowledge structure, see chapter 1, n49.
2. On standard-setting, consult Craig N. Murphy and JoAnne Yates, *The International Organization for Standardization (ISO): Global Governance through Voluntary Consensus* (London: Routledge, 2009); Valerie Sperling, *Altered States: The Globalization of Accountability* (New York: Cambridge University Press, 2009).

Ten groups of actors seem most salient, though other catalysts could be identified as well. They propel change and fuel its processes. These cosmopolitan agents are ensconced in the following institutions and milieus: (1) governments, (2) consultancies, (3) global governance agencies, (4) regional organizations, (5) accrediting bodies, (6) ranking boards, (7) higher education philanthropies, (8) think tanks, (9) technology communities, and (10) universities themselves.

While formalities like treaties, declarations, and written constitutions are in play, the intricacies and meanings are subtle. These are often informal understandings rather than recorded policies. In the jockeying among the knowledge communities noted above, standards are insinuated as narratives, practices, and norms. They may become regulatory or quasi-regulatory frameworks and means of self-regulation. The latter, soft governance, mainly relies on co-optation rather than coercion and is the more cost-effective way.

The point is that no one knowledge group or individual superintends this modus operandi. It is a matter of collective action. A quilt of designers has created and enables it.

The interconnections among diverse knowledge producers with varied interests can be opaque and flout regulation. The driving actors' interests are manifest through processes such as accreditation and rankings. These processes express interests and are not autonomous activities.

Over the last five decades, the number of players whose actions have serious consequences for knowledge governance has grown in ways that, in aggregate, are little understood. It is important to map these forces and consider the extent to which they coalesce. This chapter will thereby focus on convergence and divergence in higher education. We will proceed by examining clusters of actors and processes.

Governments and Consultants

The place to begin is with the domestic sources of education reform. Policies are rooted at the local and national levels. This is a fulcrum of restructuring universities. State funding or defunding spurs the repurposing of universities, even though the impetus is increasingly blended with extranational factors. Finances are but one of many mechanisms in this trend. State capacity, the reach of government departments and ministries, and the role of intermediary state agencies—buffers such as higher education commissions—are vital elements in regulatory reform.

States' basic principles in the area of university reform are reflected in their bilateral and multilateral education strategies. While governments name and rename their units differently, ministries of education and of international cooperation and development help formulate and execute strategies for university reform. The U.S. Agency for International Development (USAID)

Education Strategy 2011–2015, for example, gives priority to supporting good governance, effective management, and learning outcomes.[3] According to USAID, since globalization demands a more highly skilled and competitive workforce, developing countries must expand access to higher education, improve its quality and relevance, achieve greater equity, and build a research agenda. USAID maintains that it can achieve its goals by partnering with the private sector and leveraging with other donors. Additionally, USAID pledges that it will deliver assistance for knowledge-sharing in the following manner: "Mission education officers must be connected in a global network of education professionals, allowing them frequent interchange of new ideas, recent innovations, best practices, and lessons learned from other countries."[4] This involves coordinating more fully with the World Bank, because the bank is a pacemaker in university restructuring and commands substantial resources. In tandem, these organizations award government contracts to private firms and build U.S.-style universities in conflict-ridden or postconflict areas, particularly Iraq and Afghanistan.

The USAID statement cited in the preceding paragraph is significant in that the language in this script is seemingly value neutral. But it contains tropes. Partnerships among USAID, government agencies or ministries in other affluent or relatively affluent countries, and the World Bank are highly influential. With its sizable contingent of researchers and means of dissemination through training programs and advisory services, the bank promulgates values and ideas. It identifies best practices, which are for specific purposes and which accord with the lenders' missions. Operationally, they favor problem-solving knowledge rather than curiosity-driven, critical inquiry.[5]

Targeted funding rarely supports basic research, which is needed to produce advanced knowledge. These allocations also reflect the academic values of higher education institutions at home rather than in host countries. Consultants are hired on contracts to translate values into vernaculars and suggest how to implement them on the ground. They do not frame the main questions for research but work within parameters set by funders. This commissioned research can divert energy from autonomous discourses and sap critical thinking. Typically, the findings are without academic peer review. Although consultants may of course decide for themselves whether to devote their time to donors' projects, material incentives, especially at underfunded universities, are hard to spurn. Indeed, in many countries, home universities form consulting operations for selling services to funding agencies and corporations. And some intellectuals hive off from higher education institutions to establish their own consulting firms.

3. United States Agency for International Development, *USAID Education Strategy 2011–2015* (Washington, DC: USAID, 2011), 12.

4. Ibid., 20.

5. Gibbons, "Higher Education Relevance in the 21st Century," 15, 16, 55–56.

It may be argued that donors elicit local and national ownership of education projects. To be sure, many academic executives who run universities and manage faculty affairs share the values of the transnational elites in governance agencies and are also incentivized to embrace their missions. Typically, the intellectual formation of these elites in different countries bears commonality, albeit with secondary differences and occasional discord. Anchored in a knowledge structure, their training includes study-abroad, exchange programs, grants, awards, and opportunities to publish with prestigious presses or in highly touted journals. The reward system embodies best practices defined in reference to market mechanisms. And recipients of paymasters' funds are not free to spend the sums however they choose. These monies are restricted for certain uses. Eventually, the sources of revenue dry up. Donor support is fickle and likely unsustainable. In home and host countries, it is subject to political priorities and market conditions that fluctuate at the locus of decision making.

Global Governance and Regionalism

In this section, I show how donors have sought to harmonize their higher education programs and the priorities of various stakeholders. My claim is that there is a multilateral flow carrying the world-class dream. Heavily influenced by the U.S. model, it merges with varied national and regional structures and begets myriad responses. The task here is to trace this evolving pattern.

Even before the United Nations Educational, Scientific and Cultural Organization (UNESCO) was established in 1945, talk about global authority in the education arena was rife. So, too, defenders of national sovereignty have long favored funneling funding for education overseas through bilateral agencies and the World Bank. While certain international organizations like UNESCO and the United Nations Development Programme (UNDP) participate in this process, they are little by little turning into global management institutions unable to address deep structural problems. In respect to higher education, UNESCO is especially hampered by a lack of resources. And UNDP shifted from its social democratically inspired orientation to more of a monitoring role in regard to the Millennium Development Goals and, post-2015, the Sustainable Development Goals: a set of global standards and a framework for consensus centered on UN quantitative targets for advancement toward development. UNDP measures the extent to which individual countries have realized these numerical objectives.

With the rise of neoliberal globalization, organizations in the UN system traditionally charged with social policy have, on balance, played diminished roles in education reform.[6] In their stead, the World Bank Group and the

---

6. Neoliberalism is explicated in chapter 4, and subsequent chapters examine neoliberal globalization's impact on higher education in different contexts.

World Trade Organization (WTO) have been predominant trendsetters in re-structuring higher education.[7]

For the WTO, education is a service sector subject to trade liberalization.[8] The WTO administers the General Agreement on Trade in Services (GATS), which reduces trade barriers to cross-border flows of knowledge. The impediments include visa restrictions, taxation that holds back foreign institutions, accreditation schemes that benefit domestic institutions, and national or sub-national restraints on the recognition of higher education qualifications and quality assurance. A key feature of GATS is the Most Favoured Nation rule, which entails conditional and unconditional obligations to treat foreign trading partners equally, albeit with certain exemptions. In other words, all competing service suppliers in the WTO's 164 member countries must be given market access and the same opportunities available to domestic providers.

GATS is a mechanism for facilitating greater mobility of professional educators and students. It may lead to long-term migration as well. Known as "brain circulation," brain drain for some is brain gain for others. The regulatory framework for importing and exporting education services, including population flows, is of great importance in respect to licensing, accreditation, and quality assurance. It can augment national capacity but also undermine national efforts to strengthen higher education. For universities in some parts of the world, the substantial benefits offered by foreign suppliers are attractive. But others worry about the risks of Western hegemony and the dilution of local culture, particularly indigenous knowledge.

In addition, instruments for reducing trade barriers pertain to the value of the intellectual content of products and services. The Trade-Related Aspects of Intellectual Property Rights agreement addresses patents, trademarks, and copyright.[9] These pacts bear directly on instructional programs and scholarly research at universities. With the further liberalization of international trade, enthusiasts of educational globalization point to the prospects of greater opportunities for professional mobility, better working conditions, and higher salaries. But critics fret about more commodification of higher learning, diminishing national control, and the lack of accountability in a dense multilateral system with ill-defined lines of authority.

---

7. See Craig N. Murphy, *The United Nations Development Programme: A Better Way?* (Cambridge: Cambridge University Press, 2009); Karen Mundy, "Education for All and the Global Governors," in *Who Governs the Globe?* ed. Martha Finnemore, Deborah Avant, and Susan Sell (Cambridge: Cambridge University Press, 2010), 333–55; J. P. Singh, *United Nations Educational, Scientific and Cultural Organization: Creating Norms for a Complex World* (New York: Routledge, 2011).

8. The passages below on the WTO draw on Jane Knight, "Trade in Higher Education Services: The Implications of GATS," *Kagisano*, no. 3 (Autumn 2003): 5–37.

9. The protection of intellectual property rights comes under the joint purview of the WTO and the World Property International Organization.

An important aspect of this debate is the designation of higher education as a service. It is a leading export for certain countries. For the United States, education is among the top ten service exports, accounting for almost $23 billion by 2012.[10] This service involves education information, provision of distance learning, facilities, management fees, and so on. The difficulty with the WTO approach is that it can undercut the public-good aspects of higher education. If the business of higher education institutions is to nurture democratic values, critical thinking abilities, and unfettered academic freedom, the vagaries of the market inscribed in standards for international trade are not intrinsically linked to the university's basic purposes. Furthermore, it will be argued that these regulatory standards are a major factor in repurposing higher education institutions.

In international-bank talk, some multilateral initiatives are "co-brokered" by more than one organization because they include varied components of trade, finance, and development. These activities fit the blended portfolios of bilateral agencies and regional development banks.[11] The range of policy domains embroiled in such operations is vast: the interplay of laws, rules, staffing, technology, and other services.

More specifically, the World Bank's influence in higher education may be best understood in light of how it has evolved since the 1980s. After the 1981 Berg report advanced the idea of valuing higher learning on the basis of a calculated rate of return, the bank decided to concentrate its lending on the primary and secondary levels; it found that higher education has lower economic output.[12] A number of private funders followed the bank in defunding higher

10. United States Department of Commerce, International Trade Administration, "Education as a Top Service Export," *Tradeology blog*, September 4, 2012, http://blog.trade.gov /2012/09/04/education-as-a-top-service-export/ (accessed January 20, 2013), and "Can Next-Generation Education Have an Effect on U.S. Education Exports," *Tradeology blog*, September 27, 2013, http://blog.trade.gov/2013/09/27/can-next-generation-education -have-an-effect-on-u-s-education-exports/ (accessed January 20, 2013). U.S. International Trade Commission, "Recent Trends in U.S. Services 2013 Annual Report," Publication 4412 (July 2013): XV.

11. The bilateral agencies include the Asian Development Bank, the U.K. Department for International Development, Agence Française Développement, Danish Development Policy, the Australian Agency for International Development, New Zealand Aid, USAID, the Ministry of Foreign Affairs of Japan, and the European Commission. Regional development banks also promote education reform. The African Development Bank, the Asian Development Bank, the European Bank for Reconstruction and Development, and the Inter-American Development Bank seek to coordinate their programs with the World Bank. In addition, these multilateral groupings encompass subregional development banks, such as the Andean Development Corporation, the Caribbean Development Bank, and the North American Development Bank.

12. World Bank, *Accelerated Development in Sub-Saharan Africa: An Agenda for Action* (Washington, DC: World Bank, 1981); Joel Samoff and Bidemi Carrol, *From Manpower*

learning. These actions accorded with the International Monetary Fund and World Bank's structural adjustment programs (SAPs), which provided loans conditional on adopting a policy framework of privatization, deregulation, and reduction of external trade barriers. In many borrowing countries, these economic reforms, especially cuts in public spending on higher education, eased the way for foreign competitors and accelerated the brain train to the global North.

In the thick of strident criticism of the deleterious effects of its policies, the World Bank rethought its higher education strategy in the late 1990s and early 2000s. It came to regard higher education as a key factor in the global knowledge economy.[13] Meanwhile, the bank became increasingly circumspect about SAPs. By 2004, this framework fell into disfavor for three reasons: the bank's failings during financial crises, particularly in Asia in 1997–98; the rise of emerging market powers, some of which offer alternative sources of finance to borrowing countries without stringent conditions; and civil society protests against SAPs owing to their neglect of the social dimensions of reform, including gender hierarchies, marginalization, and vulnerability.[14]

Amending its narrative, the World Bank emphasized its dedication to poverty alleviation and promoted revised scripts: namely, local and national ownership, good governance, macroeconomic growth, and social sustainability. But what do these discourses mean in lived practice? While the bank prepares impact studies, its assessments are paid for, and subject to approval by, their sponsors. The bank sets standards of success or failure and then measures its own performance and that of recipients of its loans against these same categories.[15]

In higher education, the World Bank's impact largely comes from framing, developing, and transmitting knowledge—soft power traceable to technical

---

Planning to the Knowledge Era: World Bank Policies on Higher Education in Africa (UNESCO Forum Occasional Paper Series, paper no. 2, Paris, October 2003); Isaac Kamola, "The World Bank and Higher Education: From Poverty Reduction to a 'Global Knowledge Economy'" (paper presented at the annual meeting of the International Studies Association, San Francisco, April 3–6, 2013).

13. World Bank, *World Development 1998-99: Knowledge for Development* (Washington, DC: World Bank, 1998).

14. Author discussion with the president of a private firm, a former lead economist at the World Bank, Chevy Chase, Maryland, December 8, 2010.

15. The World Bank's Independent Evaluation Group reports to the Board of Executive Directors and not to the president of the bank, but critics on the right espousing free markets and on the left faulting market ideology offer external critiques beyond the parameters of internal assessment. Monitoring the bank's performance thus becomes a matter of determining the extent of this group's independence and perforce evaluating the evaluators. On varied critiques of the bank, see James H. Mittelman, "Globalization and Its Critics," in *Political Economy and the Changing Global Order*, ed. Richard Stubbs and Geoffrey R. D. Underhill (Toronto: Oxford University Press, 2005), 64–76.

assistance, policy advice (usually on a fee-for-service basis), training programs, and a website replete with vast data sets. In addition, the bank's own publications on global knowledge and education appear as a spate of books, book chapters, working papers, and scholarly articles in peer-reviewed journals. According to the bank, in one thematic area alone—the economics of education—its publications in journals are more numerous than those of fourteen leading universities, with only Harvard approaching the same total.[16] In these venues, bank staff, consultants, and networks report their research findings and tender ideas on how to realize institutional goals.

In its "Strategy 2020" agenda, the World Bank Group advocates education "system reform." This expansive concept takes in "the full range of learning opportunities available in a country" in the public and private sectors for all stakeholders from teachers and administrators to students and their families, plus ways to address barriers outside the system as it has hitherto been delimited.[17] To mobilize knowledge so broadly, the bank asserts: "It is not enough to simply get the technical details right; reforms must also navigate the challenges of a nation's political economy."[18] Concretely, this means learning from best practices, which are presented in handbooks on how to build world-class universities atop their competitors.[19] These practices are inventoried as checklists, negotiated, and stipulated in loan agreements.[20]

The World Bank Group's standardized template features greater private provision at nonprofit and for-profit institutions. It partly comes under the purview of the Bank Group's International Finance Corporation (IFC), the

16. World Bank, *Learning for All: Investing in People's Knowledge and Skills to Promote Development: Education Strategy 2020* (Washington, DC: World Bank, 2011), 53.

17. Ibid., 5.

18. Ibid., 72.

19. Peter Materu, *Higher Education Quality Assurance in Sub-Saharan Africa: Status, Challenges, Opportunities, and Promising Practices* (Washington, DC: World Bank, 2007); Jamil Salmi, *The Challenge of Establishing World-Class Universities* (Washington, DC: World Bank, 2009); Philip G. Altbach and Jamil Salmi, eds., *The Road to Academic Excellence: The Making of World-Class Research Universities* (Washington, DC: World Bank, 2011). I have gleaned information from discussions with staff members at the bank, especially Peter N. Materu, lead education specialist, World Bank, Washington, DC, December 21, 2010, and Jamil Salmi, then tertiary education coordinator, World Bank, Washington, DC, December 21, 2010.

20. For example, a "Summary Checklist" appears in Salmi, *The Challenge of Establishing World-Class Universities*, 10–11. In their formulations on how universities can achieve world-class status, World Bank research treats the race for the top as a war. Using aggressive imagery, the narrative of universities pitted against one another in "the rising international talent *war*" may be found in Jamil Salmi, "The Road to Academic Excellence: Lessons of Experience," in *The Road to Academic Excellence*, ed. Altbach and Salmi, 326, emphasis added. See also 325, and Salmi, *The Challenge of Establishing World-Class Universities*, 25.

world's largest multilateral investor in the private health and education sectors in emerging markets.[21] It is growing because public finances are not keeping pace with the demand for higher education. The IFC thus supports "educational entrepreneurs" and advances "Good Practice Propositions," to-do lists for achieving high-quality education.[22]

Added to this, global knowledge governance is interwoven with regionalism. An exemplar is the European Commission's Bologna reforms, a regulatory framework that channels globalization to member countries and attempts to mitigate its unwanted features, including what some observers deem the undue influence of U.S. norms at the expense of local values.[23] The Bologna Process is a driving force for European standards, a regional strategy wherein universities internationalize and seek to harmonize their programs.

The impetus for the Bologna policies was the desire to make European higher education more competitive globally, promote citizens' mobility, and enhance students' employability.[24] The 1998 Sorbonne Declaration called for the creation of the EHEA. It was launched as a voluntary approach the following year and now enlists forty-eight member countries. Specific measures have addressed how to make a mélange of education systems comparable and compatible. The architecture's main pillars are the standardization of a two-cycle degree structure (undergraduate and graduate), a quality assurance regime, a credit-transfer scheme, the Erasmus Programme to support mobility, and the use of learning outcomes and competence in "qualification frameworks."

Despite a common convention and protocols, the execution of the Bologna reforms in member countries has not been entirely coherent. Implementation has been uneven because of different national policies and myriad legal and institutional frameworks.[25] The two-tier bachelor's/master's structures are mostly achieved. But some countries—for instance, Germany, which faced stiff resistance from the professoriate—have slowly transitioned

21. International Finance Corporation, *IFC Annual Report 2010* (Washington, DC: IFC, 2010), http://www.ifc.org/ifcext/annualreport.nsf/Content/AR2010_HealthEd (accessed February 15, 2011).

22. John Fielden and Norman LaRocque, *The Evolving Regulatory Context for Private Education in Emerging Economies: Discussion Paper* (Washington, DC: International Finance Group, May 2008), 14–15.

23. Eva Hartmann, "Bologna Goes Global: A New Imperialism in the Making?" *Globalization, Societies and Education* 6, no. 3 (September 2008): 207–20.

24. *Bologna Declaration of 19 June 1999*, Joint Declaration of the European Ministers of Higher Education, www.ehea.info/Uploads/Declarations/Bologna_Declaration1.pdf (accessed December 10, 2013).

25. Torben Heinze and Christoph Knill, "Analyzing the Differential Impact of the Bologna Process: Theoretical Considerations on National Conditions for International Policy Convergence," *Higher Education* 56, no. 4 (October 2008): 493–510.

from the coexistence of the two cycles with its old programs, whereas the Netherlands swiftly adjusted its programs to the Bologna reform agenda.[26] Nonetheless, Erasmus has clearly facilitated cross-border exchanges, predominantly east-to-west flows within Europe. And it has spillover effects in extracurricular support: student services, counseling for those interested in study abroad, and information related to courses and other information in English.[27]

Yet in countries such as Austria and Germany, Bologna has encountered student protests in reaction to the top-down elements of a process said to be lacking democratic participation. Critics claim that "Bolognaization" is creating a mass-oriented bachelor's degree and an elite master's program, with more and more professionalization. At higher education institutions, there is concern that the Bologna Process is strengthening central management and championing market reforms, such the introduction of tuition fees and the reorganization of departments and universities, putting public education at risk.[28]

In terms of intercontinental congruence, some education policy analysts in the western hemisphere seek to learn from the European experience with reforms, though the cultural, legal, and institutional differences are of course salient, as within Europe itself. The lessons cannot be easily detached from their contextual underpinnings and transferred across the Atlantic, particularly to the United States, which takes pride in its reputed higher education excellence. That said, transnational influences from the Bologna Process and the EHEA are evident in the Asia-Pacific Quality Assurance Network, established with the backing of UNESCO and the World Bank in 2003. These measures are reflected in the goals and efforts of the Brisbane Communiqué area

26. Jeroen Huisman and Marijk van der Wende, "The EU and Bologna: Are Supra- and International Initiatives Threatening Domestic Agendas?" *European Journal of Education* 39, no. 3 (September 2004): 354.

27. *The Bologna Independent Assessment: The First Decade of Working on the European Higher Education Area*, http://ec.europa.eu/education/higher-education/doc/bologna_process/independent_assessment_1_detailed_rept.pdf (accessed December 11, 2013); European Commission, Directorate-General for Education and Culture, *The Impact of ERASMUS on European Higher Education: Quality, Openness and Internationalisation*, DG/EAC/33/20017, December 2007.

28. Sybille Reichert, "The Intended and Unintended Effects of the Bologna Reforms," *Higher Education Management and Policy* 22, no. 1 (March 2010): 14, 16; Tonia Bieber, "Transatlantic Convergence in Higher Education? Comparing the Influence of the Bologna Process on Germany and the U.S." (presentation at the American Institute for Contemporary German Studies, Washington, DC, November 10, 2011), and "Building a Bridge over the Atlantic? The Impact of the Bologna Process on German and U.S. Higher Education," http://www.aicgs.org/publication/building-a-bridge-over-the-atlantic-the-impact-of-the-bologna-process-on-german-and-u-s-higher-education/ (accessed December 11, 2013).

with twenty-seven signatory countries that stretch from Australia to Turkey.[29] Common elements linking the Bologna and Brisbane initiatives are the moves to identify best practices and harmonize quality assurance. Recognizing and periodically reviewing quality is the province of accrediting bodies and ranking systems. They set standards for programs and universities, and perform regulatory roles.

Accreditors and Rankers

Accreditation is meant to protect the rights of students and serve the public interest. This mechanism was developed to improve the caliber of higher education. In many countries, a university or program applies for official approval and if it is in compliance, receives full or provisional endorsement; if not, recommendations or requirements. The consequences for failing to meet them or not to apply at all involve ineligibility for some types of funding and apprehension among potential applicants. To satisfy accreditation agencies, universities must furnish several documents, usually including syllabi stating learning objectives and outcomes. Administrators or government designates a standard format for this exercise. The listing of objectives and outcomes can then be used as criteria in hiring and evaluating faculty members.

Speaking to these points, Ken Jones, dean of the Ted Rogers School of Business at Ryerson University in Toronto, indicated that accreditation "gives us leverage to get resources for high quality new hires."[30] Presumably he meant that it helps in negotiations with the central administration and for other sources of income. Jones also pointed out that this process has positively affected current faculty: "Everyone is working towards a common goal."[31] And when Canada's Peter B. Gustavson School of Business at the University of Victoria completed the twenty or so steps to attain accreditation from the Association to Advance Collegiate Schools of Business, university administrators found this time-consuming and expensive process to be valuable even though the school had already gained approval from a similar body, the European Quality Improvement System. According to Gustavson's associate dean, A. R. Elangovan, double accreditation signals that "you're one of the best. You are playing in the top league." As a result of this stamp of approval, "we found our ability to hire faculty and draw students was significantly enhanced."[32]

29. See Brisbane Communiqué and accompanying documents, https://www.aei.gov .au/About-AEI/Policy/Pages/BrisbaneCommuniqu%C3%A9.aspx (accessed December 12, 2013).

30. Erin Millar, "Schools Are Going for Big-League Cred," *Globe and Mail*, March 16, 2011.

31. Ibid.

32. Ibid.

Tom Scott, vice dean of the University of Alberta's school of business, added that the accreditation process "imposes self-discipline. It prevents you from becoming lackadaisical about your mission."[33]

However, accreditation is controversial because it normalizes certain practices and not others. Accreditors say that they act with integrity, provide value by ensuring that higher learning institutions furnish the public with accurate information about their programs and services, and foster accountability to an external organization. They believe that heightened government regulation over their scope circumscribes regulation by the academic sphere itself and threatens the intellectual independence of higher education. But their critics claim that they impose a hard-and-fast formula on institutions that require an accreditation committee's seal. Accreditation skeptics also say that conventional standards (for example, on tenure reviews) impede innovation, especially when technological and other forms of innovation offer opportunities to change universities and for nontraditional providers. From this perspective, accreditors are seen as powerful gatekeepers that safeguard their role as regulatory authorities so as to favor entrenched interests in fields like legal education, medicine, and engineering.

Accreditation agencies themselves can be costly, as are the steps for satisfying their standards and procedures: self-studies, recurring on-site visits by teams of experts, other peer-review methods, and action letters. The accreditation function can have stipulations for judging university libraries, percentage of full-time faculty, and research capabilities. Who then pays for accrediting and meeting its criteria? More basically, who decides on what criteria to employ?

Much depends on the country and field. Accreditation may be funded by government, user fees charged to universities, and supplements added to student tuition.

A bevy of questions arises. In view of academic freedom considerations, to what extent is and should accreditation be a governmental or nongovernmental process? Who assesses and, if need be, reforms the accrediting organizations? Are their proceedings and reports sufficiently transparent? While accreditation is largely carried out by subnational, national, and programmatic agencies in specific fields such as nursing or business, who is authorized to gauge the performance of universities' activities abroad? And in light of sometimes vast cultural, legal, and political differences between host and home countries, by whose standards of excellence? Do the regulatory authorities in varied contexts understand standards as the use of data and rubrics that define performance or as a democratic process? How to balance international and local principles on which educational excellence is judged? More and more, accreditors must look at universities' cross-border initiatives, but who

33. Ibid.

provides the remit? The integrity of this process is particularly worrisome in view of growing concerns about recruitment mills (enrolling as many students as possible regardless of their abilities and likely success), foreign degree mills (selling phony "parchment" degrees), accreditation mills (selling fraudulent accreditations), and unscrupulous for-profit providers (lacking recognition by national agencies).[34]

Similarly, as yet unsettled issues pertain to global ranking systems. Like accrediting agencies, they are regulatory instruments that give universities marks. Yet the ratings are more directly a by-product and catalyst of educational globalization.[35]

Prior to grappling with the broad import of global rankings, one should be mindful of their genesis. In the opening decades of the twenty-first century, the Shanghai Jiao Tong University Institute of Higher Education Academic Ranking of World Universities (known by its acronym ARWU) and the *Times Higher Education Supplement*'s/Quacquarelli Symonds (QS) World University Rankings (the THES) became staples of higher education. Established in 2003, ARWU is mainly centered on research indicators. And dating to 2004, the THES puts more emphasis on a survey of reputation. Since 2010, in cooperation with Thomson Reuters, it has introduced additional indices. The British company QS now produces its own world rankings, no longer published in collaboration with *Times Higher Education*. Other global-ranking scales are cropping up as well.[36]

Regional rosters for scoring the standing of universities, including the European Union's U-Map classification and its U-Multirank, are following suit, but with different methodologies. U-Multirank's website enables users to select criteria and create customized results based on comparisons of specific dimensions of institutions' performance such as teaching and learning, research, and international orientation. Sponsored by the World Bank and the Centre for Mediterranean Governance, the University Governance Screening Card Project and other schemes are similarly interactive. Yet many of these attempts at better counting, such as Webometrics Ranking of World Universities, mostly echo the ARWU, THES, and QS.

34. Jane Knight, "New Developments and Unintended Consequences: Whither Thou Goest, Internationalization?" in *Higher Education on the Move: New Developments in Global Mobility*, ed. Rajika Bhandari and Shepherd Laughlin (New York: Institute of International Education, 2009), 118.

35. Some passages below on rankings are adapted from James H. Mittelman, "Global University Rankings as a Marker of Revaluing the University," in *Global University Rankings: Challenges for European Higher Education*, ed. Tero Erkkilä (New York: Palgrave Macmillan, 2013), 223–35.

36. See Andrejs Rauhvargers, *Global University Rankings and Their Impact* (Brussels: European University Association, 2011), http://www.eua.be/pubs/Global_University_Rankings_and_Their_Impact.pdf (accessed October 29, 2012).

Diffused by new technologies, the values ingrained in global rankings bear an imprint of North American higher education. They stem from a national ranker—namely, *U.S. News & World Report* magazine, a private-sector venture launched in 1983—and the formats that inspired it. Other publishing companies in the United States, including large concerns such as Kiplinger and Forbes, soon joined *U.S. News* as competitors. And widespread use of the English language furthers the dissemination of these norm-laden systems.

In certain respects, numerical data comparing university performance can be beneficial. They convey useful information, challenge academics to improve their practices, and foster greater accountability. League tables also serve the purpose of heightening competition among higher education institutions and help differentiate them.[37]

Nian Cai Liu, director of the Center for World-Class Universities and dean of the Graduate School of Education at Shanghai Jiao Tong University, attests that in the late 1990s, China's political leaders prompted educators to prop up several world-class universities. Liu and his colleagues then launched the ARWU rankings in order to better position their university relative to the standing of competing institutions.[38] In our conversation in Shanghai, he noted that the rankers are professors of education at Shanghai Jiao who developed the ARWU system as a facet of their own research and without external funding from government or private enterprise.[39] Using third-party data sets published by Thomson Reuters and from other sources, but not universities' own statistics, they aim to measure what is measurable—mainly research output and not teaching or service.

But rankers cannot measure and compare performance in terms of the extent to which universities are building character, intellectual curiosity, and love of learning. There is not yet a way that such complexities of higher education institutions' performance on these mission-oriented issues can be captured by numerical ratings, partly because of the time lag involved. It would seem, too, that it is a matter of self-interest for any university, including Shanghai Jiao Tong, to rank itself relative to its competitors. This brings us to the high stakes in the ratings race and who is sanctioned to serve as scorekeepers.

The potential rewards or losses from ranking systems are evident in both their tangible and intangible impact. University managers employ them in updating mission statements, fund-raising, allocating resources, and offering incentives—bundles of carrots and sticks. Rankings also guide students and

37. UNESCO European Centre for Higher Education (Centre Européen pour l'Enseignement Supérieur [CEPES]), "Berlin Principles on Ranking of Higher Education Institutions," May 20, 2006, http://www.che.de/downloads/Berlin_Principles_IREG_534 .pdf (accessed March 14, 2017).
38. Author discussion with Nain Cai Liu, Shanghai, September 11, 2013.
39. Ibid.

their families when they decide where to apply for admission. Eighty-five percent of international students indicate that global rankings and reputation are key factors in their choices, and one-third say that they are the most important consideration.[40]

In addition, ranking systems are linked to the social composition of a student body in countries such as Mongolia, Qatar, and Kazakhstan, where government sponsorship and scholarships for study abroad are restricted to students who gain entry to the top 100 global universities.[41] Indonesia's Presidential Scholarships are tenable only at the world's 50 preeminently ranked universities in select countries. Norway, known for its egalitarian ethos, limits access to scholarships for study abroad to applicants who seek admission to prominent overseas universities. Rankings are pivotal for other linkages, too: Brazilian universities collaborate only with the foremost 500 universities in global rankings; Singapore, with the first 100; and the Netherlands' and Denmark's immigration laws favor international students with degrees from the world's most prestigiously ranked universities.[42] Moreover, the governments of China, Germany, Indonesia, Japan, Malaysia, South Korea, Russia, and Taiwan have pledged to boost at least one of their universities into the upper 100 rank; and Nigeria has promised to catapult two to the front 200.[43]

To realize these goals, higher education managers empanel committees or hire more administrators to design a strategy to climb the ladder to the super league of elite institutions. Their tasks are to prepare documents and reports, upgrade web presence, and curate an image. Additionally, some heads of universities receive bonuses if their institution moves up significantly in the rankings. Conversely, when a university drops in the rankings, its leader can suffer the consequences. Hence, in 2013, Sidney Ribeau, president of Howard University, abruptly announced his retirement after Howard fell sharply in a major national ranking. Coming amid fund-raising and enrollment problems, this decline from 96th in 2010 to 120th in 2013 and 142nd in 2014 marked the end of his watch.[44]

40. According to research cited in Karin Fischer, "American Universities Yawn at Global Rankings," *Chronicle of Higher Education* 60, no. 5 (October 4, 2013): A25.

41. Jamil Salmi and Alonoush Saroyan, "League Tables as Policy Instruments: Uses and Misuses," *Higher Education Management and Policy* 19, no. 2 (August 2007): 1–38, as cited in Ellen Hazelkorn, *Rankings and the Reshaping of Higher Education: The Battle for World-Class Excellence* (New York: Palgrave Macmillan, 2011), 162.

42. Ibid.; D. D. Guttenplan, "Vying for a Spot on the World's A List," *New York Times*, April 14, 2013.

43. Guttenplan, "Vying for a Spot on the World's A List,"; Fischer, "American Universities Yawn at Global Rankings," A25; Hazelkorn, *Rankings and the Reshaping of Higher Education*, 162.

44. Nick Anderson, "Howard University President Retires," *Washington Post*, October 1, 2013; Allie Bidwell, "Campus Life: Presidents in Peril," *U.S. News & World Report*, October 13, 2013.

In brief, ranking exercises are important tools for managing and marketing universities. The global rankings contribute to the denationalization of standards. By identifying Harvard, Cambridge, MIT, Caltech, or another elite university as the gold standard, these systems are ordering and decontextualizing knowledge governance. The peril of mirroring policies that conform to world ranking standards lies in a group mind-set: a globalized prototype that shapes universities' purposes. The danger of groupthink is accentuated by retrenchment following the 2008 economic collapse and the eurozone debacle, which rippled to other regions. For universities, these downturns came atop the widespread adoption of years of reformist ideas and policies.

True, university leaders have often faulted university rankings. They cite methodological flaws and the fallibility of the indicators. What should count—research, reputation, teaching, mobility, or other factors? For how much? And how to quantify them? But higher education executives still insist on objectifying these scorecards for managing their institutions. They continue to invoke global rankings to motivate faculty and staff.

While the experts who produce the numerical systems are prepared to take criticism and improve their methodologies, they firmly believe that a university's value can be counted and do not doubt whether it is inherently uncountable. But can one really compare universities' results in different historical and cultural contexts, which, after all, present their own challenges? For example, why should the performance of South Africa's postapartheid universities, which face formidable challenges in deracializing their faculty and student body, be compared to the accomplishments of Oxford or Yale? And do global rankings crowd out initiatives that do not fit the metrics of research output and reputation—say, clinical training by a law school for work in impoverished areas or for eroding gender hierarchies—and, in some cases, fail to index the prices borne by students?

Issues of domination and subordination hardly show up on global ranking systems' measures, such as Internet surveys of universities' reputations, and in their descriptive statistics. Figuratively, rankings put higher education institutions on a par with commercial services such as restaurants, cars, and hotels; they assign a number of stars to universities. So when President Barack Obama called for a government rating system for schools, Undersecretary of Education Jamienne S. Studley told college presidents that the task would be as simple as evaluating a kitchen appliance. In her words: "It's like rating a blender."[45]

A consumer-oriented university scorecard is an accounting tool for comparing data by institution on labor-market outcomes like postgraduation

45. As quoted in Michael D. Shear, "Seeking Accountability, Obama Steps into College Ratings Fray," *International New York Times*, May 20, 2014.

earnings and student-loan repayment rates as measures of the value of a degree. The analysts who calculate the wide range of complexities of higher education and convert them into global rankings may thus be likened to accountants. As with any accounting firm, their own accountability warrants attention. In the university-ranking business, to whom are the counters accountable? How are these specialists selected? What kind of oversight is exercised? Who hires and pays auditing firms to vet ranking agencies' information? Are their reports disclosed to the public, that is, transparent? Answers to these questions require contextual investigation, provided in part 2 of this book.

A common element among them is that universities self-report much of the data. The issue then becomes the consequences for misreporting, as in the United States when Claremont McKenna College, Emory University, and George Washington University inflated data, apparently attempting to game the system.[46] Will rankers consistently unrank the wrongdoing universities? Perhaps the entire transnational process of valuing resources and prestige should be fairly regulated or fundamentally rethought.

Certainly, there are winners and losers in the global ranking race. The top finisher gets the gold medal, the high standard that other contestants strive to achieve. Competitors want to be in the premier league of world-class universities.

But there is limited mobility in the race for the upper echelon of the global scorecards. Most of the same elite universities appear in this tier year in and year out. Moreover, global league tables peg just the world's top research universities, not other higher education institutions. According to Andrejs Rauhvargers's report for the European University Association, the main global rankings provide reliable data for about 700 to 1,000 universities of around 17,000 universities worldwide.[47] By rewarding or penalizing them on the basis of their categories and criteria, the ranking agencies are power brokers. They invite consent for, and participation in, repurposing universities. They extend the norms of competition. Tero Erkkilä and Ossi Piironen put it pithily: "the ideology of competition breeds rankings, and rankings uphold the ideology of competition."[48] Ranking pressures induce conformism by bandwagoning best practices, effectively punishing nonconformity, and focusing on measurable outcomes. And to confine universities to the language of counting is to fetter

46. Craig Weinberg, "GW Kicked Off U.S. News & World Report Rankings for Inflating Freshman Admissions Data," *GW Hatchet* (Washington, DC), November 15, 2012; Nick Anderson, "5 Colleges' Inflated Data Spark Debate on Rankings," *Washington Post*, February 7, 2013.

47. Rauhvargers, *Global University Rankings and Their Impact*, 65.

48. Tero Erkkilä and Ossi Piironen, "Reforming Higher Education Institutions in Finland: Competitiveness and Global University Rankings," in *Global University Rankings*, ed. Erkkilä, 140.

their purposes. Ultimately, a numerical value cannot be placed on a society's priceless cultural institutions—libraries, museums, and universities.

Higher Education Philanthropy and Think Tanks

In their support for these institutions, international philanthropy expends large sums on higher education reform. As donors, private foundations dole out funds in line with their interests and priorities, including models of best practices of knowledge production and transmission. In the main, these contributions complement the foreign policies of the government in the home country where the philanthropists are chartered. They usually share the same basic values, but, at times, diverge somewhat from official policy on specific issues such as human rights.[49]

Built on the vast fortunes of nineteenth- and early twentieth-century magnates such as Andrew Carnegie, John D. Rockefeller, and Henry Ford, U.S. corporate philanthropy is sizable compared to that of other countries. And by U.S. tax law, foundations are required to pay out at least 5 percent of the market value of their assets per year. The endowment assets of the largest 100 U.S. family foundations by giving, though not total assets, exceed the total for the United Kingdom and the rest of Europe.[50] Today, there are more than 33,000 foundations in the United States. Together, 50 American megafoundations allocated over one billion dollars to higher education in 2010.[51]

With globalizing processes, grant-making for international programming has increased substantially. Financers and technological entrepreneurs have extended the reach of American higher education philanthropy. With the earnings from their global businesses, George Soros, Bill and Melinda Gates, Warren Buffett, and others built up nouveau foundations and provide money for projects that correspond to their policy preferences. The Gates Foundation is the largest private philanthropy in the world. Smaller American foundations have also funded initiatives for higher learning reforms across national borders. For example, the Indianapolis-based Lumina Foundation sponsored a project on restructuring higher education on the basis of the experience of Europe's more than 4,000 higher education institutions. Called "Tuning USA," it sought

49. Joan E. Spero, "The Global Role of U.S. Foundations" (New York: Foundation Center, 2010), 5.

50. Cathy Pharoah, "Family Foundation Philanthropy: Report on the Giving of the Largest Charitable Family Foundations in the US, the UK and the Rest of Europe 2008," Centre for Charity Effectiveness, Cass Business School, City University London, 2008, 11, http://www.cass.city.ac.uk/__data/assets/pdf_file/0020/37280/famfoundationphil.pdf (accessed January 20, 2014).

51. Stanley N. Katz, "Beware Big Donors," *Chronicle Review* 58, no. 30 (March 30, 2012): B6–7, drawing on the Foundation Center database.

to adapt lessons from the Bologna Process.[52] In conjunction with students, faculty, and education officials from Indiana, Minnesota, and Utah, this effort aimed to create a "shared understanding among higher-education stakeholders" of "subject-specific knowledge and transferable skills in certain areas."[53]

The impact of the Bologna reforms and the tuning project is felt beyond the transatlantic area. There are efforts to apply the tuning methodology to Africa. Supported by the European Commission and the African Union Commission, the Tuning Africa pilot initiative was launched in 2011 and follows the harmonization trends in Europe and elsewhere. Like the Bologna Process, it seeks to ensure equivalency and comparability of qualifications across participating universities in Africa and to facilitate the mobility of students and faculty in the region.

In Europe and Japan, where state intervention in the economy has more scope than in the United States, private philanthropies like the Nokia and Toyota foundations, also rooted in corporate wealth, have made grants and scholarships available as well. In the global South, especially in emerging economies, newer foundations are bringing together constituencies around education reform. As in the global North, they are relieving the state of some of its responsibilities and privatizing the public sphere.[54] Notwithstanding their different legal and policy environments, global institutional funders have converged on what they regard as "strategic" challenges in higher education: access, leadership, management, technology, and, more generally, infrastructure. They are attracted to market-based approaches to issues such as mobility, benchmarks, metrics, completion of degrees, and productivity. In all, the rise of global philanthropy coincides with an increase in world income inequality and private wealth in the hands of certain entrepreneurs. Established in 2001, the Global Philanthropy Forum convened by the World Affairs Council brings these funders together each year.

On the question of foundations and their worldview, Joan Spero, a former president of the Doris Duke Charitable Foundation, maintains that "foundations are political actors pursuing foreign policies and playing an important role in the new global world." She adds: "Many old and new foundations are working together across national boundaries on global issues."[55] This

52. Lumina Foundation, "Tuning USA: Lumina Foundation Launches Faculty-Led Process That Will Involve Students and Employers in Linking College Degrees to Workplace Relevance and Students' Mastery of Agreed-upon Learning Objectives," http://www .luminafoundation.org/newsroom/news_releases/2009-04-08-tuning.html (accessed December 18, 2013).

53. Ibid.

54. William Wallis, "Rash of African Philanthropists Aims to Do More than Fill the Gap," *Financial Times*, February 8, 2013.

55. Spero, "The Global Role of U.S. Foundations," vii.

collaboration is evident in a partnership among seven American foundations seeking to strengthen higher education in Africa.[56]

Criticism of corporate grant-makers' influence centers on their nexus with the state. Some staff members have been moving back and forth between foundation and government jobs, with increased interplay of the two.[57] Although one would not expect perfect agreement between private philanthropies and the state, it is alleged that higher education projects underwritten by sizable philanthropists are skewed by the affinity of government and great wealth.[58] To assess their shortcomings and accomplishments, the foundations commission evaluations of their own projects, but independent assessments are less in evidence.

Arguably, corporate and foundation philanthropy have different aims. Corporate giving for projects in education can help improve a firm's image and is ultimately driven by the bottom line. Foundation funding, in contrast, is not bound to realizing material gain. But before putting a fine point on this distinction, one should consider the counterpoint: in allocating their money, corporations and foundations alike have the prerogative of setting priorities, excluding initiatives, and influencing outcomes. Both kinds of sponsors target advocacy research. They often provide prescriptive grants and, as noted, try to influence public policy. Moreover, the power of the purse lies in the ability to forge consensus. It is achieved by drawing together sundry organizations that do not necessarily concur with one another on higher education reform and offering incentives for concerting their interests and rewards for carrying out the provisions of a common platform. In short, corporate and foundation philanthropy are linked rather than neatly separated.

Of concern to this study is philanthropic support for knowledge production by think tanks. The thinking at these tanks may be distinguished from the long, more notional perspectives taken by many university professors. Think-tank pundits mostly engage in public policy research. They seek to shape policy on near-term problems and gain access to policymakers. By comparison, a lot of critically minded scholars maintain intellectual distance from entanglement with political authorities to whom they could be beholden.

Some policy-relevant think tanks and research institutes, such as the Finnish Institute of International Affairs (FIIA) and the South African Institute of International Affairs, are funded by governments or both governments and private donors. A variant is phantom nongovernmental think tanks that to all intents and purposes are arms of government or political parties. Other hybrids are both inside and outside government—they operate at the interstices

56. Detailed in chapter 6.

57. Marc Parry, Kelly Field, and Beckie Supiano, "The Gates Effect," *Chronicle of Higher Education* 59, no. 42 (July 19, 2013): A22.

58. Ibid., A21.

of the two realms. It can be difficult to differentiate these spheres wherein policy-research tanks and institutes are closely associated with the state and readily rotate personnel between them.

It would be a mistake to overlook think tanks' different orientations; they are on the right, center, and left of the spectrum. But in certain respects, they are alike. Their funders can color the research agenda. This is a matter of defining problems, posing the research questions that researchers are paid to answer.

In the United States, corporate donations, which can be written off as charitable contributions, come from companies like Bank of America, Citigroup, and Goldman Sachs. Along with backing by foreign governments, they may lead to biased results by hired research groups, only some of which issue disclosures.[59] The financial backers typically want the insignia of prominent think tanks, the greater legitimacy that these intermediaries lend, and returns on their investment in attaining access to power and shaping policy. For their part, the researchers seek the imprimatur of titles such as "nonresident scholar" or "visiting fellow" bestowed by think tanks. Potential for conflicts of interest is evident in that some researchers are also paid as registered lobbyists, members of corporate boards, and consultants for industry. Their studies under the auspices of tanks are used to prompt public debate and help produce a narrative for industry. In light of the close relationships between think tanks and the sponsors, including overseas organizations, questions about self-censorship, the propriety of influence-buying, and the faint line between the integrity of research and lobbying come to the fore.[60]

In addition, tanks of varied persuasions churn out an enormous amount of papers and postings. They produce rapid, useful knowledge, unlike what Flexner had in mind when he sought to justify unhurried, useless knowledge.[61] While useful and useless knowledge, applied and basic research, may be viewed as a continuum, not a sharp dichotomy, the emphasis clearly differs. Think tanks are arrayed toward one end of the spectrum and universities harbor a mix of the two.

59. Eric Lipton, "Think Tank Lists Donors, Playing Down Their Role," *New York Times*, December 14, 2013.

60. Eric Lipton, Brooke Williams, and Nicholas Confessore, "Foreign Powers Buy Influence at Think Tanks," *New York Times*, September 7, 2014; Eric Lipton and Brooke Williams, "Scholarship or Business? Think Tanks Blur the Line," *New York Times*, August 8, 2016; Eric Lipton, Nicholas Confessore, and Brooke Williams, "Top Scholars or Lobbyists? Often It's Both," *New York Times*, August 9, 2016. Cf. a response to *New York Times* allegations from Strobe Talbott, president of Brookings, and Kimberly Churches, "Safeguarding Independence in an Era of Unrestricted Giving," *Chronicle of Philanthropy*, February 2, 2016; for an additional rebuttal by Talbott, see his statement at https://www.brookings .edu/wp-content/uploads/2016/08/20160811_eo_brookings_nyt_response_corrected .pdf (accessed December 9, 2016).

61. As discussed in chapter 1, 16–17.

In sheer numbers, American think tanks, tax-exempt organizations, are predominant. According to James McGann, director of the Think Tanks and Civil Societies Program at the University of Pennsylvania, 1,830 of the world's 6,618 (27.7 percent) think tanks are located in the United States.[62] McGann and his team report that 90.5 percent of U.S tanks have been established since 1951. Valuing proximity to political power, about one-fourth of them are housed in Washington, D.C., and more than half of the total are affiliated with universities (for example, the Hoover Institution at Stanford).[63] Much like universities, think tanks are ranked worldwide, their impact measured. In the 2014 ratings, the Brookings Institution, Chatham House, and the Carnegie Endowment for International Peace were at the top of the global list.[64] And in recent years, think tanks have expanded the world round. They are present in 182 countries.[65] The Washington, D.C.-based Carnegie Endowment for International Peace has opened "global centers" in Beirut, Beijing, Brussels, and Moscow, which provide exposure to American think-thank culture. Other well-to-do tanks are following suit.

Wherever think tanks are in play, their work is rarely subject to peer review. Partly staffed by academics who have decamped, they mostly produce in-house publications that do not clear blind appraisals. Paul Krugman, a Nobel Prize–winning economist at the Graduate Center of the City University of New York and a *New York Times* columnist, put it less delicately, characterizing think tanks as "a sort of parallel intellectual universe, a world of 'scholars' whose careers are based on toeing an ideological line, rather than on doing research that stands up to scrutiny by their peers."[66] It should be said too that universities are hardly immune from funders' pressures and university researchers have their ideological biases. But, arguably, the range of views in a university is more heterogeneous and readily contested than at a think tank. Faced with instrumental demands of a different magnitude at institutions whose missions do not include academic freedom as at universities, think-tank researchers are called on to produce streams of advocacy reports, other opinion pieces that ripple through the world via media outlets, and "online

62. James G. McGann, "2014 Global Go to Think Tank Index Report," 8, http://repository.upenn.edu/think_tanks/8/ (accessed February 9, 2016).

63. Ibid., 10.

64. Ibid., 65. Such lists are mainly based on quantitative measures of inputs, among others, the number of appearances in the media, testimonies at congressional hearings, blogs, and podcasts. Less attention is paid to qualitative impact: what is done with the input, that is, the outcomes. Donald E. Abelson, *Do Think Tanks Matter? Assessing the Impact of Public Policy Institutes*, 2nd ed. (Montreal: McGill-Queen's University Press, 2009).

65. McGann, "2014 Global Go to Think Tank Index Report," 8; Lee Michael Katz, "American Think Tanks: Their Influence on the Rise," *Carnegie Reporter* 5, no. 1 (Spring 2009): 12–22.

66. Paul Krugman, "Design for Confusion," *New York Times*, August 5, 2005.

exposure" with copious blogging. And in this way, modern technology magnifies the power of utilitarian knowledge.

Technology and University Communities

The influx of technology into universities can have cascading effects on research and teaching. Its uses may oblige universities to rethink their purposes. To come to grips with this phenomenon, let us circle back to a specific issue: MOOCs and some of their antecedents.

Started at the turn of the millennium, the open courseware movement, an easily accessible form of publication, has catalyzed change. Adding to distance learning, it has made available web-based teaching materials for courses presented in a standard format. This initiative links universities around the globe, many of them in the OpenCourseWare Consortium.

Leading universities have pumped large sums into developing new technologies used to improve teaching methods and for bringing them to their campuses. For example, Harvard and MIT invested heavily to set up edX, a nonprofit organization. Established in 2012, edX's mission is to build up an open-source technology platform and offer online courses available throughout the world.

Universities and ed-tech providers have joined with venture-capital firms to spark innovation, linking knowledge and social production. For-profit corporations are proceeding apace to upgrade MOOCs. Coursera, Udacity, and others attract investments from companies like the Silicon Valley–based Kleiner Perkins Caufield & Byers. They have gained a share of the academic market, including with university publishers, some of which believe that MOOCs can enable them to sell books to a wider audience. It is too soon to know exactly how MOOCs make money. Their sponsors have the potential to secure revenue by charging for commercial advertisements, access to student profiles, content licensing, and professional development. Already, Coursera decided to award certificates in data science, mobile-app development, and cybersecurity to students who complete its program, called Specializations, at a cost of $200 to $500.[67] These firms can also phase in fee-based services to clients such as government agencies and private companies seeking technical support and other solutions to problems.

Entrepreneurial professor-technologists are challenging the traditional modalities that universities have used to deliver education. Coursera's founders, Daphane Koller and Andrew Ng, former professors at Stanford who started the company in 2012, piloted streaming tutorials and auto-grading.

---

67. Steve Kolowich, "Completion Rates Aren't the Best Way to Judge MOOCs, Researchers Say," *Chronicle of Higher Education* 60, no. 20 (January 31, 2014): A3.

Along with other technology advocates, they hold that MOOCs can reconfigure learning and contain costs. Irrespective of geographical constraints, students can download lectures while their own instructors handle face-to-face communication. It is also said that the global learning platforms are a means of furnishing opportunities for students who cannot pay for expensive institutions. They are seen as a way to overcome barriers to distributing global knowledge.

Technology critics, however, contend that MOOCs are a business model of higher education, impeding diverse viewpoints by teaching the same course at far-flung universities. Remembered as a great supporter of technological innovation on campuses, Vest, the MIT former president who had pioneered the university's OpenCourseWare project, told me in a conversation in 2013, shortly before his passing, how he viewed the promise of MOOCs. He remarked that while they reach a large audience, the *quality* of interactions among students and with their professors remains crucial. Vest added: "I had a nightmare that students across the world watch one big lecture."[68] Concerns are also raised about the prevalence of plagiarism in MOOCs and a course completion rate of 10 percent or less. A risk is that learners without a lot of self-discipline are left behind.

Too, MOOCs skeptics maintain that third-party online providers are contributing to the privatization of public universities and jeopardizing the residential university. This setting is where students and faculty informally exchange views, often outside the classroom, and where cross-pollination among disciplines can flourish. In lieu of residency on campus, some students find that working independently, with the option of online chat sessions with their instructors, is more convenient and affordable.

To assess ways in which technological innovation is spurring university reform, more hard evidence and systematic analysis are needed. Funded by the Bill & Melinda Gates Foundation, research on the use, efficacy, and improvement of MOOCs is underway.[69] In a preliminary assessment, John Hennessy, a computer scientist and president of Stanford University until 2016, adjudged MOOCs as failing on two criteria: mass and open. He observed that they are too large to motivate most students and that the majority of those who sign up for them do not even view the first lecture. According to Hennessy, the courses appear to be more of a private product and ineffective for a general

68. Author discussion with Vest.

69. The Gates Foundation MOOC Research Initiative supports projects, currently at the University of Michigan, Duke University, and elsewhere, for collecting and analyzing data. The results become papers, some of the best ones in the peer-reviewed journal *International Review of Research in Open and Distance Learning*. Steve Kolowich, "Researchers Push MOOC Conversation beyond 'Tsunami' Metaphors," *Chronicle of Higher Education* 60, no. 16 (December 20, 2013): A8.

audience.[70] And even if they are completed, the culmination is without a university degree.

For now, blends of new forms of learning and traditional instruction seem to be the way to go. The unanswered question is how best to blend them without adopting a stenciled form of educational programming. My view is that the most recent educational technology by itself will not transform higher learning; the precursors heralded as system-changers have not done so. Some newly developed technological panacea is not *the* key to the problems besetting universities. The gateway is to better educate students to exploit technological forces. And for the resuscitation of higher education, transformation is more a matter of the socioeconomic environment in which the latest formats are situated and less a question of technique. The environment must enable a technology so that it becomes organic to a knowledge structure.

In increasingly entrepreneurial milieus, an array of academic administrators, students, and faculty provides impetus for shifts in knowledge production and dissemination. Adopting innovative technologies is but one part of this multifaceted dynamic.

To cope with internal and external pressures from university trustees and pecuniary needs, managers are adopting tools such as Academic Analytics, which melds large databases and predictive modeling, a form of actionable intelligence for decision making. These corporate-originated instruments are used for marketing the university's products at home and overseas. University administrators also employ them for cost savings by measuring faculty productivity on a yearly basis, designating underperforming individuals.[71] Facing intense competition, university executives have their eyes on positional movement for their institutions, tracked by ordinal number schemes.

Charged with this task and loath to be heard on big public issues, such as war and social justice, education leaders' offices often respond to queries on such matters by saying that the president cannot be reached for comment. Today, university presidents spend the bulk of their time attending to numbers, especially for the profit-and-loss performance of their respective institutions. Few of them have the pluck to step up on difficult public controversies facing the nation. Many of these chief executives are risk averse and assume technocratic stances, lest they run afoul of political authorities, university trustees, and other funders.[72] To be sure, the web of constraints on the heads

70. Andrew Hill and Richard Waters, "Problems Identified with MOOC Courses: Too Massive and Too Open," *Financial Times*, February 3, 2014.

71. Paul Basken, "As Concerns Grow about Using Data to Measure Faculty Members, a Company Changes Its Message," *Chronicle of Higher Education* 63, no. 8 (October 21, 2016): A14.

72. See Scott Sherman, "University Presidents—Speak Out!" *The Nation*, March 11–18, 2013, 18–23.

of universities is formidable: outright political interference in the mission of some institutions, onerous regulations, rising costs, intense competition, and students' wants. But this does not excuse a lack of principled leadership, a skittishness that lapses into stony silence. It can come at the cost of impoverishing societal debates on crucial issues of the times.

Understandably focused on their immediate needs and goals, many students adopt a business and policy orientation in their education. They are, for the most part, intent on what is on offer on the market. True, some of them protest societal problems like economic inequality and climate change. Their presence was felt in the Occupy movement, the Arab Spring, and other civil-society actions. Unlike their parents, the younger generation faces the rise of the richest 1 percent, income stagnation among the middle classes in some economies, and high unemployment rates. Given this landscape, how many students pursue academic programs that develop high-order thinking and critical reasoning? Then again, the availability of such courses is a matter of resources to support these offerings and of curricular decisions by faculty, who in turn are also implicated in repurposing universities.

There are at least three reasons why intellectuals comply with the drift in universities' missions. One explanation for consent is socialization: the training wherein personnel learn the normal disciplinary protocols of academic culture, including its regulations for rank order on tenure and promotion. Professors used to grading are accustomed to marks, and most of them strive for high ones according to established criteria and subject to performance review. Rankers spotlight the route, showing standards for excellence. Second, employees are reluctant to bite the hand that feeds them. And an increasing proportion of instructors are working off the tenure track. Without job security, they are vulnerable to personnel actions. Third, playing by the rules offers the promise of research funding and recognition. So, too, riding globalizing processes can provide additional tangible rewards like opportunities for travel, privileges for which administrators create incentives. When individuals are ever more susceptible to competitive, globalizing market forces, coercion can take the form of penalties for nonconformity, including job loss or heavier teaching loads at institutions that fare poorly in rating systems and contests for external revenue.

A Confluence of Factors?

In the absence of a single locus of educational reform, a plurality of actors and processes is propelling this shift. These forces are diffuse. But do they coalesce?

They come together around meeting challenges of globalization and neoliberal reforms. The range of actors noted above shares common reference points: broader scope for internationalization of the university, a more utilitarian approach to research, greater professionalization of degree programs, and an emphasis on science and technology. We have seen that, time and again, specific instruments of reform include best practices, new forms of assessment, measurable learning outcomes, and quality assurance. Locales in different continents have had diverse experiences with the metrics, but few national systems of higher education have been able to avoid them.

True, as Allan Goodman, president and CEO of the Institute of International Education (IIE), observed, "international education is not lurching in any direction." [73] But even if the lurch is not down a single path, it would be remiss to fail to note that this early stage of educational globalization is marked by growing intersubjectivity. Across borders, transnational elites are propagating discourses that reflect sameness. Amorphous catchphrases like "training for global leadership" and "pursuing excellence" are without substance unless this antiseptic wording is made specific. Some of the affinity among elites is a nascent yet insipid consensus whose lure comes from constant and authoritative repetition of keywords to the point that educators hardly notice this cloning and imbibe a way of thinking. Exercising influence in this manner is thus not a matter of straightforwardly prescribing the content of courses. The latter would likely infringe academic freedom, heighten contestation, or trigger defiance.

While creating consensus on higher education reform is not orchestrated, a *confluence of forces* may be discerned at three junctions. They may be regarded as venues for repurposing universities. Most visibly, these may be categorized as working sessions of international nongovernmental associations; major convocations that advance higher education reform; and backstage conversations on how important participants in this process can strengthen linkages and build up American-style support services. Let me be concrete about each of the three types.

A spate of international nongovernmental associations is promoting higher education reforms, often with the support of formal intergovernmental organizations. Examples of these initiatives abound. Among them:

- UNESCO provides the headquarters for the institutions and organizations from over 120 countries that form the International Association of Universities.
- Established with support from UNESCO and the World Bank, the 83-member Asia-Pacific Quality Network has its executive office in the Philippines and encourages good practices for quality assurance agencies in the world's most populous region.
- With a secretariat in Barcelona and more than 250 members, the International Network for Quality Assurance Agencies in Higher Education

73. Author discussion with Allan E. Goodman, Washington, DC, February 10, 2011.

(INQAAHE) also develops and disseminates information on good practices and standards among quality assurance agencies, for instance, with regard to accreditation.

• Its secretariat located in Warsaw, and registered in Brussels, the International Ranking Expert Group Observatory on Academic Ranking and Excellence is an ongoing forum in which rankers and ranking analysts share ideas with one another and with policymakers, including university administrators; they make actionable recommendations on issues such as auditing procedures to their own executive committees.

At points of articulation, large forums assemble knowledge communities from different countries. Emblematic of these gatherings are conferences of the European Universities Association, the All-Africa summit aimed at reaching a consensus for revitalizing higher education on the continent, and the annual World Innovation Summit for Education (WISE). The latter is supported by the Qatar Foundation and held annually in Doha. Akin to the World Economic Forum, which convenes leaders of the global economy to brainstorm in Davos, Switzerland, each year, WISE is designed to be the Davos of education—a parley for ministers of education, heads of universities, foundation officers, professors, and student representatives. It gives prizes for best practices, encourages models of sustainable and scalable ventures, and finances projects. In a sense, it seems odd to think of representatives of conservative, undemocratic governments converging in Doha, with sponsorship from Qatar, as promoting university repurposing. Yet this kind of repurposing can serve the interests of illiberal regimes by diverting attention from the inconvenient issue of open discussion and free expression on home campuses.[74]

At WISE and elsewhere, key players hold consultative meetings on higher education reform. The World Bank invites groups of U.S. private foundations to Washington, D.C., for closed-door sessions. The agenda is about process in higher education reform; the goal, to earmark common interests and possible avenues of collaboration.[75] The bank provides funds and its endorsement, facilitating some of the nongovernmental initiatives and assemblages mentioned above. These forms of cross-fertilization establish genial arenas where consensus can be hammered out. Just as U.S. universities are expanding their programs and campuses around the world, so the American model of student services has spread. Buttressing this tendency, rising tuition and fees mean that students believe that universities should offer more benefits. As a result,

74. I am grateful to Nicholas T. Smith for raising this point, email message to author, January 20, 2013.

75. Author telephone discussion with New York–based foundation program officer, January 3, 2011; author discussion with New York foundation officer, Kampala, Uganda, May 21, 2013.

many countries have introduced a U.S.-kind of career services, mental health counseling, and leadership training. The International Association of Student Affairs and Services, launched in 2010, advances this trend; it includes 1,200 members from 75 countries.[76] Historical and cultural differences are of course central considerations. Nevertheless, a premise underlying student development philosophy is that the university should extend its reach in intellectual formation to the extracurriculum and be more directly involved in personal development.

The subtext in these moves is about realignments of regulation and self-regulation. They can stretch all the way to mentalities in the sense of basic outlook and orientation, as well as permeate the private lives of members of the academy. In this fashion, repurposing higher education inculcates disciplinary power in daily existence.

Yet the constellation of actors and processes delimited in this chapter are weakly ordered. The institutions and organizations cooperate in certain instances but also compete with one another for resources and prestige. In terms of process, the monitoring of higher education reform is irregular, replete with tensions about scope, prerogative, and funding among national and international, public and private, authorities. To take a flagrant example of uncertain and sometimes contested jurisdiction, this discussion has touched on, and subsequent chapters will revisit, the question of who should be empowered to assess academic programs and campuses overseas and judge their standards on issues such as gender and mental health. In view of different historical trajectories and cultural variation, should universalizing narratives cover the whole gamut? Or how can balances between the local and global be struck?

At this stage, the connective tissue in a web of cross-continental educational reform is not substantially joined but gradually spreading. This webbing is not carefully spun and unlike the deliberate way in which planners design their work. Architects and engineers, for instance, are systematic and use blueprints. Notwithstanding strategic planning at individual universities and organizations, transformations in higher education are occurring without an overall master plan. The strategic dimension pertains to accommodating global pressures and local trends.

Globally, higher education reforms approximate the French structural anthropologist Claude Lévi-Strauss's concept of bricolage, which signifies more than going along without forethought.[77] Like the ten groups of actors making

76. Sara Lipka, "Campuses Engage Students, U.S.-Style," *Chronicle of Higher Education* 58, no. 28 (March 16, 2012): A1, A12, A14, A16, A17; http://iasas.global/ (accessed October 11, 2016).

77. Claude Lévi-Strauss, *The Savage Mind* (Chicago: University of Chicago Press, 1966). This paragraph recalls theses in James H. Mittelman, "Global *Bricolage*: Emerging Market Powers and Polycentric Governance," *Third World Quarterly* 34, no. 1 (February

the net of reform, bricoleurs use imagination and deploy whatever tools are at hand. They proceed in a mostly spontaneous and pragmatic manner. In contemporary higher education, this means that managing practical problems trumps purposeful, long-range planning. Most often, the reorganization of academic and administrative units proceeds apace under the banner of consolidation, cost containment, and efficiency.

Adding to Lévi-Strauss's insight, the poststructural philosopher Jacques Derrida applied the concept of bricolage to unpick dominant discourses.[78] In Derrida's usage, bricolage is not then only improvisation or a jumble of ad hoc processes but also a way to parse texts, speech, and political institutions. One might go even further to ponder educational bricolage: narratives that center on innovations in the purposes of universities. Intellectual bricolage would extend to new ways of thinking, including reassemblages that confer meaning and relate cognitive processes to material power.

Now, to round up my main points. The patterns that comprise university repurposing are not linear. They are multidirectional and without one-way causality. The visible agendas are more about process than content and fundamentally about securing consent on paradigmatic matters like positivism, preferred methodologies, entrepreneurship, and particular narratives. Along with incentives and punishments, their unremitting reiteration has a bandwagon effect, bringing aboard more academics.

Educational bricoleurs are the change agents identified in this chapter. They have produced a new common sense about universities. Comprehended the world over, the language accompanying it has strong communicative pull, attracting many to think normally in these terms. Figures of speech like best practices, benchmarking, and branding are simple proxies for a broad conception of accommodation to globalizing pressures. At a practical level, these accommodations are ways to build a lattice of world-class universities wrought by a cast of actors and powerful structures that are transforming higher education. This transformation is plodding, with fits and starts, rather than a sudden mutation.

The scripts are subject to institutional adjustments and local policy intellectuals' ideas. They manifest concretely, with tangible effects. To grasp them, we will be mindful of granularity and rely on the texture of historically informed case studies.

2013): 23–37. Also see Martin B. Carstensen, "Paradigm Man vs. the Bricoleur: Bricolage as an Alternative Vision of Agency in Ideational Change," *European Political Science Review* 3, no. 1 (March 2011): 147–67.

78. Jacques Derrida, *Writing and Difference*, trans. Alan Bass (London: Routledge, 2001).

PART II

Case Studies

CHAPTER FOUR

The Neoliberal Model: The United States

IN THE UNITED STATES, celebrating the reputed preeminence of the nation's universities is commonplace. So too many university executives in other countries are in thrall to the narrative that takes the Ivy League and other American elite universities as the standard-bearers. Although it would be a mistake to devalue distinctive national and regional histories, the trajectories of some higher education systems outside the United States suggest that they have come to parody aspects of the American pattern. They revel in an imagery of the world-class university, for the neoliberal paradigm generates a story about best practices that has gone global.

Since the 1980s, neoliberalism has been the major precept for organizing state-society-economy relations in the United States. It is a philosophy developed by economists, notably the Nobel Prize winners Friedrich von Hayek and Milton Friedman, at the University of Chicago. Their free-market ideology became ascendant in the home countries of students trained under the aura of the Chicago school and its disciples. By definition, neoliberalism is a set of ideas and a policy framework that centers on deregulation, liberalization, and privatization. President Ronald Reagan, along with Prime Minister Margaret Thatcher, popularized this thinking and spearheaded its implementation as public policy. Emanating from this foundation, neoliberalism coupled with financialization, a combination that moved front and center in not only markets but societies and polities. In an age of volatile financial securities, asset bubbles, toxic lending for mortgages, and the failure of big banks and investment houses destabilized economies and precipitated the 2008 global crisis. In university life, the financialization of education has ramified widely, as evidenced by mounting problems of affordability and student debt.

The complexities of this history may be grouped in the following periods, each one animated by the social forces that shaped it: the colonial and initial postcolonial era (1636–1789); secularization and professionalism (1790–1944); massification (1945–94); and the expansion of technologies in the run-up to, and the aftermath of, September 11 (1995–the present).

Connecting threads are woven into the fabric of reform. Traced in this chapter are four strands: socioeconomic hierarchy, executive power, regulatory adjustment, and global reach. Tangles in interweaving them will be identified. For instance, insularity inscribed in American representations of unparalleled excellence, on the one hand, and the emergent outward orientation of its universities to the global arena, on the other, are at odds. In some respects, nationalism and globalization are divergent forces. But with globalizing education, they also converge.

This seesaw slants according to the balance of social forces. It swings with the political ballast, tipping between an inward disposition favoring an ethnocentric form of patriotism and homeland concerns, on the one side, and cosmopolitanism, manifest, for example, in today's emphasis on worldly careers, on the other. Tracking these shifts will complicate the dominant narratives about U.S. universities.

American Narratives

The American nationalist discourse does not lack prominent purveyors. Bok, the former Harvard president, extols the achievements of "our scientists and researchers who remain unequaled."[1] He is not alone in articulating this sentiment. In an impressive book on graduate education and the research university, Cole, Columbia's former provost, charts the evolution of the research university in the United States, which has resulted in "the greatest system of knowledge production and higher learning that the world has ever known."[2] He holds that "our finest universities are . . . the envy of the world."[3] And in his acclaimed work *College: What It Was, Is, and Should Be*, Andrew Delbanco, professor of American studies at Columbia, champions the U.S. undergraduate liberal arts experience and makes the case for American excellence.[4]

Exponents of U.S. higher education exceptionalism are prideful but hardly complacent. They recognize deficiencies in this vaunted system. Their

1. Bok, *Higher Education in America*, 410.

2. Cole, *The Great American University*, 13. In *Toward a More Perfect University* (New York: PublicAffairs, 2016), Cole develops this point with respect to highly selective, research-intensive universities.

3. Ibid., 5. Tempering his point about American preeminence, Cole maintains that scholarly advance around the world would be good for all (469–70, and discussed in chapter 7, 210–11, of this volume).

4. Andrew Delbanco, *College: What It Was, Is, and Should Be* (Princeton: Princeton University Press, 2012).

celebratory statements are modulated by concerns about growing challenges and threats to its standing. The narratives convey worries about domestic trends and intense competition from overseas institutions and governments, which seek the economic advantages and prestige that strong universities can confer. In this vein, historian James Axtell salutes the accomplishments of higher education in the United States but notes that federal largesse bears costs.[5] He traces the case of Stanford's climb to academic renown to illuminate the larger issues of the price that research universities pay for military and corporate sponsorship. Axtell highlights the pernicious tendencies of lessening autonomy to set intellectual agendas, widening distinctions between entrepreneurial "haves" and the "have-not" departments without outside funding, and the increasing propensity of doctoral students to choose dissertation topics likely to appeal to external patrons. While admiring American elite universities, Axtell's erudite account indicates that these trends have fed into the shift from basic to applied research and the decline in university support for the humanities and other "softer" fields.

At the same time that U.S. higher education is experiencing public retrenchment, governments in Germany, Russia, China, and some other Asian countries are trying to upgrade their universities and escalating spending on them. Moreover, in a reverse brain drain, an increasing number of students from abroad who earn PhDs in the United States choose to return home because of better opportunities there and greater rewards for their expertise. Following September 11, 2001, with the USA Patriot Act and the Public Health Security and Bioterrorism Preparedness and Response Act, they face tight restrictions on immigration and hostility from some on the right of the political spectrum. At the same time, the tapered level of U.S. government support for basic relative to applied research is but one sign of the position that fundamental inquiry is a cost to be borne privately and not as public investment in the future.[6] Finally, some observers acclaim American elite universities but are also concerned about their close synergy with private corporations and the military.

Educational leaders who laud *U.S. universities as number one* are half right, half unpersuasive. Since their story acknowledges contingencies and is diffuse, it can be best chronicled by tracing chains of historical development and deciphering how the publicity operates.

True, U.S. research universities dominate global rankings. In the 2013 Shanghai ranking, for example, American universities took 17 of the 20 top spots. But if one looks at the tallies for the first 200 and compares them to the scores in previous years, data show that U.S. institutions may be slipping

---

5. James Axtell, *Wisdom's Workshop: The Rise of the Modern University* (Princeton: Princeton University Press, 2016), 333–39.

6. In addition to the texts cited above, author telephone discussion with Duderstadt.

relative to overseas universities in the global pecking order.[7] On the one hand, the leading university *system* in the 2014 U21 Ranking of National Higher Education Systems is the United States. It is followed by countries with much smaller economies and populations: Sweden, Canada, Denmark, Finland, Switzerland, the Netherlands, the United Kingdom, Australia, and Singapore. China is quickly moving up in this table, climbing eight notches from the 2013 rankings.[8] Yet when performance is adjusted for level of economic development and gross domestic product (GDP) per capita, the results differ. The top 10 countries are, in rank order, Sweden, Finland, Denmark, Serbia, New Zealand, the United Kingdom, Canada, China, Portugal, and the Netherlands. The United States drops to 15th place.[9] Similarly, Ellen Hazelkorn, policy advisor to the Higher Education Authority in Dublin, Ireland, looks at the system level and finds that about 6 percent of U.S. higher education institutions appear among the top 500 in the three main global rankings, where about 22 percent of Ireland's public higher education institutions place. The United States spends a larger percentage of GDP on education than does Ireland and enrolls only a small minority of students at its leading universities.[10]

The question is why, given substantial resources in the United States, would American universities as an aggregate be losing their standing and fail to correspond to the narrative of preeminence typically projected from the top of its educational hierarchy? Apart from one hundred or so high-end research universities—the Harvards, Princetons, and Stanfords—a range of other institutions in the United States is trying to cope with the interlocking synergies of low degree completion rates, chronic attrition, exorbitant student debt, and affordability. Heads of many of these institutions remonstrate that in the current environment, their universities are starved of funding.

Beyond the campuses, U.S. policymakers perceive that the country's universities are falling short. Many political officials share military leaders' worry that an underperforming education system weakens national security.[11]

7. Fischer, "American Universities Yawn at Global Rankings," A23, A25.

8. Universitas, "U21 Ranking of National Higher Education Systems," http://www .universitas21.com/article/projects/details/152/u21-ranking-of-national-higher-education -systems (accessed May 18, 2015). These scores are compiled by researchers at the University of Melbourne.

9. Universitas, "U21 Ranking of National Higher Education Systems," http://www .universitas21.com/article/projects/details/158/overall-2014-ranking-scores (accessed May 18, 2015).

10. Hazelkorn, "Could Higher Education Rankings Be Socially Transformative?"

11. E.g., U.S. Secretary of Education Arne Duncan, "Education and International Competition: The Win-Win Game" (Remarks to the Council of Foreign Relations, October 19, 2010), http://www.ed.gov/news/speeches/education-and-international-competition-win -win-game-secretary-duncans-remarks-council-foreign-relations-new-york-city (accessed April 21, 2015).

With nearly 5,000 of the world's roughly 17,000 universities, the size and scale of American higher education is vast.[12] So, too, is the range of its institutions: as mentioned (page 7), public and private, rich and poor, secular and faith-based, for-profit and nonprofit, mixed-gender and single-sex, historically black and Native American, specialized (art, Bible studies, design, mining, music, technology) and comprehensive, and so on. It includes several networks: consortia such as the Ivy League, the Big Ten, the National Association of Schools and Colleges of the United Methodist Church, and the Association of Jesuit Colleges and Universities.

Compared to that of most other countries, the U.S. structure, with its flagship campuses, is decidedly hierarchical and decentralized, with higher education institutions subject to the laws of fifty states and municipalities within them. Public and private universities are substantially funded by private capital markets, lightly regulated, and infused with a culture of individualism. This configuration has been developing incrementally for more than three centuries. By 1940 its structural elements crystallized as a multilayered, segmented system.[13] And, to punctuate a point, it is important to grasp how the past informs the present, as in the ensuing discussion.

The Formation of Higher Education Institutions

THE COLONIAL AND EARLY POSTCOLONIAL PERIOD

In 1636, English immigrants established a college at a site that came to be known as Cambridge, Massachusetts.[14] A Puritan merchant and a graduate of Cambridge University, the Reverend John Harvard, entrusted his library and half of his estate to this fledgling institution for the purpose of advancing

---

12. The number of universities in the United States and worldwide varies widely by source, the criteria, and methodology. In comparison to the figures presented by the U.S. Department of Education, National Center for Education Statistics (2013), *Digest of Education Statistics, 2012* (NCES 2014-15), http://nces.ed.gov/fastfacts/display.asp?id=84 (accessed April 24, 2015), Webometrics finds fewer U.S. universities (3,289 universities) among a total of 23,887 in the world. Webometrics, "Countries Arranged by Number of Universities in Top Ranks," January 2015 edition, http://www.webometrics.info/en/node /54 (accessed April 30, 2015).

13. Roger L. Geiger, *The History of American Higher Education: Learning and Culture from the Founding to World War II* (Princeton: Princeton University Press, 2015), 507, 532–39.

14. The following historical overview has benefited especially from careful work by Axtell, *Wisdom's Workshop*; William G. Bowen and Eugene M. Tobin, *Locus of Authority: The Evolution of Faculty Roles in Governance* (Princeton: Princeton University Press and ITHAKA, 2015), a book ostensibly about decision making but of wider import; Geiger, *The History of American Higher Education*; Laurence R. Veysey, *The Emergence of the American University* (Chicago: University of Chicago Press, 1970).

learning in North America. Named in honor of this benefactor, Harvard College began to award degrees in 1642, and was originally governed by two bodies, the Board of Overseers and the President and Fellows, also known as the Corporation. And as a result of 1865 Massachusetts legislation, laymen came to replace clergy in governance.

To the south, William & Mary, the second oldest college in the American colonies, was chartered in 1693. The beginnings of other colonial colleges followed in the eighteenth century: Yale, created with the help of Elihu Yale's munificent gift; the College of New Jersey, eventually Princeton; King's College, now Columbia; the College of Philadelphia, later the University of Pennsylvania; the College in the Colony of Rhode Island and Providence Plantations, which assumed the family name of a major donor, Nicholas Brown; Queen's College, subsequently Rutgers; and Dartmouth, at first a missionary school intended to serve Native Americans, though, in practice, they gained few benefits from it. After national independence, beginning 1819, public universities granted state funding—among others, Virginia, designed by Thomas Jefferson at Charlottesville, and North Carolina—sought to foster an educated citizenry and trained professionals. Consonant with their Protestant faiths but increasingly to support the scientific and technical infrastructure of the times, these nascent institutions embraced the visions of their founders. Drawing on a combination of private and public funds, they provided an education at a price that few could manage.

In his account of this historical path, Frank Rhodes, a long-serving president of Cornell University (1977–95), remarks: "The colonial college, large in aspiration but small in size and modest in the range of its curriculum, was unambiguous in its educational purpose, selective in its admissions, and homogeneous in its student body."[15] In the colonial era, students pursued a classical curriculum and were required to attend chapel. Dedicated to the aims of church and state, higher education was for white Protestant boys.

College administrators admitted students according to the mores of their times: slavery, the depredation of indigenous American cultures, and the exclusion of women from leadership positions. They courted well-to-do colonial families—among them, merchants and planters who profited from the slave trade. Colonial colleges propagated the idea of white America.[16] Race was treated as a science. In "anatomical studies" at medical schools, academics examined cadavers, some of them stolen from cemeteries, and tanned skin to justify subordinating black people. Craniologists measured and exhibited skulls, purportedly showing the inferiority of blacks and contributing to the

15. Frank H. T. Rhodes, *The Creation of the Future: The Role of the American University* (Ithaca: Cornell University Press, 2001), 8.

16. See Craig Steven Wilder, *Ebony & Ivory: Race, Slavery, and the Troubled History of America's Universities* (New York: Bloomsbury Press, 2013).

racial narrative. With missionary zeal, colonizers trained pupils in religion and civilization, relegating indigenous people and the descendants of slaves who practiced faiths other than Protestantism to the role of infidels.[17]

In their private capacities rather than under the aegis of their colleges, individual academics generated research on human variation. Their findings on race were introduced at court trials and used as evidence. Professors, graduates, and scientific societies furnished witnesses, giving expert testimony. Race science made an impact on not only law but, more broadly, policy. The social construction of the biological basis of citizenship owes much to scholars whose work was used as a touchstone for discrimination against African Americans, Native Americans, Asians, Irish, and Jews, as well women in general.[18]

SECULARIZATION AND PROFESSIONALISM

After the United States attained political independence in 1776, the governance of colleges and universities trended toward secularization, which became more evident toward the end of the nineteenth century and the initial decades of the twentieth century. Merchants, some of whom profited from the slave trade, and professionals became numerous on boards of governors and replaced many of the clergymen.[19] Their representation in prominent university positions symbolized the permissibility of a system of enslavement, until the end of the Civil War. Slave trading by members of a governing board is thus deeply implicated in a higher education institution and exposed other members of the university to a way of thinking.

The captains of institutions of higher learning were accountable to their boards, made up of moneyed interests in the post–Civil War period of burgeoning commercialism. Ascendant social forces shaped educational institutions. Manufacturing and industrialization spurred greater social differentiation, seen in the governance of knowledge structures. In an evolving capitalist order, the affluent such as Carnegie, Hopkins, Rockefeller, and Stanford provided funds to run universities, which, in turn, offered training and a scientific infrastructure.[20] They buoyed an entrepreneurial spirit and the value of competition, which, even back then, was part of the chase for prestige and riches.

17. Ibid., 156, 193, 200, 208; Sean M. Heuvel and Lisa L. Heuvel, *The College of William and Mary in the Civil War* (Jefferson, NC: McFarland, 2013), 17.

18. Wilder, *Ebony & Ivory*, 211–12, 273.

19. Arthur Cohen, *The Shaping of American Higher Education: Emergence and Growth of the Contemporary System* (San Francisco: Jossey-Bass, 1998), 86.

20. Clyde W. Barrow, *Universities and the Capitalist State: Corporate Liberalism and the Reconstruction of American Higher Education, 1894–1928* (Madison: University of Wisconsin Press, 1989). I am grateful to Kees van der Pijl for bringing works by Barrow and Abbott (n28, below) to my attention.

On campuses like Rutgers in free states, universities were auspicious venues for the idea of resettling slaves and former slaves in Africa. After Charles Fenton Mercer, a Princeton graduate, helped plan the establishment of Liberia, a number of students came to share his belief in the policy of sending black Americans to Africa. Many of these students professed devotion to the importance of making the United States white. By the 1830s, colonization societies at about thirty-six higher education institutions were active in this movement.[21] Antislavery sensibility spread at U.S. universities in the North. One could be both against slavery and for resettlement. They went hand in hand. The decline of slaveholdings among Northern faculty and administrators abetted this alignment.[22] These student movements betray an incipient awareness of cultural and economic links between the local and the global, an understanding of transnational forces furthered by social movements on campuses in the twentieth and twenty-first centuries.

Amid struggles surrounding race and class, and the waning of the church's influence on universities' aspirations, the drive to build up the American state fed into the growth of higher education. The federal government found that universities provided not only training but also support for modern industry and national defense. From the age of the Puritans during colonial times to the Civil War years, the purposes of U.S. universities fluctuated. With vast changes in the composition of American society, higher education institutions came to encompass more engagement in public life and greater social responsibility.

The 1862 Morrill Act laid a foundation for public higher education and incentives for research. More specifically, it granted federal land for states to set up public universities and colleges to meet citizens' needs in fields deemed of practical utility—agriculture, home economics, mechanical arts, and military tactics—along with liberal arts. Soon after, land-grant schools—Kansas State University, Michigan State University, Pennsylvania State University, and others—came into existence, some of them enlarging extant agricultural schools. In addition, the federal government created the National Academy of Sciences (1863) and adopted the Hatch Act (1867), which offered funds for agricultural research and produced mechanisms for expert advice.[23]

The land-grant movement of the nineteenth century and the legislation that immediately followed represent major steps to expand educational opportunities and push higher education institutions along the path of producing useful research and knowledge workers for the market.[24] Justin Smith Morrill, a Vermont congressman and senator, sought to facilitate access to universities for the industrial classes. The purposes of the act were to integrate

21. Wilder, *Ebony & Ivory*, 248, 259, 262–63.
22. Ibid., 243–45.
23. This paragraph borrows from Cole, *The Great American University*, 28–29.
24. Geiger, *The History of American Higher Education*, 282–84.

practical arts with classical studies and advance applied research for boosting the local and national economy.[25] But Morrill's intentions were not entirely fulfilled. Texas and some other states set up new agriculture and mechanical units such as Texas A&M University, founded in 1871 and opened in 1876, alongside universities. During the Reconstruction period, a few southern states used the Morrill Act as a way to award grants to education institutions for African Americans so as to keep them separate from all-white universities.[26] Herein lies a tension that played out in later years: massification evolved as an attempt to maintain the core purposes of higher education *and* to orient universities toward practical ends. It embodied different sets of purposes. We will return to the question of whether these missions are compatible or at cross-purposes.[27]

After the Civil War, roughly from the 1870s to the early 1990s, university faculty carried out their studies on more specialized topics in their respective fields. New graduate programs were created. The curriculum and the research enterprise were professionalized in the sense of competition for funding and peer review. From the 1890–1910 period, disciplines, in the contemporary sense of academic units, delineated the structure of knowledge in American higher education. Departmental lines were drawn, though the timing of their emergence varied by discipline. In the United States, the growth of universities and career mobility among them meant that the knowledge structure required internal order. Disciplinary networks were channeled according to a division of labor. The market supplied jobs for academics whose intellectual life was organized into units of study. In view of objections to disciplinary specialization and the impetus for interdisciplinarity, multidisciplinarity, and, more recently, transdisciplinarity, it is important to recall this original move away from general education and toward a disciplinary system. To this day, academics have encamped in its territories, wherein they become versed in their rules, cultures, and codes, and seek the rewards.[28]

By the turning of the century, the American university had formed. It blended the English undergraduate residential college and German higher education's stress on research and graduate study. Variations on this model may be discerned at institutions such as Cornell and Johns Hopkins. Founded in a picturesque rural setting in upstate New York in 1865, Cornell was established as a combination of federal–land grant colleges and privately endowed colleges. The university's namesake, Ezra Cornell, made his fortune as a stockholder in Western Union and provided money to start the school. He shared

25. Ibid.

26. Ibid., 285, 297ff.

27. A theme in chapter 7.

28. Andrew Abbott, *Chaos of Disciplines* (Chicago: University of Chicago Press, 2001), 121–36, and as discussed in chapter 3 of this volume.

his vision with Andrew Dickson White, the university's first president, who likewise wanted to create "an institution where any person can find instruction in any study."[29] Ezra Cornell had in mind rich and poor, women and men: "the whole colored race and the whole female sex," as White put it.[30] Converting these ideas about the university's mission into curricular reform, Cornell University admitted women in 1872 and built Sage College for women, which opened in 1875.[31]

Another genus of the American university is represented by Johns Hopkins, opened in urban Baltimore in 1876. Its name recognizes a gift from a local investor in wholesale groceries and then multiple other companies, including the Baltimore & Ohio Railroad. Inspired by the Humboldtian spirit of research-based higher education, the university is devoted to the purposes of advanced scholarship and graduate studies and also offers an undergraduate degree.

Thus drawing on facets of universities in other countries, the United States adapted them to its own social context. It developed a national system and, over time, added distinctive ideas and practices.[32] Some leading educators and senior scholars make the opposing argument that given extraordinary differences among its universities, the United States does not have a system of higher education.[33] A countervailing view, however, is that the evolution of these institutions reflects a shared national culture and a common history marked by momentous events such as the Civil War, world wars, and waves of migration, constituting a multilayered system with many subsystems.[34] Yet by 1940, it became more fragmented and hierarchical. In view of the scope of the free market and relatively weak regulatory authority, it is hardly surprising that American higher education is fluid and largely unplanned. On balance, one can recognize a kaleidoscope of patterns and still find order in, and distinctive characteristics of, the U.S. system.[35]

At issue then are the different ways that individual institutions are embedded in university systems marked by their educational cultures, sense of moral purpose, and historical underpinnings. Let us now continue tracing the history.

From the end of World War I on, a panoply of state agencies provided increasing financial support for research and national needs in agriculture,

29. As quoted in Rhodes, *The Creation of the Future*, 5.

30. Ibid.

31. Morris Bishop, *A History of Cornell* (Ithaca: Cornell University Press, 1962), 148, 150.

32. Cole, *The Great American University*, 44; Rhodes, *The Creation of the Future*, 6–7.

33. Author discussion with Hunter Rawlings, then interim president of Cornell University, Ithaca, New York, November 10, 2016.

34. Geiger, *The History of American Higher Education*, 536–40.

35. Ibid.

defense, health care, and economic development. Private philanthropies, such as the Ford and Rockefeller foundations, fueled the growth of the American university system. This complex represents extreme concentrations of wealth: the holdings of large dynasties like the Carnegies, Mellons, and Rockefellers. As indicated, these funders, by dint of their support for certain academic programs and some genres of research but not others, have played a major role in shaping the structures of American universities.

Another key element in this matrix is the practices and laws of individual states, especially regarding the race factor. In the early twentieth century, Anglo-Saxon clubs emerged on campuses such as William & Mary, the University of Virginia, and Washington and Lee.[36] In a landmark decision, *Plessy v. Ferguson* (1896), the Supreme Court upheld the constitutionality of state laws on "separate but equal," authorizing segregation in public facilities. This move sanctioned the partition of races, including at state universities. African Americans in the South encountered not only legal but financial hurdles in trying to attain higher education at underfunded schools, particularly during the Great Depression. In an effort to mitigate this problem, George Patterson, president of Tuskegee Institute (later renamed Tuskegee University), founded the United Negro College Fund. It mobilized resources through charitable contributions and distributed them to historically black colleges on the basis of their enrollment.[37] Other initiatives followed World War II.

MASSIFICATION

The Servicemen's Readjustment Act of 1944, known as the GI Bill, enabled members of the armed services returning from the war to readjust to civilian life and helped them prepare for the job market. It granted stipends for tuition and living expenses at college or trade schools. In effect until 1956, this bill permitted nearly ten million veterans to gain further education, boosting the American economy.

The GI Bill not only augmented enrollment in higher education institutions but also added diversity to the student body. In principle, it increased university access for all veterans. Although the bill's provisions were egalitarian, African Americans faced barriers in their attempts to utilize them. Implementation of the bill was entrusted to state and local governments or third-party institutions such as schools and banks, some of which discriminated among veterans who qualified for their programs. In practice, the authorities divided applicants into white and non-white compartments.[38]

36. Heuvel and Heuvel, *The College of William and Mary in the Civil War*, 163.
37. Kathleen J. Frydl, *The GI Bill* (New York: Cambridge University Press, 2009), 240.
38. Ibid., 222.

To avoid integration and maintain a Manichean order, some states in the South subsidized black students' tuition in other states. For veterans who had received a stipend resulting from the GI Bill, the home state also paid for a train ticket to an out-of-state institution.[39] But as a result of GI enrollment, attendance at historically black universities soared. The training offered by Howard University and other historically black institutions fed into the civil rights movement. The Howard School of Law, for example, provided expertise for fighting legal battles during this turbulent period of American history. Kathleen Frydl makes the point that by benefiting some historically black universities, the GI Bill was however used to sponsor segmented avenues of higher education.[40]

Another landmark is the Supreme Court's 1954 ruling in *Brown v. Board of Education*, which overturned *Plessy v. Ferguson*, declaring that state laws establishing separate public schools for black and white students are unconstitutional. But *Brown* met resistance in the South and evasion in some localities elsewhere. It was more than a decade later before large-scale school integration was underway. Importantly, the momentum of the *Brown* case aided women working to change misconceptions and pursuing equal rights. The *Brown* decision thus widened space for public discussion about inequalities affecting myriad groups in the realm of higher education.[41]

A series of executive orders, laws, and court decisions barred race and ethnicity as legitimate means of excluding people from education and jobs. The Civil Rights Act of 1964 reinforced these measures and laid a foundation for affirmative action, enacted during Richard Nixon's years in the White House. The American Disability Act of 1970 and the Rehabilitation Act of 1973 then afforded access to a wider swath of disadvantaged citizens. The normative questions surrounding this legislation and publicly debated at the time are still with us today: Whom should federal, state, and local dollars assist? What are the responsibilities of taxpayers? And who should be left on their own?

By the mid-twentieth century, opening the doors to universities entailed an increase in public support for higher education. Postwar federal funding for basic research stemmed from the mid-1940s vision of Vannevar Bush, an advisor to President Franklin D. Roosevelt and the first director of the Office of Scientific Research and Development.[42] It was subsequently marshaled by other forward-looking policymakers. A substantial part of this research was carried out at Cold War universities, which forged alliances with industry and the

39. Ibid., 240.
40. Ibid., 244.
41. Elizabeth Davenport, "*Brown* and Gender Discrimination," in *Brown v. Board of Education: Its Impact on Public Education*, ed. Dara N. Byrne (New York: Thurgood Marshall Scholarship Fund, 2005), 77–80.
42. Vannevar Bush, *Science, the Endless Frontier: A Report to the President on a Program for Postwar Scientific Research* (Washington, DC: GPO, 1945).

military.[43] Drawing attention to this relationship, President Dwight Eisenhower warned that the "government contract becomes virtually a substitute for intellectual curiosity" and has grave consequences for the scholarly community.[44] And Senator J. William Fulbright later added foreboding about what was happening to the academy's sense of purpose: "When the university turns from its central purpose and makes itself an appendage to the Government, concerning itself with techniques rather than purposes, with expedients rather than ideas, dispensing conventional orthodoxy rather than new ideas, it is not only failing to meet its responsibilities to students; it is betraying the public trust."[45]

With the rush to bolster universities during the Cold War, it is hard to say whether Eisenhower's and Fulbright's apprehensions drew notice. From midcentury, the National Science Foundation was one of sundry governmentally funded institutions that granted research awards and graduate assistantships. Other government agencies, such as the National Aeronautics and Space Administration and the National Institutes of Health, also funneled revenue to universities. Little by little, the federal arms of higher education expanded their scope, as with the National Defense Education Act of 1965 and the Higher Education Act of 1965. Under Title VI, support for foreign language and area studies was readily available during the Cold War.

In the late 1960s and into the 1970s, the Vietnam War years, military spending crowded out substantial domestic expenditure. These decades were marked by student dissent, challenging authority. Many young Americans who sought to escape the military draft received a deferment by entering graduate school or finding a medical reason for not serving.

Then, with Reagan in the White House (1981–89), reductions in spending at home deepened. Yet a surge in university enrollments continued. The growth of universities led to more specialized units of study, fields of instruction, and research programs. Educational coherence became increasingly problematic. Institutions of higher education were more differentiated by orientation, a shift facilitated by new technologies.

TECHNOLOGICAL INNOVATIONS
AND ACCESS TO ACQUIRING THEM

Over the last quarter century, research universities have developed applications of new communications technology to countless aspects of daily life:

43. As noted in Michael M. Crow and William B. Dabars, *Designing the New American University* (Baltimore: Johns Hopkins University Press, 2015), 10, citing Stuart W. Leslie, *The Cold War and American Science: The Military-Industrial Complex at MIT and Stanford* (New York: Columbia University Press, 1993), 2.

44. As quoted in Leslie, *The Cold War and American Science*, 2.

45. As quoted in ibid., 13.

banking, entertainment, shopping, travel, health care, and, particularly after September 11, security in the form of surveillance. It is difficult to evade this compass.

In the academy, computerized technologies are revamping instruction, as with interactive online formats and the dissemination of learning materials. They can make content into a form of play as opposed to a didactic exercise and kindle creativity. In addition, they reconfigure the business and management functions of universities. Digital technology and the skills that go with it facilitate liaisons with other universities and corporations around the world. The new tools offer many possibilities, including digital libraries, digital media, and digital activism. They are vital to building research and professional communities and providing access to different knowledge cultures. Technological and entrepreneurial innovations enable universities to assume greater purchase on globalizing processes.

Technology has become a necessary but not sufficient means of improving universities' performance. Since the transformative potential cannot be fully known at this time, it would be wrong to underestimate the roles of information communications technology in higher education. But one should not overrate the gains either, especially if the benefits are exclusionary. And it would be a mistake to skirt the issue of who is being served by modern technology. To what extent is everyone able to share its rewards? Do underrepresented minorities?

Long after the Jim Crow era (the period from the 1880s to the 1960s, when state and local laws enforced racial segregation), its legacy is still strongly felt at American universities. Uneven access to up-to-date technology and the opportunities afforded by it are structured by university admissions procedures and the gateways to graduation. Without entering the minefield of debates on race-conscious admissions—the use of quotas including the question of upper limits for groups such as Asian Americans and affirmative action as a means of overcoming racial adversity—one can take California as an example and look at its 2009 going rate (the most recent data available), calculated by "dividing the number of entering students from each ethnicity and gender, by the total number of graduates by each ethnicity/gender combination."[46] At the University of California, the rate for African Americans is 4.1 percent; Latinos, 3.8; Caucasians, 5.9; and Asians, 25.9 percent. For California State University, these group percentages are 9.8, 10, 10, and 13, respectively. And for California community colleges, they are 22.1, 24.9, 20.5, and 23.3, also respectively.[47] The

46. California Postsecondary Education Commission, "College Going-Rates to Public Colleges and Universities," http://www.cpec.ca.gov/StudentData/CACGREthnicity.asp (accessed March 3, 2015).
47. Ibid.

figures show that students who identify as Asian or white are more likely to go to the University of California, where the largest share of resources in the system per student capita are found, while, proportionately, African Americans and Latinos are more numerous at community colleges, which utilize digital technology but are not as richly equipped as the other two echelons of the California system.

Another indicator of differential access to acquiring the skills offered at the nation's universities is four-year BA graduation rates, by race. According to 2014 data, the rate for African Americans is 20.8 percent; American Indian/Alaskan Natives, 23; Hispanics, 29.8; Asian/Pacific Islanders, 46.2; and Caucasians, 43.3.[48] In view of comparable statistics for 1996, the 2014 figures indicate that African Americans' gains on this measure are small relative to those of other groups; and the numbers for five-year graduation rates are not significantly different. Similarly, a 2015 Brookings Institution study finds that African American students comprise only 4 percent of registrants in the top decile at four-year colleges, gauged by midcareer alumni earnings. By comparison, 26 percent in the bottom group of colleges are African American.[49] While societal impediments encountered in precollegiate education may partly explain the below-average rates, the conundrum for universities is how to provide all their students with the proficiencies needed for a lifetime of curiosity-driven knowledge. This betterment is a matter of demonstrating institutional advancement, fulfilling a moral responsibility, and adhering to the cardinal purposes of the university.

While higher education institutions are striving to meet a large variety of performance standards set by internal and external bodies, American universities are also owning up to their past. In 2009, William & Mary's Board of Visitors acknowledged the college's part in exploiting slave labor and, in the postbellum years, supporting Jim Crow practices. Its Lemon Project: A Journey of Reconciliation (named for one of the people enslaved by William & Mary) investigates the college's role in sustaining slavery and racial discrimination.

---

48. Institute of Education Science (IES), National Center for Education Statistics, Digest of Education Statistics, "Graduation Rate from First Institution Attended for First-Time, Full-Time Bachelor's Degree-Seeking Students at 4-Year Postsecondary Institutions, by Race/Ethnicity, Time to Completion, Sex, Control of Institution, Acceptance Rate: Selected Cohort Entry Years, 1996 through 2007," table 326.10, http://nces.ed.gov/programs/digest/d14/tables/dt14_326.10.asp? current=yes (accessed March 4, 2015), cited in U.S. Department of Education, National Center for Education Statistics, Integrated Postsecondary Education Data System (IPEDS), Fall 2001 and Spring 2007 through Spring 2014, Graduation Rates component.

49. Brookings Institution, "Black Students at Top Colleges: Exceptions, Not the Rule," February 3, 2015, http://www.brookings.edu/blogs/social-mobility-memos/posts/2015/02/03-black-students-top-colleges-rothwell (accessed June 8, 2015).

Faculty and student researchers are exploring this painful history. Stakeholders at William & Mary are also addressing symbols of the past, such as a Confederate plaque displayed on one of the buildings. At other universities in the South and the North, a contentious issue is the monikers of edifices that commemorate white supremacists.[50]

Studies at Yale and Brown have sparked debate about their connections, some of them via trustees, benefactors, and alumni, to slavery and the abolition movement. Inquiries at Princeton, Emory, and other institutions have followed. Professors and students at Columbia are looking into the donations it received from families that profited from the slave market in lower Manhattan, the cotton trade, and plantations in the West Indies. In 1730, 42 percent of households in New York City's population owned slaves, and by the mid-eighteenth century, this market was second in size to only Charleston's slave market.[51] Georgetown University has acknowledged that in 1838, the Jesuits in charge of the college sold 272 enslaved African Americans to finance the institution's operations. Georgetown University now collaborates with a nonprofit group, the Georgetown Memory Project, which assists in identifying descendants of the families.

The research, a form of critical self-reflection on the university's participation in the institution of slavery, promises to have substantial pedagogical value as a way to ground analysis of history and ethics and learn methodologies. It also points to the question of what can be done to rectify the record in a manner consonant with the university's basic purposes. The higher administration agreed to remove the names of two early Georgetown presidents involved in the slave trade from campus buildings. Other proposed forms of redress include a formal apology from university authorities, a new research center for the study of slavery and its legacies, scholarships for the descendants, and a memorial to those enslaved.[52] Perhaps more far-reaching in its potential impact would be the establishment of a truth and reconciliation commission.

Going forward, the reformist framework represents a collective effort to reset priorities in U.S. higher education and update the system to meet the challenges of a globalizing order. Now, I want to angle off the route to neoliberal reforms and identify what these practices effectively mean.

50. Heuvel and Heuvel, *The College of William and Mary in the Civil War*, 16, 167.
51. Sylviane Diouf, "New York City's Slave Market," New York Public Library, 2015, https://www.nypl.org/blog/2015/06/29/slave-market (accessed November 23, 2016); see also Eric Foner, "Columbia University and Slavery: A Preliminary Report," file:// /C:/Users/jmittel/AppData/Local/Microsoft/Windows/INetCache/IE/Z0FRU0SH /PreliminaryReport.pdf (accessed March 7, 2017).
52. Pending at the time of writing.

Characteristics of Reform

SOCIOECONOMIC HIERARCHY

We can grasp emerging patterns by remembering that American universities reflect their histories and larger societal trends. The long arc is from the enrollment of Protestant boys during the colonial era to the growth of public provision for a somewhat more varied but still restrictive cohort in the nineteenth and mid-twentieth centuries to an even more complicated, differentiated system in the last few decades. Notably, institutions of higher education have evolved distinctly from the ethos of the 1862 Morrill Act granting land for public education and the subsequent expansion of mass education. Since the 1980s, parallel to growing nationwide income inequality, the university system has become increasingly segmented. At one end of the continuum are wealthy institutions, which are mostly privates, and, at the other pole, poor universities, some bled for resources as a result of public defunding and the 2008 financial crisis.

That said, universities are more than mirrors of social conditions. In the 2000s, when the United States is beset by low social mobility relative to the vertical changes in Canada and many Western European societies, American universities can provide opportunities to offset the tendency for the rich to get richer. In theory, they have the potential to equip large numbers of the less privileged with the knowledge for repositioning themselves.

While some public higher education institutions in the United States, such as Michigan State, changed the emphasis in their financial aid criteria from need to merit in the second half of the 1900s, many of them followed suit in the twenty-first century. This shift serves to attract students with better scores, which ratchets up a university's ranking. It also draws applicants from affluent families (a pool of potentially large donors) as well as from out of state and overseas who pay higher tuition. According to Thomas Piketty, author of the best-selling *Capital in the Twenty-First Century*, which argues that the rate of capital return in developed countries exceeds the rate of economic growth and causes widening wealth inequality, the parents of Harvard students earn, on average, approximately $450,000 per year, placing them in the top 2 percent of the income hierarchy in the United States.[53] This income in turn affords direct and indirect educational benefits to their offspring, which other strata find hard to gain. True, some well-endowed elite universities have scholarships for middle- and low-income students. But the latter cohort's numbers remain small. On this point, William Julius Wilson notes that his university, Harvard, has a program providing free tuition for students with disadvantaged

---

53. Thomas Piketty, *Capital in the Twenty-First Century*, trans. Arthur Goldhammer (Cambridge, MA: Harvard University Press, 2014), 485.

backgrounds. He also invokes statistics that indicate 67 percent of the entering first-year students at the most selective institutions in 2010 represented the top quarter of the earnings distribution, but just 15 percent were from the bottom half of the income distribution.[54] The same is true for students who enjoy generous financial provisions at corresponding selective private institutions, which want to keep up with their competitors and buttress their case for continuing tax exemptions.[55]

Like Harvard, other elite universities are part of the movement to increase economic diversity in their student bodies. Stanford, for example, issues tuition waivers to students whose parents have an annual income and assets of less than $125,000 and free room and board for those making under $65,000. But its total enrollment remains starkly skewed toward wealthy families whose children are raised in neighborhoods with highly educated people and top schools. They have benefited from households with the resources to invest in pre-K programs, tutors, SAT preparation courses, enrichment activities, summer camps with academic curriculum, and worldwide travel. These activities systemically advantage applicants from privileged backgrounds and play a large role in boosting their qualifications for higher learning.

Over the years, institutions such as Oberlin College in Ohio and Amherst College in Massachusetts have bucked the trend of the growing economic divide. Founded in 1837 by Presbyterian ministers, Oberlin was the first institution of higher learning in the United States to regularly admit black students and women. It continues to be known for its policies of affirmative action in admissions and realizing diversity. Amherst devotes more resources to grants rather than loans, offers scholarships to low-income international students who are ineligible for Pell funding, admits most of its transfer students from community colleges, and looks favorably on underprivileged applicants with high SAT scores. While these measures could be catalysts, they have been adopted at small colleges and, in the main, are anomalies in the United States. By themselves, these incongruent instances have had little impact on the national educational scene.

Coincident to a drop in state funding for higher education, the cost of tuition is up 500 percent since 1986. Private citizens have shouldered the brunt of it. The average borrower owed $25,100 in 2013. Total student-loan debt has

54. William Julius Wilson, "The Role of Elite Institutions," *Chronicle Review* 58, no. 40 (July 6, 2012): B9. See Anthony P. Carnevale and Jeff Stroh, "Separate and Unequal: How Higher Education Reinforces the Intergenerational Reproduction of White Racial Privilege," Georgetown Public Policy Institute, Center on Education and the Workforce, July 2013, https://cew.georgetown.edu/wp-content/uploads/2014/11/SeparateUnequal .FR_.pdf (accessed June 15, 2015).

55. William Deresiewicz, "How to Lower the Cost of Higher Ed," *The Nation* 300, no. 29 (July 20/27, 2015): 29.

soared to over $1.2 trillion, more than double the amount of 10 years ago. Students are paying more largely because state spending is shrinking. For all 50 states, the average allocation per student from the onset of the financial crisis in 2008 to 2015 dropped from about $9,000 to approximately $7,000, the least in 30 years.[56] Under these circumstances, students are gravitating away from the humanities because of increasing university enrollments, encompassing more less-privileged students, many of them via community colleges; job opportunities in practical fields; and universities' decisions to admit fewer entrants in humanities programs. More are majoring in subjects such as business and economics that lead to career prospects in the relatively lucrative fields of finance and consulting.

While American universities continue to be mechanisms of stratification, academe is promising to address inequalities, including in its own ranks. Nonetheless, the power and pay hierarchies within universities themselves persist. Take gender dynamics. The available data reveal that although women's enrollment in the student body surpasses that of men, women on the faculty are underrepresented, especially at the senior levels. Men outnumbered women by three to one among full professors at doctoral universities in 2013–14, with women earning, on average, 91 cents per dollar paid to male faculty members. By comparison, women account for more than half the faculty at two-year colleges. But the pay differences for men and women are also evident there, albeit at smaller levels and at lower salaries.[57]

The stratification among universities is linked to endowment inequality. Pointing to Harvard's immense endowment, Cole cites the large comparative advantage of elite research institutions. Noting the high correlation between the reputed quality of these universities and the magnitude of their endowments, he highlights the leverage: "The private American universities with the top six endowments were all ranked as being within the top ten universities in the world."[58] Further, Cole conjectures that the annual *growth* in Harvard's endowment could become greater than the *total* endowment of its competitors, which, except for a handful, are being reduced to "a farm system" of talent.[59] This inequality can be viewed in terms of endowments *per student*: in 2014, $1.709 million at Harvard, and $2.621 million at Princeton (the latter with a much smaller enrollment than at the former).

56. Rana Foroohar, "How the Financing of Colleges May Lead to Disaster!" *New York Review of Books* 53, no. 15 (October 13, 2016): 29, drawing on Beth Akers and Matthew M. Chingos, *Game of Loans: The Rhetoric and Reality of Student Debt* (Princeton: Princeton University Press, 2016).

57. "Women Face More Disparity in Pay and Representation at Academe's Top Levels," *Chronicle of Higher Education* 60, no. 30 (April 11, 2014): A26.

58. Cole, *The Great American University*, 475.

59. Ibid., 475, 477.

By comparison, consider the levels at public universities, even leading ones, for example, $0.041million at Berkeley and $0.223 million at the University of Michigan.[60]

Correspondingly, Piketty also calls attention to university endowments as an engine of inequality. He maintains that the most sizable fortunes generate the highest rates of return on capital.[61] The top-ranked universities—Harvard, Princeton, Yale, Stanford, and so forth—with the largest endowments get the biggest increases. Piketty finds that for Harvard, Yale, and Princeton, taken together, the yield was 10.2 percent from 1980 to 2010, twice as much as the gains at lesser-endowed institutions. For universities with funds of $1 billion or more in assets, 10-year returns averaged 7.2 percent in 2015, while those with $100 million or less averaged no more than 6 percent.[62] In the United States, the median university endowment has $115 million in assets.[63] Higher education institutions with average or small endowments are unable to compensate their teams of portfolio managers handsomely in the manner of opulent universities like Harvard and other Ivy League schools: typically 2 percent for annual management and 20 percent of the investment profits for plotting strategies and investing funds. The most prosperous institutions can afford to pay fees that their competitors are unable to provide. In addition, expensive accountants and high-priced law firms work out ways for their clients to avoid heavy tax burdens. Inequalities among institutions, then, are to a great extent attributable to earnings on capital, which amplify the affluence of prestigious universities.[64]

Recent data (2014) on the 20 universities with the biggest endowments support Cole's and Piketty's observations about the distance on the scale of endowments, as table 4.1 shows. Strikingly, of the 20 universities with the largest endowments, 15 have top 20 U.S. rankings. Harvard's endowment, which commands the topmost spot, is 42 percent greater than that of the runner-up, Yale, and 51 percent more than that of the University of Texas *system*, with about 227,848 students, around eight times Harvard's enrollment of 29,652

60. National Association of College and University Business Officers and Commonfund Institute, "U.S. and Canadian Institutions Listed by Fiscal Year (FY) 2014 Endowment Market Value and Change in Endowment Market Value from FY2013 to FY2014" (revised 2015), http://www.nacubo.org/Documents/EndowmentFiles/2014_Endowment _Market_Values_Revised.pdf (accessed June 15, 2015). Used as a basis of computing per-student endowments.

61. Piketty, *Capital in the Twenty-First Century*, 449.

62. Stephen Foley, "Endowments Failed by Reality of Low Returns," *Financial Times*, February 1, 2016.

63. Ibid., drawing on an annual study of investment returns by the National Association of College and University Business Officers.

64. Piketty, *Capital in the Twenty-First Century*, 449–54; Victor Fleischer, "Stop Colleges from Hoarding Cash," *New York Times*, August 15, 2015.

Table 4.1. Top 20 U.S. Endowments and Rankings

Endowment Ranking 2015	University	Endowment Size 2015	National University Ranking 2015
1	Harvard University	$36.45	2
2	Yale University	$25.57	3
3	University of Texas System	$24.08	Austin, 53
4	Princeton University	$22.72	1
5	Stanford University	$22.22	4 (tied)
6	Massachusetts Institute of Technology	$13.47	7
7	Texas A&M System	$10.48	College Station, 68
8	Northwestern University	$10.19	13
9	University of Pennsylvania	$10.13	8 (tied)
10	University of Michigan, Ann Arbor	$9.95	29
11	Columbia University	$9.64	4 (tied)
12	University of Notre Dame	$8.57	16
13	University of California System	$8.00	Berkeley, 20; Los Angeles, 23; San Diego, 37, Davis, 38; Santa Barbara, 40; Irvine, 42; Santa Cruz, 85
14	University of Chicago	$7.55	4 (tied)
15	Duke University	$7.30	8 (tied)
16	Washington University in St. Louis	$6.82	14
17	Emory University	$6.68	21
18	University of Virginia	$6.18	23
19	Cornell University	$6.04	15
20	Rice University	$5.56	19

Source: Compiled from "Almanac 2016–17," *Chronicle of Higher Education* 62, no. 43 (August 19, 2016): 54; "National University Rankings," *U.S. News & World Report*, September 9, 2014, http://colleges .usnews.rankingsandreviews.com/best-colleges/rankings/national-universities (accessed April 13, 2015).

Note: 2015 university rankings are based on Fall 2014. Endowment sizes are in billions of dollars.

in mid-2016.[65] Note that 15 of the biggest 20 endowments are held by private universities. And of the five public institutions, three are statewide systems; two, the University of Michigan–Ann Arbor and the University of Virginia, single campuses. The disproportion in the size of endowments between private and public universities is apparent too in the endowment per student. Leaving aside Rockefeller University, which has about 200 MD-PhD students, all postgraduates, and is devoted to biomedical research, Princeton ranks first

---

65. "College Navigator," National Center for Educational Statistics of U.S. Department of Education, http://nces.ed.gov/collegenavigator/ (accessed September 9, 2016).

in endowments per student by an amount that exceeds that at any public university by a factor of ten.[66]

While the wide chasm in resources between the most touted universities, including the aforementioned ones, and other higher education institutions is evident, the backstory is important. The other institutions, some of them having minuscule endowments, cater to the general populace, 80 percent of which receives its higher education at public institutions. In the socioeconomic hierarchy, community colleges enroll about 45 percent of students seeking higher degrees. The enrollment at public community colleges is six times as much as at private research universities. Whereas education-related spending per student at the former is slightly above $10,000, it is nearly $36,000 at the latter.[67] That said, community colleges can be pathways to four-year programs, themselves segmented into small private colleges, midsize state institutions, and for-profit institutions.

Overall, the United States has a growing divide between students attending rich and poorly financed institutions. Given high tuition fees, student debt, and the distribution of parental income, the university system in the United States pledges, but is not vectoring toward, equal access. Longitudinal data show that American universities have become increasingly stratified.[68] Equal opportunity remains an aspiration. It is a high ideal, a dream, rather than an actuality. Political and managerial leaders are wrestling with how to fulfill it.

EXECUTIVE POWER

In decision making on academic life, the power of the executive is rising relative to that of the faculty. Executives use the dwindling of public funding as an occasion to spearhead reforms in university governance. Their rationale is the need for greater autonomy to improve personnel management and gain flexibility. In states such as Wisconsin, the governor also advocates limiting public sector unions and weakening the tenure system. And some state legislators favor zero funding.

On the whole, executive control of exercising oversight itself is opaque. The power of politicians, the governing board, and the university president is contested, as demonstrated in the struggle over the attempt to oust President

66. Calculation based on the most recent data available, published in "Almanac 2016–17," *Chronicle of Higher Education* 62, no. 43 (August 19, 2016): 54–55, and in "College Opportunities Online Locator," National Center for Educational Statistics of U.S. Department of Education, September 9, 2016, http://nces.ed.gov/collegenavigator/ (accessed September 9, 2016).

67. Delta Cost Project (American Institutes for Research, Washington, DC, 2015), http://www.deltacostproject.org/ (accessed June 18, 2015).

68. Ibid.

Teresa Sullivan at the University of Virginia. This brings to light the contention between outside and inside executives—those external to the university and those internal to it—though collusion happens as well. Their normative values and philosophical commitments become educational policy differences, as the controversy surrounding Sullivan demonstrates.

In 2012, the Board of Visitors ordered her to design a strategic plan that would "examine our very purpose and reason for being" and provide "a roadmap for our future." The president's special committee, steering committee, and seven working groups involved more than ten thousand students, staff, alumni, and others in this exercise aimed at securing board approval.[69] The challenge was to come to grips with the multiple purposes of the university and make them operational. This is fundamentally a matter of who or what does the scripting and how it works.

Unhappy with President Sullivan's performance, members of the board, appointed by the governor and confirmed by the state legislature, forced her resignation, only to reinstate her after protests by faculty and opposition from alumni, students, and donors. There was widespread concern that the board had overstepped its statutory bounds in assigning specific goals to the president and that it had failed to follow its governance requirements. The Southern Association of Colleges and Schools Commission, the accrediting body, accused the board of compromising the university's integrity and placed this prominent institution on warning for one year. In essence, these tumultuous events suggest that executive authority is riven by deep tensions affecting society more generally and that its rise is not limitless. They epitomize the disruption caused by engrafting a business model that emphasizes achieving near-term, utilitarian results on the long-honored purposes of the university. Inasmuch as both Sullivan and her detractors on the board favored market culture, but advocated different strategies to this end, the contention, too, hovered around which and whose business model to adopt.

In another case, efforts by Texas governor Rick Perry, supported by the university system chancellor, Francisco G. Ciagora, to remove the president of the University of Texas at Austin, William C. Powers, came to a head in 2014. The battle was over their different views of the purposes of the university.

69. Teresa A. Sullivan, letter to members of the University of Virginia Board of Visitors, July 29, 2013, http://www.virginia.edu/bov/meetings/13aug%20Retreat/Letter%20from %20President%20Sullivan%20to%20the%20Board%20of%20Visitors%20-%20Strategic %20Plan%20Update.pdf (accessed December 13, 2013), and "Update Regarding the Strategic Direction of the University," December 2, 2013, http://www.virginia.edu/president /speeches/13/message131202.html (accessed December 13, 2013); "U-Va. Board Approves Basic Framework of Strategic Plan," *Washington Post*, November 17, 2013, which draws on *U.S. News & World Report* rankings wherein the University of Virginia tied the University of California at Los Angeles for the number two spot among public universities and came in twenty-third among all public and private universities in the United States.

Governor Perry held that universities should publish balance sheets that show the amount of money that individual faculty members raise and cost the institution; grant faculty bonuses based entirely on student evaluations; and offer a $10,000 degree, without specifying standards for awarding it. For the governor, chancellor, and an outspoken trustee, Wallace L. Hall Jr., the emphasis in running the university ought to be on efficiency and customer satisfaction rather than, as President Powers advocated, the academic values of faculty autonomy, research excellence, and undergraduate teaching. In the face of a public backlash against firing the president, it was mutually agreed that Powers would retire nearly a year later, at the time he had requested.[70] As in Virginia, the clash in Texas engulfed values, governance, and budgeting.

Many university campuses are utilizing a form of decentralized budgeting that provides incentives, fosters entrepreneurship, and spurs competition among cash-strapped academic units. More attention is given to revenue and costs, which, critics allege, pushes the university's mission toward making money as its bottom line.

Under these conditions, institutional spending patterns are changing rapidly. Professional and administrative hiring outpaces the rate of growth of full-time faculty and increases in student enrollment. New billets are established for vice presidents, assistant vice presidents, deputy provosts, their assistants, and the like. Support positions include directors of financial operations, risk managers, human resources coordinators, admissions officers, computer analysts, counselors, athletics coaches, and health workers. The Delta Cost Project of the American Institutes for Research, a nonprofit social science organization, reports that from 1990 to 2012, the number of full-time faculty and academic staff members per professional and managerial administrator declined 40 percent at public higher education institutions, and to slightly fewer faculty and staff per administrator at private universities.[71] All the while, full-time faculty salaries remained flat for several years and then, since the 2013–14 academic year, showed an uptick.[72]

The reasons usually given for the spike in noninstructional jobs are austerity in state appropriations and heightened expectations of universities.

70. Jack Stripling, "Rogue Trustee in Texas Stirs Debate on His Role," *Chronicle of Higher Education* 60, no. 2 (April 25, 2014): A3–4; Hunter R. Rawlings III, "Texas Makes an Appalling Mess of Education 'Reform,'" *Chronicle of Higher Education* 60, no. 41 (June 18, 2014), http://chronicle.com/article/Texas-Makes-an-Appalling-Mess/147561/ (accessed March 6, 2015).

71. Delta Cost Project, "Labor Intensive or Labor Expensive?" (Washington, DC: American Institutes for Research, 2014), 14, http://www.deltacostproject.org/sites/default/files/products/DeltaCostAIR_Staffing_Brief_2_3_14.pdf (accessed June 25, 2015).

72. Ibid., 15; "Professors Pay Has Rebounded Strongly since the Recession, Faculty Association's Annual Survey Shows," *Chronicle of Higher Education* 62, no. 32 (April 22, 2016): A14.

Institutions of higher education are increasingly called upon to provide student services such as psychological and career counseling, offer a wide range of cocurricular activities like remedial skills to make up for deficiencies in precollegiate education, respond to pressure from parents and policymakers, comply with labyrinthine federal and state regulations in areas ranging from student privacy and sexual misconduct to disability accommodation, mount new technology platforms, raise more funds to offset the ebb of public subsidies, and face up to mounting overseas competition. More managers are needed to minister the explosion of data on these tasks. Noticeably, this resembles the proliferation of "stats" in the national pastime, baseball, prone to a form of unofficial regulation maintained by self-interested technologists. But universities should not be akin to big-time sports competition: businesses that generate large profits. In academe, whether the trend of expanding the number of professional and administrative positions is excessive or justified is subject to debate. Surely this polemic can deflect attention from the guiding purposes of universities.

A prime responsibility of a university chief goes beyond ensuring that an institution's engine runs; she must keep it on track to realize the grand purposes of education. She should prompt constituents and the public to reflect on what learning is all about. An educational leader can inspire them to think deeply about transcendent questions and soulful concerns. Her pulpit is a station for kindling the imagination, for setting an agenda with elevated discourse. It is not overly preachy to call on students to be mindful of abiding principles and social justice when the world is in the throes of transformations in technology, the environment, and the social economy. More often, however, presidents' preoccupations are mundane; pecuniary matters busy their minds and dominate the daily schedule.

University CEOs are compensated handsomely for their work. The direction is toward seven-figure salaries for high-ranking university administrators, sums defended by trustees on the basis of what they think the market demands and denounced by critics as outsize in times of pinched budgets, tuition increases, and escalating student debt. Large executive pay packages are needed, governing boards say, if a university is to be competitive with its peer institutions and other industries, where CEO-to-worker pay ratios exceed those in higher education.[73] The number of million-dollar presidents at private universities reached 39 in 2014.[74] Counting signing and moving bonuses, as well as severance payments, the salaries of five public-university

73. Executive pay at companies listed in the S&P 500 for 2014 averaged 204 times median worker pay, https://www.glassdoor.com/research/ceo-pay-ratio/ (accessed November 10, 2015).

74. Dan Bauman, "Executive Compensation at Private Colleges," *Chronicle of Higher Education* 63, no. 16 (December 9, 2016): A16–18.

presidents surpassed $1 million in 2015.[75] And when E. Gordon Gee exited the presidency at a public university, Ohio State, in 2013, he reportedly received a package of more than $6 million from this tax-exempt institution.[76] The nominal base salaries of many presidents are supplemented by not only severance but also deferred compensation and extra dollars for their participation on corporate boards. Added to this, when institutions of higher education are struggling to meet their financial obligations, high-power sports coaches draw multimillion-dollar remuneration: in 2014, University of Alabama football coach Nick Saban's contract topped $6.9 million per year for the next eight seasons. Jim Harbaugh, football coach at the University of Michigan, received a higher salary, reportedly $9 million in 2016. He is one of 72 coaches who make more than $1 million per year, a level of compensation, their employers explain, justified by the amount of revenue produced, market competition, and the going way to convert a brand name into national power.[77]

CEOs at for-profit universities collected an average of $7.3 million in 2010, and Robert S. Silberman, Strayer Education's chief executive, garnered $41 million in 2011, including stock options.[78] Owned by publicly traded companies and private equity firms, these institutions educate 12 percent of students enrolled in U.S. higher education institutions. The best known of these, the University of Phoenix, operates programs at multiple locations in the United States and overseas. Sylvan Learning Systems, Inc., has a network of campuses in Latin America and China. They serve nontraditional students such as active-duty personnel on military bases and veterans, and have come under public scrutiny for pocketing federal aid from Pell grants and thus taxpayers' money, unscrupulous recruiting, and misreporting data. Accused of fraudulent practices, Corinthian Colleges, with 72,000 students and 12,000 employees, went bankrupt in 2016. Now, new for-profit products sold by outside companies such as Pearson and Civitas Learning include "course-in-a-box kits" and "dashboards," which can be offered by temporary or part-time instructors who receive minimal pay.[79] Meanwhile, traditional universities are developing their own for-profit, web-based subsidiaries. These online programs are in keeping with other for-profit tools imported from the business world.

75. Dan Bauman, "Bonuses Push More Public-College Leaders Past $1 Million," *Chronicle of Higher Education* 62, no. 41 (July 22, 2016): A17–22.

76. Frank Bruni, "Platinum Pay in Ivory Towers," *New York Times*, May 20, 2015.

77. Lawrence Biemiller, "Million-Dollar Salaries," *Chronicle of Higher Education* 63, no. 10 (November 4, 2016): A4.

78. Tamar Lewin, "Senate Committee Report on For-Profit Colleges Condemns Costs and Practices," *New York Times*, July 30, 2012.

79. Goldie Blumenstyk, "How For-Profit Education Is Now Embedded in Traditional Colleges," *Chronicle of Higher Education* 62, no. 18 (January 15, 2016): A13.

But do for-profit and nonprofit universities really need to pay their presidents five, ten, or more times the salaries earned by those who teach students and carry out research? On average, full-time male professors received $91,994 in 2012–13; women, $73,982 in the same year.[80] And do presidents need to accept the big raises offered? In a shining example of an effort to keep administrative salaries down, Gregory Fenves rejected an increase from about $425,000 to $1 million per year when he was promoted from provost to president at the University of Texas at Austin and agreed to $750,000.

The trouble with the palpable divergence between executive compensation and remuneration for faculty and staff is that it can cut against a sense of community. The pay ratio between upper-level administrators and other employees hurts morale. It is out of proportion and symbolizes market values that stray from the purposes to which higher learning is dedicated. It is at cross-purposes with the university's mission and jeopardizes its core principles. It influences the ethos of higher education, increasingly that of winners and losers. And it correlates with other shifts in the academic workforce.

Under the auspices of their boards of directors and presidential leadership, senior managers are pulling back authorization and budgets for tenure-track positions. A growing share of faculty job openings are for contingent workers: temporary full-time instructors on term contracts, part-time adjuncts, and graduate student employees. Figure 4.1 depicts the casualization of academic labor. Full-time tenured and tenure-track faculty declined from 56.8 percent of the total in 1975 to 29.8 percent in 2011. And full-time non-tenure-track increased from 13.0 to 19.1 percent in the same years. Meanwhile, part-time faculty jumped from 30.2 to 51.1 percent. The rest of the teaching was done by graduate assistants. In all, contingent faculty surged from 43.2 to 70.2 percent during this period. The latter figure is considerably greater than the representation of contingent workers in the overall American labor force, now 40 percent. The proportion of total growth from 1975 to 2011 attributable to contingent appointments came to 91.5 percent.

Although the data on these trends vary by source and according to the definition of categories, the overall pattern in academic labor markets is arresting. Reporting that between 1969 and 2009, tenured and tenure-line faculty tumbled from 78.3 percent of all faculty to 33.5 percent—a reversal in the ratio—Bowen and Tobin note that "this shift in the mix of teaching staff is truly *revolutionary* (the right word here, as it is often not) and shows no sign of abating."[81] Adding to their point: from the mid-1970s to the present day, the percentage of tenured and tenure-eligible faculty relative to contingent faculty

80. "Average Salaries of Full-Time Faculty Members, by Rank and Type of Institution, 2012–13," *Chronicle of Higher Education Almanac 2013–14* 60, no. 46 (August 23, 2013): 6.
81. Bowen and Tobin, *Locus of Authority*, 153, emphasis in original.

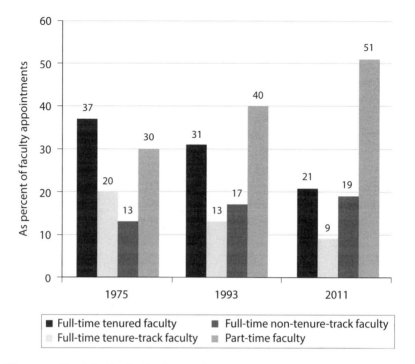

Figure 4.1. Trends in Faculty Employment Status, 1975–2011.
Source: Figure 4.1 is a slightly modified version of U.S. Department of Education, National Center for Education Statistics, "IPEDS Fall Staff Survey"; published tabulations only. Compiled by the AAUP Research Office, John W. Curtis, Director of Research and Public Policy, Washington, DC, March 20, 2013, http://www.aaup.org/sites/default/files/Faculty_Trends_0.pdf (accessed April 1, 2015).

Note: Figures for 2011 are estimated national totals for all degree-granting institutions. Percentages may not add to 100 due to rounding.

has flipped. The 70 percent tenured and on a tenure track has contracted to 30 percent while 70 percent is now a contingent workforce.

American higher education's instructional personnel have become a more differentiated system of haves and have-nots. Tenured faculty, 20.7 percent of the 2011 teaching cadre, enjoy job security, a steady salary, and benefits; 79.3 percent do not. The lot of people who teach at a university without contractual assurance is subject to increasing scrutiny. A 2014 study, "The Just-in-Time Professor," by the U.S. House Committee on Education and the Workforce, details the situation for more than one million adjunct and other non-tenure-track faculty.[82] With median pay of about $2,700 for a three-credit course,

82. U.S. House of Representatives, Committee on Education and the Workforce Democratic Staff, "The Just-in-Time Professor" (Washington, DC, 2014), http://democrats .edworkforce.house.gov/sites/democrats.edworkforce.house.gov/files/documents/1.24.14 -AdjunctEforumReport.pdf (accessed June 29, 2015).

adjuncts often teach several classes, frequently commuting to different universities, in order to make a living. They report annual salaries of $5,000 to $55,000 per year, many of them below the federal poverty line for a family (of three, $19,530, or four, $23,550), necessitating reliance on a spouse's income and, in some cases, food tamps.[83] Relishing academic life, many part-timers have a teaching load of five courses per term, cover the cost of their own travel between campuses, and use a car as an office. They cannot find time to carry out research and for publication, crucial for landing a full-time position, and do not receive support to attend the conferences where recruiting takes place.[84] It is difficult for them to hold office hours, meet with students outside class, and find time to write letters of recommendation.

In an eforum organized by the House Committee, one part-time instructor's poignant story epitomizes this saga.

During this [experience working at universities], we lost our home. We could no longer afford to make the payments on my poverty wages and my domestic partner's wages from her job. We moved in with a friend and now had to commute an hour each way and a half hour between schools. I was driving three hours a day and teaching five days a week switching colleges during the day. I had no office space, so I often carried all of my work with me. Piles and piles of manilla [sic] folders in the back of my failing car. A car I couldn't afford to take care of but was basically working out of. It is a run down Nissan that cost $60 a tank to fill and I was filling it two to three times a week, paying for childcare for my son who made it out of the hospital in good health and paying for my child support for two boys. I was now making $3000 a class and able to make $15000 for that semester.[85]

More than a description of an individual's predicament, this communiqué suggests that universities not only are home to faculty who love learning and are devoted to exchanging knowledge with colleagues and students but also can be alienating places for unprotected intellectual workers. Their precarious existence shortchanges students saddled with mounting tuition and debt, many of them seeking attentive, caring mentors.

To advocate for contingent academic workers, the New Faculty Majority formed in 2009. This activist group's aims are to set standards and put pressure on employers. Their leaders convoke meetings with university administrators to propose concrete, low-cost ways for better supporting part-time employees and recount remedial measures adopted by peer institutions. In addition, adjunct unions' initiatives mesh with some of the more-established

83. Ibid., 6, 9.
84. Ibid., 23.
85. Ibid., 8.

strategies of the AAUP, the American Federation of Teachers, and the Service Employees International Union for attaining health insurance, retirement benefits, livable wages, basic institutional support, and full-time contracts. The overall objective is to alter a system in which some instructors become second-class citizens.[86] Following a 2016 ruling by the National Labor Relations Board that requires private universities to bargain with labor unions representing graduate-student employees, political and managerial executives now must either muster new funding or reallocate extant revenue to improve temporary employees' conditions of employment.

The risk with officials' bids to strip faculty protections of tenure and shared governance is that it can compromise judgment and restrain political voice. This is particularly worrisome in a country where McCarthyism has threatened academic freedom: the rights and responsibilities of both faculty and students in the pursuit of knowledge without fear of persecution and without regard to background or orientation. To this day, McCarthyite incidents recur, as I know from personal experience.

I encountered casualization and constraints on intellectual autonomy before I received tenure and, later, as a full professor and university administrator. Initially hired as an assistant professor on a one-year contract at an elite university, I came under fire when asked to teach "Contemporary Civilization" in the core curriculum.[87] Noting that the list of readings prescribed for this course failed to include a single work by a non-Western author, I decided not to deviate from the required texts but to supplement them with books by authors from the global South. Toward the end of the term, a senior professor responsible for the "Contemporary Civilization" program told me not to assign the additional books. Seeking to be nonconfrontational and find common ground, I pointed out that my syllabus included all the material that instructors of the several sections were expected to incorporate. In my defense, I insisted that students were supposed to learn about "Contemporary Civilization," not only "Western Civilization," and suggested that the reading list should be broadened to take into account the diversity of the world.

My next brush with a clampdown on academic freedom occurred shortly after I was appointed professor and dean of international studies at another private university. The attack was triggered by a government official who, with taxpayers' money, hired a consultant to write a report on a unit for which I was

86. See David Dobbie and Ian Robinson, "Erosion of Tenure and the Unionization of Contingent Faculty," *Labor Studies Journal* 33, no. 2 (January 2008): 117–40; Peter Schmidt, "Adjunct Advocacy: Contingent Faculty Are Demanding—and Getting—Better Working Conditions," *Chronicle of Higher Education* 61, no. 26, Trends Report (March 11, 2015): B27–30.

87. The passages on academic freedom in this chapter echo Mittelman, "Who Governs Academic Freedom in International Studies?"

responsible. The document alleged that our curriculum was faulty because it reflected a liberal bias and, late in the Cold War, fostered "capitulationist" attitudes.[88] The statement condemned as pacifistic an inventory of strategies of conflict resolution that included nonviolence, bargaining, and compromise. It held that teaching about foreign cultures damaged American values and encouraged "moral relativism." Another indictment was the omission of the biblical concept of creation, prenatal justice, and the rights of unborn children.

In the face of a threat from the largest donor to withdraw funds if the problem was not resolved, the chancellor of the university and the Board of Trustees made no attempt to defend our curriculum, publications, or personnel. On the contrary, the chancellor issued a gag order to prohibit staff from commenting in public on the controversy and called for a watchdog committee to inspect the *balance* of instructional programs, delayed faculty appointments, and failed to respond to inquiries about this issue from legislators.

The chancellor claimed to be walking a tightrope between the fiscal health of the university and the principle of academic freedom. The vice chancellor for academic affairs asked me to respond in writing to a series of questions formulated by the chancellor: Why does the faculty give priority to the suspect themes of global conflict analysis and international development? Why is the school of international studies hiring non-U.S. nationals? Why is the school of international studies preoccupied with the Third World?

In the end, the university mounted a weak defense against the wanton violation of academic freedom by its chief executive, a political official, and a private donor, and even compromised and collaborated with these forces. After trying to establish middle ground and negotiate with the central administration, I tendered a letter of resignation, expressing anguish at the adverse actions that degraded the freedom of the university:

> The core of academic freedom is the unrestrained and diverse pursuit of ideas. . . . I profoundly disagree with your professed stance of "walking a tightrope" between the donations of conservatives and the principle of academic freedom. The foremost responsibility of the chancellor of the university is to defend the right to pursue ideas without infringement.[89]

I cite these events not because my biography is intrinsically interesting but to show that academic freedom can be threatened from different quarters: the state, donors, university executives, and academics themselves. Without invoking a spate of more recent cases of abuses that have caused controversy,

88. Gregg L. Cunningham, "Blowing the Whistle on Global Education," report prepared for Thomas G. Tancredo, Secretary's Regional Representative, Region VIII (Washington, DC: U.S. Department of Education, 1986).

89. James H. Mittelman, personal letter, June 4, 1987.

my point is that academic freedom remains fragile. It must always be won and rejuvenated. Academics bear responsibility for safeguarding dissent, critical thinking, and the autonomy of the institutions in which they work and study. While welcoming observations from outside groups, universities are, in the first instance, accountable to themselves. The way to ensure this accountability, though imperfect, is through a multilayered system of checks and balances: investigations of alleged misconduct by committees, self-studies, peer review of scholarly manuscripts, multilevel assessments for hiring and promotion, student evaluations of courses, research oversight by institutional review boards, financial audits, grievance procedures, appeals to ombudsmen, and accreditation via regulatory bodies. Accountability and accreditation go hand in hand, both vital aspects of regulation.

REGULATORY ADJUSTMENTS

A distinction can be made between two types of regulation. One is explicit. It is recorded in laws, rules, and guidelines for conduct. Explicit regulation is a formal process within the remit of government, accreditation agencies, and universities themselves. The other type is tacit regulation, much of it self-regulation, understood not merely as the sanctioned codes that higher education institutions adopt for their official bodies such as academic senates. Rather, it is informal, driven by the market, politics, and ideology. Self-regulation is governmental in the Foucauldian sense of normalizing certain values that are translated into policy and as incentives for structuring behavior.[90] And as with Foucault's Panopticon, a central facility at an institution like a prison wherein its operators remain invisible but can watch and discipline inmates, university managers surveil faculty and staff. Today, the use of information technology, including computerized monitoring and online reporting systems, renders university employees relatively docile. While explicit regulation meets the eye, tacit regulation is the more subtle, covert practice. At issue is how the mix of the two forms of regulation gels in different contexts.

To be concrete, the norms of competition are manifest in ranking systems and the global race for the top. The rankings hinge on competition because, as said, not all players can be above average, let alone in the upper tier. To heighten competition, the power of discourse sounds the same norms and keywords highlighted earlier in this book—counting, measuring, rating, branding, performing, benchmarking, following best practices—and instills them into the mentalities of knowing subjects. The medium drills dominant narratives into university culture and forms common sense.

---

90. Michel Foucault, *Discipline and Punish: The Birth of the Prison*, trans. Alan Sheridan (New York: Vintage Books, 1995).

As they embark on academe, the younger generation of faculty and students by and large absorb these ingrained narratives, imagining them to be normal conduct. Taught to conform to the methods and mores of their chosen discipline, graduate students are subject to discursive power.

Since Congress wields the power of the purse, its support for students is crucial. But this was not always so. The legislature laid groundwork for the formal role of the federal authorities in accreditation when it passed the Korean War GI Bill in 1952, signed into law by President Harry Truman. By stipulating that veterans could use their education benefits only at federally accredited institutions, this legislation initiated the government's recognition procedure. Under the Higher Education Act of 1965, institutional eligibility for federal student aid programs such as grants and loans is adjudged by the accrediting agencies recognized by the U.S. secretary of education. And in 1992, Congress defined as law the standards for assessing quality at higher education institutions. Through this process, the U.S. Department of Education exercises regulatory authority over the administration of federal funds for student assistance.

Essentially, government has reserved the right to grant or withhold the accreditation of accreditors. They are in turn tasked with applying standards, which may vary by region, state, and program of study. In doing so, the accrediting bodies serve as gatekeepers for federal Title IV funds.

Contention over the performance of accrediting organizations arises when it is time for Congress to reauthorize the Higher Education Act. Now, attempts to reform traditional accreditors stem from concerns that they block new players such as noninstitutional providers that offer alternatives like competency-based education in lieu of prescribed courses for a predetermined number of credits. Accreditors' critics admonish them for usurping institutional autonomy in formulating recommendations and by dictating mission. Too, the naysayers hold that accrediting agencies need to delink from regulating access to funding.[91]

Meanwhile, in this maelstrom, accrediting bodies come under fire from the corporate sector for their staid approach. A proposal for meeting industry standards and improving oversight, used by employers and accounting firms such as Ernst & Young, is to introduce an alternative structure. The suggestion is that an audit model for monitoring quality and gaining access to federal student assistance would replace or complement the current system of accreditation.[92]

91. I am cobbling together criticism presented by Anne Neal, president, American Trustees and Alumni, and other participants at the Council for Higher Education Accreditation conference titled "Innovation, Disruption and the Status Quo: What Do We Want for Accreditation?" Washington, DC, January 27–29, 2014.

92. Goldie Blumenstyk, "Forget Accreditation: Bring on the College Audit," *Chronicle of Higher Education* (October 28, 2016): B6–8.

Stoking this debate about regulation and accreditation, President Obama's 2013 proposal for the establishment of a government rating system for universities, judged by measurable factors, implied changes in the ways in which accreditation requirements are set. By Obama's thinking, the goals are to provide consumer information, protect taxpayers, and enable them to better evaluate institutions. However, his overture gained little traction in Congress or from grassroots higher education reformers. As previously alluded to (chapter 3), the Department of Education then constructed a new set of customizable quantitative metrics, a consumer tool for comparing universities available at a government-run website known as the College Scorecard.[93]

This initiative calls into question the role of nongovernmental accreditors. A principal group opposing calls to roll back their scope is the Council for Higher Education Accreditation (CHEA), which regards itself as a national voice for quality assurance. It represents about three thousand degree-granting colleges and universities and sixty accrediting organizations. In response to what it views as federal encroachment, CHEA objects to overreach by government, its regulatory intrusion, and expansion of oversight. Agreeing that accreditors must do more to fulfill their mandate, CHEA seeks to maintain the domain of nongovernmental organizations in quality control of higher education and institutional autonomy under the leadership of the academic community.[94]

To unspool this back-and-forth, it is important to emphasize that in principle, accreditation is voluntary. But in practice, universities comply with its strictures, for noncompliance would deny access to federal money for students and research. And if a higher education institution is without accreditation, far fewer students would apply for admission. Its enrollment would dwindle.

To secure accreditation, universities are expected to continuously upgrade their academic programs and garner revenue. These desiderata can lead to complex trade-offs between an institution's hallowed academic purposes and the commercial value of its initiatives. And to tap new sources of revenue, technology managers on campus are negotiating deals with outside companies like Intellectual Ventures, a patent aggregator. Such firms engage in technology transfers that offer to bring profits to partner universities, but some academics and advocacy groups are wary of the opaque nature of their operations. Contracts and consulting for these private businesses provide opportunities to enhance technical competence, training that jibes with the university's commitment to serve the public. The skills captured are for job preparation involving specific tasks, mostly knowledge for technical matters.

93. See https://collegescorecard.ed.gov/.

94. For a reply to accreditation skeptics, see Judith S. Eaton, president, Council for Higher Education Accreditation, "It's Time to Speak Out: Accreditation, Its Critics and Its Future," *Inside Accreditation* 9, no. 4 (June 25, 2013).

However, as Einstein counseled, the drawback to giving wide scope to specialization is that its excesses diminish the sense of common educational purpose, including its emphasis on aesthetics and ethics.[95] In recent years, the wave of professionalism—referred to by critics as vocationalism—sweeping campuses has sparked debate about hyperspecialized, applied fields. Entering the fray, Rhodes, Cornell president emeritus, applauds the exchange of ideas between professional studies in subjects such as medicine and the basic sciences but stresses that growing professionalism of the university weakens the moral assumptions and ethical context of higher education. Although his message hardly captures a new phenomenon, it remains apt:

> *Professionalism has shifted the allegiance of the faculty away from the university.* Consultancy arrangements, company directorships, royalty and patent rights, clients who are wealthy and influential, benefactors bearing gifts, coveys of assistants, generous fees from professional practice, enviable research support, favorable salaries, popular books, successful videotapes, the international lecture circuit, superior working facilities—these are all typical involvements and enjoyments of the most successful members of the professional faculty. . . . Their allegiance is not to their institution, not to their college, not primarily to their students, but to their profession, their guild, their colleagues, most of them beyond the campus, and to their clients.[96]

While faculty have long sought career advancement through organizations beyond the confines of the university, Rhodes's apprehension signals that professionalism ripples through university culture and is objectified in the curriculum.

For example, the field of international development is fundamentally about ethics. As the work of the economist, philosopher, and Nobel laureate Amartya Sen indicates, development raises the questions of how to realize the good life and what is just distribution at a world level.[97] Burrowing deeply, he is asking readers to ponder development for what. But in universities today, this course of studies is oft converted into specialization in development management wherein the emphasis is on immediate useful knowledge and technical skills.

Digital technologies have abetted a similar shift in cognate fields. Classically, the humanities imparted an appreciation of close reading of texts—a deeply pensive and solitary engagement with meanings. In contrast, the digital humanities feature distant reading. This approach views books from afar,

---

95. As discussed in chapter 2, 39, 58.

96. Rhodes, *The Creation of the Future*, 36, emphasis in original.

97. Amartya Sen, *Development as Freedom* (New York: Oxford University Press, 1999), and *The Idea of Justice* (Cambridge, MA: Harvard University Press, 2009).

is data driven, and draws on computational methodologies.[98] Digitization is used instrumentally as a way to shore up the status of literature studies.

The academy's embrace of even more applied training and technical skills is based on its perceptions of how to satisfy employment markets. However, its reading of demand contradicts empirical research on employers' assessments of their own needs. To take one of several empirical studies, a survey commissioned by the Association of American Colleges and Universities asked 302 executives at private and nonprofit organizations what attributes they seek in new hires and how universities can best prepare graduates for career success.[99] The proportion of employers who believe that universities should place more emphasis on written and oral communication is 89 percent; on critical thinking and analytical reasoning, 81 percent. Trailing these top two needs are the application of knowledge and skills though internships or other hands-on experience, 79 percent; complex problem-solving and analysis, 75 percent; and ethical decision making, 75 percent.

The misperception that prizes techno-professional studies over other kinds of learning circles back to accreditation. Pressured to give more weight to innovation, notably programs that favor technological development and professional training, nongovernmental accreditors and government officials are engaged in a lot of give-and-take, diverging from one another over the powers and extent of what I have called explicit regulation. Much of the discord pivots on political control: whether nongovernmental or governmental regulators are too far-reaching and straying from their mandate. The two parties meet little dissent from universities, which, after all, are self-interested actors intent on receiving funding. Conceding the leverage of gatekeeping in the form of accreditation, universities are not about to spite themselves. When it comes to this process, they have not dared challenge proneoliberal reforms. The main plank of the proneoliberal platform is that universities can stem austerity cuts and receive more public support if they mainstream market-based, privatizing measures geared to standardized metrics and monitored by government-sanctioned accrediting agencies. While universities in general are conditioned by this regime, one might expect them to be oriented somewhat differently from governmentally chartered accreditors.

What appears as divergence on mechanisms for gauging quality is however largely a convergence of views on repurposing higher education. In tandem with universities, nongovernmental accreditors and governmental authorities come together in swinging toward a techno-professional posture. Without malice, they are on a course of tacit, self-regulatory reform and buy into a

98. See Franco Moretti, *Distant Reading* (London: Verso, 2013).

99. Hart Research Associates, "Raising the Bar: Employers' Views on College Learning in the Wake of the Economic Downturn," a survey among employers conducted on behalf of the Association of American Colleges and Universities (Washington, DC, 2009), https://www .aacu.org/sites/default/files/files/LEAP/2009_EmployerSurvey.pdf (accessed July 8, 2015). This survey corroborates findings in the 2013 report cited in chapter 1 of this volume (35n62).

trilateral consensus on what accreditation seeks to accomplish: in an unacknowledged bargain, government delegates specific tasks to *quasi-regulators*, nongovernmental accrediting agencies with which they share a normative worldview, and elicit universities' consent. These partnerships are marked by respectful conversation. Befitting a democracy, it features some dissent. Intramural debates constitute healthy tension among epistemic elites whose job is to question and find nuance, lending legitimacy to them. Noticeably, too, the resultant intersubjective framework is veering toward the global.

GLOBAL REACH

Like university ranking systems, which originated in the United States, accreditation regimes have spread across national borders and are linked to the American experience. And contemporary globalization is changing their workings.

Accreditors in different countries and regions are pushing for quality assurance mechanisms at their locally based knowledge institutions. They are adopting guidelines for compliance and standards for equivalence. Global governance organizations such as UNESCO and the World Bank distribute tool kits for quality assurance in sundry ways, including as templates for reports, via joint reviews of learning objectives and outcomes, and by visiting teams. Accrediting agencies hold university programs accountable for implementation of quality assurance protocols. While vowing to be sensitive to a range of cultural heritages and historical legacies, they generally base their recommendations for recognition and reaccreditation on criteria developed in the United States: an elaborated mission statement, a strategic plan, an efficient means of administering funds, an assessment procedure, and so on.

Under INQAAHE and kindred transnational networks, quality assurance instruments are, in the main, promoting convergence among universities. Indeed, they subscribe to much the same standards. Yet when it comes to distance education, overseas branches of universities, and programs desiring the brand name conferred by accreditation organizations in other parts of the world, frequently North America or Europe, the lines of national and transnational jurisdiction are blurred.

The drive to internationalize academic programs involves establishing more branch campuses and increasing the mobility of students and scholars. In the competition to thrust out and scale up, U.S. universities are the largest source of international branch campuses, with 78 in 2011, followed by France in second place with 27, and Britain third at 25, in the same year. The top host countries for branches are United Arab Emirates, 37; Singapore, 18; and China, 10, also according to data for 2011.[100] The principal destination

100. "Top Source and Host Countries and Territories for International Branch Campuses, 2011," *Chronicle of Higher Education Almanac 2013–14* 60, no. 46 (August 23, 2013): 72.

countries for American students are in Europe (Britain, Italy, Spain, and France) and China in the fifth spot.[101] The countries sending the most students to the United States are different, though, with China, India, South Korea, Saudi Arabia, and Canada in the lead.[102] The number of international students in the United States grew to a record high of 886,052 in the 2013–14 academic year, hovering around 20 percent of the world's 4.5 million globally mobile university students, more than for any other country.[103] Meanwhile, 289,408 Americans were studying abroad for academic credit—a figure that has more than tripled over the last two decades.[104]

These flows bring not only intellectual gains in learning and research but also material rewards. International students contributed $35.8 billion to the U.S. economy in tuition, fees, and living expenses in 2015. The proceeds have had a multiplier effect in supporting 340,000 jobs in accommodations, dining, transportation, and retail.[105] Plus, there are sums accruing to the United States for management contracts at overseas branch campuses, the transfer of technology, and other services. Nongovernmental organizations such as IIE and International Researches and Exchanges Board provide sponsorship for university administrators from overseas to study management, as it is done at American institutions of higher education, and keep account of their progress. For government, the U.S. Department of Commerce tracks the trade surplus from higher education and, as indicated in chapter 3, reports that it is among the country's top ten service exports.[106] To boost this commerce, the department markets American higher education abroad, making it part of the portfolio of trade specialists in its offices at home and at U.S. embassies. And as active traders, American higher education institutions are venturing new forms of global engagement. For example, NYU, which defines itself a "Global Network University," generates revenue by creating what it calls full-service

101. "One-Year Change in Number of U.S. Students in Top 25 Destination Countries, 2009–10 to 2010–11," *Chronicle of Higher Education Almanac 2013–14* 60, no. 46 (August 23, 2013): 66.
102. "Change in Number of Students Sent to U.S. by Top 10 Sending Countries, 2007–8 to 2011–12," *Chronicle of Higher Education Almanac 2013–14* 60, no. 46 (August 23, 2013): 67; Institute of International Education, Open Doors Data, http://www.iie.org/Research-and-Publications/Open-Doors/Data (accessed July 10, 2015).
103. Institute of International Education, Open Doors Data, http://www.iie.org/Research-and-Publications/Open-Doors/Data (accessed July 10, 2015).
104. Ibid.
105. U.S. Bureau of Economic Analysis, "Table 2.1. U.S. Trade in Services, by Type of Service," http://www.bea.gov/iTable/iTable.cfm?ReqID=62&step=1#reqid=62&step=9&isuri=1&6210=4 (accessed October 26, 2016); Association of International Educators, "The Economic Benefit of International Students," http://www.nafsa.org/_/File/_/eis2014/USA.pdf (accessed July 10, 2015).
106. Francisco Sanchez, "No Better Export: Higher Education," *Chronicle of Higher Education* 57, no. 31 (April 8, 2011): A43.

campuses abroad, allowing students to circulate among sites in an integrated system around the world.

Although greater cross-cultural understanding can enhance national security, universities' increased global reach also strikes terror in the minds of the guardians of homeland security. They are alarmed at the risks associated with the flows of international students and faculty. Policymakers have thus tightened procedures for issuing immigrant and nonimmigrant visas to them. There has been furor among students and scholars over restrictions on mobility and academic freedom when professors and practitioners are invited from abroad to air unpopular views on controversial topics such as conflicts in the Middle East and then denied visas. In notorious cases, Tariq Ramadan, a Swiss philosopher offered a tenured position at the University of Notre Dame and now a professor at Oxford University, and Adam Habib, the current vice chancellor at South Africa's University of the Witwatersrand, who had earned his PhD at the Graduate Center of the City University of New York, were barred entry to the United States because of alleged links to terrorism.

Moreover, open-inquiry tensions continue to arise concerning American universities' involvement in illiberal societies and in regard to the influence of foreign donors, some of them governments in the Middle East, on academic programs and on closely aligned, sometimes in-house, think-tank projects. It is alleged that the sponsors limit topics of research, diminish confidence in its quality, and compromise intellectual independence. Some faculty worry that their home universities, impelled by the fund-raising imperative, relax their standards of free inquiry in order to maintain partnerships in places like China and Singapore. Nevertheless, universities pursue such opportunities far and wide, seemingly without an overall plan.

Searching for Purpose

Before his passing in 2003, Clark Kerr, the first chancellor of the University of California at Berkeley, subsequently president of the University of California, started to consider how higher education could respond to the pressures of globalization and technological development. Earlier, he was the architect of the California Master Plan for Higher Education. This document responded to, and anticipated, challenges of the times—the transition from the 1950s to the turbulent 1960s, marked by the free speech movement, the civil rights struggle, and protests against the Vietnam War. Imaginative thinking about whole systems of education, not only a flagship campus, informed the 1960 Master Plan. A bold and original document, it instituted structural reform and has influenced the course of higher education elsewhere in the United States and overseas.

Resting on democratic ideals, the California Plan embodies a commitment to both advanced research and equality of opportunity. It wraps three levels of education under a single structure: the University of California, for doctoral and professional studies and cutting-edge research; state colleges, which admit students from the top one-third of high school graduates and offer degrees through the master's level; and community colleges, to take in any students over eighteen seeking two years of training so as to enable them to comprise a more skilled labor force. Building in mobility among these three levels, the arrangements allow students to transfer from a community college to a four-year university. And to further access, public institutions in California have wide geographic spread.[107]

In contrast to Kerr's innovatory and integrative model, today's de rigueur exercises known as strategic planning typically represent bricolage. They consist of lists of often distantly related, unrelated, or vaguely formulated goals and inventories of ways to achieve them. In all, the projection of long-range objectives and strategies for meeting them has been problematic, as it has turned out in California. Then governor Ronald Reagan and the Board of Regents' conservative leadership fired Kerr in 1967 despite the chancellor's and the faculty's support for him, and the university turned to bricoleurs in his stead. The state slashed the budget for its higher education system, and the campuses have had to devise short-term, ad hoc measures to cope with dire shortages. Although state funding for public universities rose slightly after the 2008 recession, it is not back to the proportionate level of a quarter century ago.

Since Kerr piloted structural reforms, other university leaders have tried to step up as master planners. In an ambitious effort, Michael Crow, president of Arizona State University, has advocated a new model for the purposes of providing wide access to higher education, with a student body representative of a diverse nation. Other objectives are to link teaching to the frontiers of research and emphasize the generation of new knowledge.[108] Crow wants the university to achieve "national standing in academic quality and impact" and establish a "global center" for "use-inspired research."[109] Further, Arizona State is redesigning the traditional disciplines and commingling them in technology-driven academic units.

Crow has prospected near and far for riches to support this mission, including from corporations such as Starbucks, whose employees are offered incentives to enroll in the university. Much is to be said for Crow's fetching argument that the success of a university is not how exclusive it is, judged by a low rate of acceptance of applicants, but rather its inclusiveness. He is thinking daringly about the way ahead and how to tackle systemic challenges. But the jury is out on the extent to which he is going beyond tinkering with the system and

107. Clark Kerr, *The Gold and the Blue: A Personal Memoir of the University of California, 1949–1967*, vol. 1 (Berkeley: University of California Press, 2001).

108. As elaborated in Crow and Dabars, *Designing the New American University*, 61.

109. Ibid., 61–62.

rebranding it. The challenge for Crow and his colleagues is to do more than marketing makeshift reforms in a shrewd way while relying on standard neoliberal formulas and "efficiencies" like contingent labor to mount mass-scale education.

Paralleling reforms by universities themselves, associations of universities, national commissions, and national academies such as the National Research Council have put forward numerous policy recommendations.[110] They have presented concrete proposals for allaying the public's concerns about accountability, affordability, opportunity, performance, and quality. Asked about converting their vision to action, principals in these groups say that the rollouts are still coming in and that some of their recommendations, for example, on financial aid, have been adopted.[111] The difficulty, however, is that many of their prescriptions are at variance with the political fracturing in Washington, the conviction held by many that higher education should be a private cost borne by students and their families, and continual resource constraints after the 2008 economic meltdown. Absent the nation's political will, the bulk of the commissioners' ideas remain wishful thinking.

Meanwhile, some states and localities are attempting to tackle the problems of higher education. For instance, Oregon is developing a "Pay It Forward, Pay It Back" financing scheme under which students do not pay tuition while they are enrolled in school. After graduation, they remit a flat 3 percent of their income for two or so decades to support the cost of education for future students. Third-party lenders, including the big banks that have sustained student debt, are thereby taken out of the picture. And locally, communities in Syracuse and Buffalo have gone beyond tuition deferment and raised funds to help graduates of their public school systems cover the cost of tuition and on-campus housing at in-state public universities. Nonprofit groups like Say Yes to Education have conceived ways to organize these self-reliance initiatives.[112]

But what kind of students are universities accrediting? According to William Deresiewicz, a former professor at Yale and a literary critic, first- and second-tier elite universities are producing students with "a stunted sense of purpose," driven to perform and seeking to be high achievers but lacking

110. Among the reports are U.S. Department of Education, Commission on the Future of Higher Education, "A Test of Leadership: Charting the Future of U.S. Higher Education," 2006, http://www2.ed.gov/about/bdscomm/list/hiedfuture/reports/final-report.pdf (accessed July 17, 2015); American Association of Universities, Task Force on American Innovation, 2008, *Policy Recommendations for President-Elect Obama*, http://www.aau.edu /policy/task_force.aspx?id=7286 (accessed September 17, 2012); U.S. National Research Council, *Research Universities and the Future of America: Ten Breakthrough Actions Vital to Our Nation's Prosperity and Security* (Washington, DC: National Academies Press, 2012), http://www.federalrelations.wisc.edu/docs/FutureofAmericaU.pdf (accessed July 17, 2015).

111. Author telephone discussion with Duderstadt; discussion with Vest.

112. Say Yes to Education, a national group with chapters in different cities in the Northeast, http://www.sayyestoeducation.org/ (accessed July 16, 2015).

intellectual curiosity and without awareness of why they are on this course.[113] With a nod to exceptions to this portrayal, he casts today's students as unhappy, cynical, and fearful of the future. Many of them suffer from depression and high anxiety, reflected in alarmingly high suicide rates. They regard the university as a checklist to be completed. Construed as an organization that stocks an inventory of degrees, it grants the credentials needed to embark on a career and is not chiefly viewed as a haven for mindful exploration and discovery of the inner self. Moreover, according to Deresiewicz, universities are complicit with other societal institutions, forming a "machine" for churning out generally uniform graduates.[114] He notes that this process starts not with higher education but child-rearing when bedrock norms are taught and students prepare for advancing in their roles in society, albeit without cognizance of purpose. Having put the onus for programming youth on society, not only on the universities that manufacture graduates, Deresiewicz maintains that the way to escape this trap is for individuals to divine solitude by taking charge of their own purposes in education and nurturing the life of the mind. He places great faith in individual agency and assumes that each person has the ability to make autonomous decisions.

Ruminating on this perspective, I asked an accomplished student on the eve of completing his PhD if the author's thesis is on the mark or too disparaging. In no uncertain terms, he said that students do see university education as a checklist. He told me that his cohort is rational in its response to the crushing environment around them. Having navigated his undergraduate, master's, and doctoral studies on scholarships, along with unpaid internships and volunteer work overseas, he recounted his own discouraging, ongoing experience on the job market. After applying for sixty positions and landing just one interview, he anticipates a series of short-term contracts, temporary positions, and abrupt relocations among locales. This story is one of anguish, insecurity, and profound uncertainty.

Deresiewicz's telling, then, is fodder for probing more deeply than the normal metrics of learning objectives and outcomes allow into what qualities the university aims to nourish and how it can help students appreciate the joy of their own minds. He scrutinizes a major stakeholder in university repurposing, clearly characterizing some, but not all, students. Deresiewicz paints a portrait with a broad brush, yet the subjects are more varied, including at the elite institutions on which he focuses, than he acknowledges; their relationships to the university are more nuanced than he grants. Yes, students must steer their own education, even go underground, so to speak, as some of my very best students have done when they organized seminars, to my great

113. William Deresiewicz, *Excellent Sheep: The Miseducation of the American Elite and the Way to a Meaningful Life* (New York: Free Press, 2014), 3.

114. Ibid.

delight, to supplement our fourteen weeks of coursework. However, I fear that the general atmosphere of societal busyness is overtaking this kind of collective self-initiative.

The basic environment for the knowledge structure is changing, especially with increasing public mistrust of political institutions. Empirical evidence points to an erosion of trust between the government and universities since the 1970s, a trend reflected in public attitudes toward institutions of higher education.[115] Polarization, sharp partisan divides, and coarsening of political discourse in Washington feed into this overall loss of confidence in mainstay organizations. The rise in incivility countrywide marks the harsh climate in which universities must operate.

Locating them in their milieu, a series of national surveys conducted by the National Center for Public Policy and Higher Education shows that 60 percent of Americans feel that institutions of higher learning are more concerned with the bottom line on their balance sheets than on the educational experience of their students.[116] These polls indicate that the number of people who take this view is on the upswing—eight percentage points over three years. In addition, a Lumina Foundation study of American public opinion reports that the proportion of its respondents who say that the quality of higher education in the United States is better than in other countries is just the same as for those who think that it is no better than elsewhere: 46 percent in each category.[117] Lumina's concluding observation is that most Americans would be receptive to a redesign of higher education degrees.[118]

Underpinning this finding are some of the main points in this chapter: in a country that prides itself on the excellence of its universities, the magic of the marketplace works in strange ways. The authorities are giving higher education a beating, whittling per student state funding and replacing full-time, tenured faculty, a cornerstone of the university, with precarious knowledge workers. Additionally, a boom in executive power, hikes in senior managers' salaries, and serial hiring of administrators are accompanied by rising tuition

115. "Troubled Waters: Higher Education, Public Opinion and Public Trust," Higher Education Strategic Information & Governance Working Paper #2 (HESIG, William J. Hughes Center for Public Policy, Richard Stockton College of New Jersey, 2013), compiles the results of survey research drawn from several sources.

116. John Immerwahr and Jean Johnson, with Amber Ott and Jonathan Rothkind, "Squeeze Play 2010: Continued Public Anxiety on Cost, Harsher Judgments on How Colleges Are Run," National Center for Public Policy and Higher Education and Public Agenda, 2010, http://www.highereducation.org/reports/squeeze_play_10/squeeze_play _10.pdf (accessed July 18, 2015).

117. Lumina Foundation, "America's Call for Higher Education Redesign," 6, http:// www.luminafoundation.org/files/resources/americas-call-for-higher-education-redesign .pdf (accessed February 2013).

118. Ibid., 9.

and skyrocketing student debt. The effects of these trends are ramifying, heightening the public's discontent with institutions of higher education.

Subject to prevailing conditions, universities are losing their way because they neglect their sometimes uncomfortable but important histories, allow market-based narratives to dominate the discussion of their missions, and fail to convince the public of the need to redeem the purposes at their core. The neoliberal paradigm is indubitably tugging universities among different purposes. With long-established central principles on the wane, new ones are being born.

The next two chapters examine the extent to which these patterns obtain in other world regions and pick up on their texture and vernaculars. To prefigure the conclusion, part 3 of this book will delimit the new principles and show how they are advancing on the old.

CHAPTER FIVE

A Social Democratic Path: Finland

LIKE THE UNITED STATES, Finland is a participatory democracy experiencing multiple pressures on its universities. With a small population of 5.4 million, it is trying to strike a balance between its historically social democratic values and demands to repurpose universities. The Finnish Constitution enshrines basic education as a right, but this public-good component of the welfare state is contracting relative to its private-good elements. For higher education institutions, the dilemma is how to maintain Finland's homegrown practices of democratic training, critical inquiry, and academic freedom, and cope with globalizing tendencies such as externally defined world-class and quality assurance protocols.

In an EU policy framework arcing toward heightened neoliberalism, Finnish universities are tuition free, though from 2017, students from outside the EU and European Economic Area (EEA) faced tuition fees for certain MA programs taught in a language other than Finnish and Swedish. These students are eligible for scholarships, and Finnish students receive financial aid in the form of study grants, housing supplements, government-guaranteed loans at favorable rates, and now-diminished subsidies for meals and some study-abroad programs. For those who incur it, approximately one-third of students, accrued debt is relatively low, averaging 5,010 euros in 2012 (US$6,937 at the current conversion rate).[1] Although the country has not had private universities since the 1970s, far-reaching reforms in 2009 advanced privatization within institutions of higher education. And while all Finnish universities

---

1. *Tilastokeskus: Velkaantumistilasto 2012* (Helsinki: Statistics Finland 2012, updated January 23, 2014), 7, http://www.stat.fi/til/velk/2012/velk_2012_2014-01-23_tie_002_fi .html (accessed April 29, 2014).

continue to receive the bulk of their funding from the state, regulatory policies have brought changes in their governance and legal status.

This chapter examines these dynamics, their impact, and the mechanisms of university repurposing. The place to begin is with long historical trends. Following this history shows myriad influences on institutional development: storied national traditions, the power of ideas, and varied interests. These elements not only are integral to the here and now but also can shape the future.

Reform at Finnish universities may be bracketed in four periods: Russian rule (1809–1917), political independence and the reorganization of the university (1917–1960s), expansion of *national* higher education (1960s and 1970s), and adjustments to a rise in *globalizing* processes (1980s into the 2000s). Five interlocking themes mark reformation in the latter phase: managerialism, competitiveness, autonomy, equity, and globalization of export services (or internationalization, as it is generally called at Finnish universities). We will now delve into the intricacies of repurposing Finland's universities and focus on the state-market-university triangle. The culturally specific features of higher education in this country are key aspects of an explanation of its historical transformation.

Historical Trajectory

RUSSIAN RULE

University reform dates from 1640 with the founding of the University of Turku, known as the Royal Academy of Åbo, when the Kingdom of Sweden ruled Finland.[2] The Royal Academy's mission was to train civil servants, physicians, officers, and clergy for the Lutheran Church. An early shift in the conception of the academy came as a result of the 1809–12 Napoleonic wars; Sweden transferred Finland to Russia and it became a Grand Duchy with autonomy in internal matters, including at the university.[3] During the reign of Russian emperor Alexander I, the initial reforms in higher education enlarged the Imperial University, as it was then called, and transformed it into more of

2. This section draws on stellar research assistance by Jan Westö at the University of Helsinki. I am grateful for our many conversations, his deep knowledge of political history, translations of Finnish-language sources, and unpublished background paper, February 20, 2014. Important sources on the history of universities in Finland are Matti Klinge, *Helsingin yliopisto 1640–1990* (University of Helsinki 1640–1990) (Helsinki: Otava, 1989), and Jussi Välimaa, "Nationalisation, Localisation and Globalisation in Finnish Higher Education," *Higher Education* 48, no. 1 (July 2004): 27–54. In addition, Nicholas T. Smith helped greatly, especially in generating data and figures 5.1 and 5.2 (unpublished background paper, October 14, 2013).

3. For an overview of Finland's political struggles and involvement in wars, see Fred Singleton, *A Short History of Finland* (Cambridge: Cambridge University Press, 1998).

a Finnish rather than Swedish institution. Its mission was to guide the moral standards of students, groomed to become the Grand Duchy's state officials. As in some other parts of Europe, Humboldtian ideas (also known as German humanism) of moral growth and academic freedom contributed to shaping the evolving purposes of the university.[4]

After the great fire of Turku in 1827, the emperor moved the university to Helsinki, the de jure capital of Finland since 1819, and renamed it the Imperial Alexander University. Although the European revolutions of 1848–49 did not actually flare up in Finland, there was concern about potential upheavals spearheaded by students. To avert them, the university reform of 1852 augmented professors' control of potentially radical student associations. Also, building a Finnish national identity took on greater scope. It was resolved, for example, that Russian would not be the language of instruction. Embodying the Hegelian tradition of the realization of ideas in the spirit of the state, the philosopher-statesman Johan Vilhelm Snellman and his compatriots comprising the Finnish cultural movement produced folklore and poetry. It was embraced by political nationalists who promoted the use of Finnish language and literature. (The upper classes mainly spoke Swedish as their mother tongue.) At the university, the combination of cultural and political nationalism increasingly oriented elites' preparation for governmental duties and leadership. The dawn of the twentieth century then brought the decisions to adopt Finnish as a second official language, alongside Swedish, in university administration, admit a larger number of Finnish-speaking students, and establish more professorial positions.

POLITICAL INDEPENDENCE AND THE REORGANIZATION OF THE UNIVERSITY

Following the Bolshevik revolution, Finland attained political independence for the first time in 1917. This was a period of growing commercial activity, concomitant needs for a differentiated labor force, and mounting class stratification. Having been fertile ground for Humboldtian and other inspirations from Germany about educational mission, the Imperial Alexander University closed during Finland's 1918 civil war between the Reds and Whites, the latter supported by German troops.

Subsequently, state-building included a new university law that addressed the language question and, implicitly, the content of Finnish nationalism. The national university retained its bilingual culture. In 1923, legislation delineated a numerical division of language positions allocated for professors (72, Finnish

4. Klinge, *Helsingin yliopisto 1640–1990*, 46; Välimaa, "Nationalisation, Localisation and Globalisation," 33.

speakers; 29, Swedish speakers; and 3, fully bilingual).[5] The university also continued to maintain substantial autonomy, with professors as the dominant force in decision making and represented by a counselor vis-à-vis the state. The university's internal structures forged objectives and ways to conduct its business while the Ministry of Education implemented policies. Then a minor governance body, the ministry provided little independent initiative.[6]

By the 1950s, a national system of higher education had not yet crystallized. In the wake of World War II, Finland was in transition from an agricultural nation to an industrialized society. Higher education institutions enacted their own statutes at the Swedish-speaking Åbo Academy (established circa 1918) and the Finnish-speaking University of Turku (founded circa 1920), the new state university in Oulu, the Jyväskylä Pedagogy College (later a university), the College of Social Sciences (thereafter the University of Tampere), and subsequently polytechnics expected to train a skilled workforce.[7] Next, the challenge was how to configure mass higher education.

EXPANSION OF NATIONAL HIGHER EDUCATION

In the 1960s and 1970s, the shift toward a national system of higher learning involved several steps. An increase of educational places for students brought more standardization of academic programs at Finland's different universities. The country's regions with burgeoning businesses and industries sought to create their own higher education institutions as signs of development and to fuel economic growth. Regionalization then came to mean that the provinces could set up and build their respective universities.

In the politics of higher education, the premier status of the University of Helsinki was a source of unease. So, too, the balance of power between academic elites at this flagship institution and government ministries caused concern. One observer described the situation as "free-falling without any central government . . . its development was about to get out of hand and [was] too loosely regulated and unpredictable."[8] In view of this drift, the perceived need for coordination of educational mission and policy was palpable.

Additionally, disturbances at many universities throughout and beyond Europe erupted in 1968, including in Helsinki, with the occupation of Old

5. Westö, unpublished background paper, 15.

6. Osmo Lampinen, *Suomalaisen korkeakoulutuksen uudistaminen—reformeja ja innovaatioita* (The Development of the Finnish Higher Education System—Reforms and Innovation) (Helsinki: Finland Ministry of Education, 2003), 25.

7. Finland has retained its dual system of universities and polytechnics. This chapter will focus on the universities and treat the polytechs only incidentally.

8. Jaakko Numminen, *Yliopistokysymys* (The University Question) (Helsinki: Otava, 1987), 40.

Student House, and resulted in reforms. At the time, administrative reforms at Finland's universities appeared without nationwide legislation. And the University of Helsinki's power in making decisions about higher education was, to a greater extent, now shared with government and other academic institutions.

Partly due to their financial problems, private universities were nationalized, as were their capital and debt.[9] This move coincided with discussions about how best to utilize the country's resources. The outcome was a series of Higher Education Development acts starting in 1967, augmenting access to the universities and opening space for government to steer education reform.[10]

Against this backdrop, the Nordic welfare model of social democracy made an imprint on Finnish policymaking, including in academe. While the welfare state allows for differences among Nordic societies, a common element is its emphasis on social cohesion. Grounded in class compromises, this framework for managing market capitalism stresses state involvement in the economy and egalitarian norms.[11] With regard to Finland, the term "social democratic model" should nonetheless be used advisedly, especially when government coalitions dominated by conservatives or the center-right periodically hold power.

In the Finnish case, academic values there are to varying degrees shared throughout the Nordic region. As many analysts have affirmed, the trademark features of Finland's schools are cooperation and equity.[12] This is not to overlook ongoing debates and counterthinking. Indeed, universities' core missions of training for democratic citizenship, encouraging critical thinking, and protecting academic freedom foster a plurality of views.

The imbroglio is that the traditions of autonomy and pluralism, evident in the coexistence of Swedish- and Finnish-speaking institutions of higher education, suggest divergence, but a system of national planning involves more standardization, that is, convergence of educational institutions. For political actors, the task of balancing convergence and divergence has presented complexities. While they have sought to establish equilibrium, changing conditions

9. Ibid., 37–38; author discussion with Turo Virtanen, adjunct professor, Department of Political and Economic Studies, Faculty of Social Sciences, University of Helsinki, Helsinki, April 22, 2014.

10. Jussi Välimaa, "Social Dynamics of Higher Education Reform: The Case of Finland," in *Reform and Change in Higher Education: Analysing Policy Implementation*, ed. Åse Gornitzka, Maurice Kogan, and Alberto Amaral (New York: Springer, 2005), 248.

11. The academic literature on this model is voluminous. For an elaboration of its characteristics, see, for example, Gøsta Esping-Andersen, ed., *Welfare States in Transition: National Adaptations in Global Economies* (Thousand Oaks, CA: Sage, 2004).

12. Sahlberg, *Finnish Lessons*, 9.

on a world scale stood to modify the equation. For Finland's higher education institutions, commingling the local and global became a thorny issue.

ADJUSTMENTS TO A RISE IN GLOBALIZING PROCESSES

In line with the growth of neoliberal ideas and policies worldwide during the 1980s, and consonant with the goals promulgated by the Organisation for Economic Co-operation and Development (OECD), Finland relaxed central authority over universities so that they would have more leeway to set their own course. This self-direction was intended to enhance productivity, efficiency, and demonstrable outcomes. Reporting and evaluations were means to check progress toward ends. Government offered resources, even annual increases in appropriations, in return for universities' support, though some contrary views emerged as well.

The Higher Education Development Act of 1986 embraced the principle of profitability. More than a cost-benefits calculation, what I have called a principle has also been described as doctrine: "This doctrine emphasizes the university's role as a service institution that has to react and respond to society's needs and to produce wanted services."[13] It heralded a reformulation of the purposes of Finnish universities and defined them as service providers. Implementation of this notion came amid a severe economic recession triggered by a banking crisis in Finland and budget contractions at its universities in 1993. With adjustments in welfare state policies, cutbacks in public funding for higher education prompted exhortations for private provision for universities. Both private and public authorities called for even more stringent assessment procedures and stiffer competition among and within institutions of higher learning. Corresponding to these expectations, the budding polytechnics, also known as universities of applied sciences, formed in 1991, allowed for additional teaching, greater specialization in higher education, and heightened, albeit informal, stratification among academic providers. So, too, evaluation of their performance became more systematic, especially with the launch of the Finnish Higher Education Evaluation Council (FINHEEC) in 1996.[14] A public agency under the auspices of the Ministry of Education and Culture (MEC), FINHEEC has assisted with reviewing universities. It helped frame education issues and links Finnish universities to reforms elsewhere in Europe.

13. Osmo Kivinen, Risto Rinne, and Kimmo Ketonen, *Yliopiston huomen: Korkeakoulupolitiikan historiallinen suunta Suomessa* (The Future of the University: The Historical Direction of Higher Education Policymaking in Finland)(Helsinki: Hanki ja Jää, 1993), 221–27, as quoted in Lampinen, *Suomalaisen korkeakoulutuksen uudistaminen*, 29.

14. As a result of a 2014 merger with the Finnish Education Council and the National Board of Evaluation, FINHEEC became known as the Finnish Education Evaluation Centre.

Concurrently, Finland's 1995 accession to full membership in the EU posed new global challenges. Together with Europe's 2000 Lisbon Strategy, a ten-year program aimed at refueling economic growth in a global information society (though without explicit plans for higher education), the government in Helsinki encouraged stakeholders to invest in a high value-added and knowledge-intensive economy. Since the turn of the millennium, Finland has sought to upgrade its telecommunications industry, originally with the aid of the Nokia Corporation, and to emphasize knowledge development as a pathway to economic well-being. Universities were seen as a key part of this strategy.

Along with other European higher education institutions, Finland's universities thus entered the era of best practices, results-based funding, and decentralization of decision making. The Ministry of Education had already set up a database, KOTA (replaced later, partly, by Vipunen, another database), for collecting information on costs and results. It facilitated analysis of profit and loss and comparisons among universities. A new Higher Education Development Act for the period 1998–2004 sanctioned greater international cooperation with other institutions of higher learning and enabled more administrative autonomy at Finnish universities. It enlarged the scope for principals and deans and allowed for board members who came from outside the academy. The steering mechanisms of higher education were thereby reset.

On the basis of the history sketched above, let us look at repurposing universities in terms of continuities and discontinuities. The ensuing discussion will show how higher education institutions in Finland are attempting to stay on the national historical path while actively engaging globalizing forces. Certainly, the drivers of university reforms are not primarily internal *or* external to Finland but a distinctive combination of them. The mix is fluid; the balance, unsteady. Instruments of global knowledge governance such as ranking systems are increasingly impinging on local dynamics and following transnational trends. To trace the interactions, I will deal with each of the five interrelated themes (p. 138 of this chapter) in repurposing Finnish universities.

Themes

MANAGERIALISM

In higher education, managerial reforms may be understood as an effort to accommodate rising market pressures and are linked to the new public management (NPM) framework. It emerged from the Anglo-American experience during the 1980s when Prime Minister Thatcher and President Reagan held the reins of power and sought to apply business techniques to public service.[15]

15. Beginning in the early 1990s, President Bill Clinton and Vice President Al Gore embraced the NPM. Their initiative to reform and streamline the U.S. federal government was known as the National Partnership for Reinventing Government.

The NPM aims to reduce the size of large bureaucracies, bring efficiency to government agencies, promote competition among them and with private companies, and develop a consumer orientation. It also calls for government contracts with private-sector firms and the adoption of market mechanisms in the public sector: competitive bidding and performance-based standards, including league tallies, merit pay, and incentive systems. While different world regions and countries have adapted the NPM in varied ways, a commonality is the application of a set of corporate techniques for running organizations, including at universities, in spite of their dissimilar missions, histories, and cultures.

At British institutions of higher learning, this process involves assigning points for imputed excellence and for allocations of funds. It is known as the national Research Assessment Exercise and the Research Evaluation Framework. Irrespective of multiple critiques of the impact of this managerial framework on the grounds that it skews the discovery of new knowledge and that academics follow the money, the structure can reconstitute the business of the university.[16] Skeptics allege that it advances corporate, top-down governance without serious reflection on the long-running goals of higher education.

The NPM discourse and its practices have had great appeal to policymakers and funders in many countries. It is firmly implanted in ministries of education and universities around the world, especially when markets have cycled down, as in Europe during the twenty-first century.

Like its neighbors, Finland has had to address the effects of the 2008 worldwide economic crisis and the eurozone mayhem. For European countries, including the ones with their financial houses in order, these slumps have meant a buildup of sovereign and private debt, mounting unemployment, and bailouts or other emergency measures to stabilize the faltering economies of Greece, Ireland, Portugal, Spain, and Cyprus.[17] While the EU and IMF have negotiated and monitored austerity programs in these countries, some politicians in Europe, including in Finland, seized the occasion to advocate an austerity budget at home. Their goal is to reduce social expenditure and effectively withdraw a large portion of this funding from the public sector.

Meantime, Finland has a sluggish economy and more strain on its public-sector finances and welfare state institutions. The demand for paper, an export commodity, has dropped and the pulp industry is down. And trade with neighboring Russia plummeted because of diminished oil prices, Western sanctions triggered by Moscow's incursion in Crimea, and "Cold War" tension in the region.

16. Charles Husband, professor emeritus of social analysis at the University of Bradford, UK, email message to the author, April 10, 2014.

17. A detailed discussion of the effects of these crises on Finland would take us astray. For a careful account, see Heikki Patomäki, *The Great Eurozone Disaster: From Crisis to Global New Deal* (London: Zed Books, 2013).

The crown jewel of the Finnish knowledge-intensive industry, Nokia, had already experienced massive disruption when its mobile device business stagnated. With about 60 percent of its export revenue derived from the technology industry, and 75 percent of R&D investments by Finnish firms concentrated in this sector, it is pivotal to the fortunes of the national economy.[18]

Upstarts in online gaming and green technology have come on the scene, but these industries are not large. Rovio, the gaming firm with the Angry Birds franchise, is struggling financially. Supercell, another Finnish concern, produces Clash of Clans, a mobile game that is also encountering difficulty maintaining momentum in a transient business environment. So, too, old pulp, mining, and metal enterprises have sought to convert to the new economy yet show only small advances. Meanwhile, Nokia and other Finnish companies face cutthroat competition from European rivals such as Ericsson and China's Huawei and ZTE.[19] To better compete, Nokia sold its mobile phone unit to Microsoft and integrated with the French telecommunications equipment maker Alcatel-Lucent. After Microsoft then terminated Nokia-brand smartphones, Nokia licensed its brand to manufacture new smartphones and tablets to Foxconn, a large Taiwanese technology company, and HMD Global, a Finnish concern. In this crowded market, global players adopted strategies of creative destruction and consolidation. Worldwide, mergers often became management's preferred option: a lesson heeded by education managers.

For higher education institutions then, the political pressure coupled with state disinvestment is to expand privatization. In the Finnish case, what Gorz called reformist reforms (chapter 2) were *initially* gradual and top-down. These measures gained impetus in the 2000s. MEC and the Ministry of Finance have sought to align Finland's education policy with the *Europe 2020—Strategy*, which maps the EU's efforts to coordinate economic development and employment.[20] In accord with these guidelines, several European higher education institutions with olden practices, such as in Austria, undertook au courant university reforms—moves that Finnish authorities duly noted.

18. Turo Virtanen, "Merging and Privatising to Reach for the Top: A New Finnish University of Technology, Business, and Art and Design," in *University Reform in Finland and Japan*, ed. Timo Aarrevarra and Fumihiro Maruyama (Tokyo: Center for National University Management and Finance, 2008), 62, citing http://www.teknologiateollisuus .fi/english/index.php.

19. David J. Cord, *The Decline and Fall of Nokia* (Helsinki: Schildts & Söderströms, 2014); Daniel Thomas and Richard Milne, "Nokia Goes in Search of New Cash Machine," *Financial Times*, April 30, 2014.

20. Ministry of Finance, Republic of Finland, *Europe 2020—Strategy: Finland's National Programme* (Helsinki: Ministry of Finance, 2012), http://ec.europa.eu/europe2020 /pdf/nd/nrp2012_finland_en.pdf (accessed April 8, 2014).

That said, one of MEC's major concerns is that a shortage of qualified workers will undermine a revival of economic growth.[21] On this ground, and relative to other OECD countries, the national government in Helsinki has continued to provide a large portion of university funding (see figure 5.1): at present, 64 percent in direct financing. Public sources of support are, however, down from 84 percent of total university funding in 1990.[22]

Under the current arrangements, state funding is renewable every four years and comes in a lump sum without earmarks for specific educational or research activities. External funding for research projects is available on a competitive basis. Added to this, the government offers increments as incentives for tapping supplementary resource streams. It also subsidizes entities such as the Academy of Finland, the Finnish Funding Agency for Technology and Innovation, the Finnish Innovation Fund, and the Technical Research Centre of Finland, which support research projects.

In figure 5.1, World Bank data indicate that in comparison to the rest of the Euro area, the United States, and elsewhere in the world, Finland's public spending on education in relation to the nation's GDP is significantly above average.[23] Since 1985, Finland has led the United States, the Euro area, the OECD, and world averages in public spending on education as a percent of GDP.[24] Toward the end of the 1981–2010 period, Finland's public spending on higher education hovered around 6.85 percent of GDP (figure 5.1). The Universitas 21 ranking of 48 national higher education systems corroborates this World Bank finding.[25]

Yet by 2012, Finland's Ministry of Finance decided on "adjustment measures" and "a programme of structural reforms also aiming at closing the general sustainability gap" to be phased in.[26] This gap in financing is linked to the rate of population aging. Significant change in the latter weakens public finance because age-related disbursements grow while the working-age

21. Ministry of Education and Culture, Republic of Finland, *Education and Research 2011–2016: A Development Plan* (Helsinki: MEC, 2012), 12, http://www.minedu.fi/export /sites/default/OPM/Julkaisut/2012/liitteet/okm03.pdf (accessed April 8, 2014).

22. Jussi Välimaa et al., "Discussion: Finnish Higher Education Faces Massification and Globalisation," in *Finnish Higher Education in Transition: Perspectives on Massification and Globalisation*, ed. Jussi Välimaa (Jyväskylä, Finland: Institute for Educational Research, University of Jyväskylä, 2001), 214.

23. World Bank, *World Development Indicators*, last modified April 19, 2014, http:// databank.worldbank.org/data/views/variableSelection/selectvariables.aspx?source=world -development-indicators (accessed April 10, 2014).

24. But when private expenditure is factored in, funding is highest in the United States, Korea, Canada, and Chile. Universitas 21 and the Melbourne Institute of Applied Economics and Social research, *U21 Ranking of National Higher Education Systems 2012*, University of Melbourne, http://www.universitas21.com/article/projects/details/152/u21 -ranking-of-national-higher-education-systems (accessed April 21, 2014).

25. Ibid.

26. Ministry of Finance, Republic of Finland, *Europe 2020—Strategy*, 23.

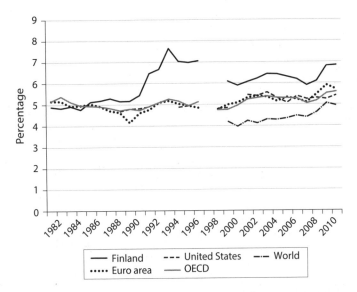

Figure 5.1. Public Spending on Education as a Percentage of GDP, 1981–2010.
Source: World Bank, World Development Indicators, last modified April 9, 2014, http://databank
.worldbank.org/data/views/variableSelection/selectvariables.aspx?source=world-development
-indicators (accessed April 10, 2014).

Note: Data for 1997 and 1998 are unavailable. Also, expenditure on tertiary education is not
disaggregated from spending on primary and secondary levels.

population declines.[27] A rise in the proportion of retirees means that more
senior citizens are drawing state expenditure relative to those who are contributing to the welfare system.

Figure 5.2 shows the magnitude of demographic pressure on public
finance. For the 1981 to 2012 period, the proportion of the population aged
65 or older rose from 12 to 18 percent. During the same years, Finland experienced a reduction in the size of its 15- to 64-year-old age group, from 68 to 65
percent of the population.

Meanwhile, the Finnish system of public universities has faced the challenges of integrating new technologies into its academic programs. Since the
country has its own information and communications technology sector, technological innovation is not at all a newcomer to higher education in Finland.
Nevertheless, the rise of public-private partnerships, knowledge nodes at science parks, development companies, business incubators, and thus competing
claims on funding programs have hastened the reconfiguration of universities.
In addition to MEC and institutions of higher learning themselves, elements
of the knowledge structure have included myriad players: among them, the

27. Ibid.

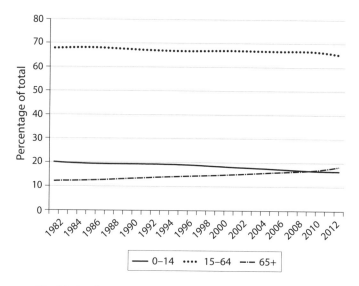

Figure 5.2. Finnish Age Groups, 1981–2012.
Source: World Bank, World Development Indicators, last modified April 9, 2014, http://databank
.worldbank.org/data/views/variableSelection/selectvariables.aspx?source=world-development
-indicators (accessed April 10, 2014).

Ministry of Finance, the Ministry of Employment and the Economy, the Science and Technology Policy Council (renamed the Research and Innovation Council), and the Technical Research Centre of Finland. The task became how to prevent the interconnections among them from becoming too unruly.

More than a matter of coordination, a larger issue was how to deal with the tangle of market, political, demographic, and technological forces influencing Finnish universities. They have had to address the disruption brought by a rapidly changing global environment. The response is embodied in the 2009 new Universities Act, which, in concert with the European Commission's Lisbon Strategy, OECD measures, and the Bologna reforms, was conceived as a way to gain competitive advantage in global markets. The purpose of the legislation is to make higher education institutions more businesslike in their approach to research and teaching. The objective is to consolidate universities and rationalize administrative structures. The reforms are premised on the belief that large organizations have more resources than do small, fragmented institutions. The value added would be greater interface with firms and stronger linkages with the global knowledge economy.

COMPETITIVENESS

Planning the 2009 act was in train for several years. The run-up to this law included discussions at the Ministry of Education, small expert groups, background memos, evaluations of Finland's prior university reforms, analysis of steering mechanisms in higher education politics, and discussion forums.[28] By 2007, the Ministry of Education started to prepare legislation for the new reforms.[29] After the bill was signed into law, implementation began in 2010. Stakeholders in Parliament, ministries, trade unions, and academic communities themselves had yet to work out many practical issues. In these arenas, the purposes and business of universities were to be negotiated.

Mindful of public regulation of competition among higher education institutions, institutional designers set their sights on the aims of the regulatory reforms. The regulations were intended to elevate standards and guarantee that variation among universities is not tantamount to variation in quality. In this respect, competition is restrained.[30] Still, being more globally competitive is a central theme in university mission statements. While saluting the University of Helsinki's traditions and values, its rector (the president) accordingly indicated: "Our strategic objective is to be counted among the 50 leading universities in the world by directing resources to the development of a *world-class* research and teaching infrastructure."[31] Already ranked in the top 100, the University of Helsinki is reaching for a higher echelon. While striving for this uppermost tier of elite universities, its 2013–16 strategic plan is in step with the three main regulatory reforms brought by the 2009 act.

First, the universities are no longer state entities and have become "independent legal entities." As public corporations, they can own and manage their own buildings, make investments, and use profits to support their academic activities. Two of Finland's fourteen (previously twenty) universities constitute foundation-based institutions. In the Finnish context, a foundation is a nationally registered entity in charge of its funds and empowered to deploy them for specific purposes, such as scientific research or museum activities. Aalto University, a merger of three universities amid a series of mergers, and Tampere University of Technology are foundations in keeping with private law. By

---

28. Osmo Lampinen, *Suomalaisen korkeakoulutuksen uudistaminen—reformeja ja innovaatioita* (Reform of Finnish Higher Education), No. 25 (Helsinki: Ministry of Education, 2003), 4; Erkkilä and Piironen, "Reforming Higher Education in Finland," 133; author discussion with Virtanen.

29. Council of State, Republic of Finland, "University Law Reform Is under Preparation," press release, June 7, 2007, http://www.minedu.fi/OPM/Tiedotteet/2007/06/Yliopistolain_uudistusta_valmistellaan.html (accessed March 2, 2014).

30. Turo Virtanen, "The Finnish Model of Higher Education Quality Assurance in International Perspective," in *Higher Education Reforms in Finland and China: Experiences and Challenges in Post-Massification Era*, ed. Yuzhuo Cai and Jussi Kivistö (Tampere, Finland: Tampere University Press, 2011), 179.

31. University of Helsinki, *Strategic Plan for the University of Helsinki 2013–2016*, 7, http://www.helsinki.fi/strategia/pdf/strategia_2013-2016_eng.pdf (accessed April 29, 2014), emphasis added.

statute, then, faculty and administrators at all fourteen universities have ceased to be civil servants; they are under contract with their employers. Effectively, management has gained flexibility in hiring and firing its employees. The particular managerial arrangements are not uniform and vary by institution.

Second, the University Board is now the primary decision-making body at the universities.[32] It is responsible for university business and strategy. By mandate, the size of these boards is smaller than previously constituted. At least 40 percent of board members are external representatives, that is, they come from outside the university. Down from 50 percent in draft legislation, these stakeholders constitute, at minimum, a minority vote while the majority is drawn from the academic community. Further, the board nominates the rector, who was previously elected by university staff and students. The 2009 reforms augment her power. The rector effectively becomes the executive of a university corporation and is obliged to carry out the board's decisions. For all intents and purposes, this shift in governance reduces internal democratic decision making. Traditionally, the University Collegium—a tripartite structure of professors, other teaching and research staff, and students—has played a vigorous role, but the new legislation limits its bounds.[33]

Third, in accordance with the NPM approach, greater emphasis is placed on performance review and performance-based funding. There is more and more reporting. University management is results oriented because it has to negotiate agreements with the government for renewed funding, faces mounting pressure to compete for outside revenue, and has embraced the ethos of an audit culture in which transparency is highly valued.

The consequences of this set of reforms include more mergers of academic units within and among universities, folding extant institutions into a single structure or as members of consortia. There is increasing reliance on term rather than permanent contracts. At all levels, Finnish scholars say that endless reporting reduces time devoted to research and teaching. The prevailing view is that the need to keep applying for secure positions and funding detracts from scholarship.

Together, these processes reward the achievements of winners over losers, not collective performance, which is stressed in Finnish pre-university education. This disjunction is accompanied by another shift: a rise in executive

32. See Jarkko Tirronen and Terhi Nokkala, "Structural Development of Finnish Universities: Achieving Competitiveness and Academic Excellence," *Higher Education Quarterly* 63, no. 3 (July 2009): 219–36; Jussi Välimaa, "The Corporatization of National Universities in Finland," in *Universities and the Public Sphere: Knowledge Generation and State Building in the Era of Globalization*, ed. Brian Pusser et al. (New York: Routledge, 2012), 101–19.

33. Timo Aarrevarra, "Oh Happy Days!—University Reforms in Finland," in *Cycles of University Reform Japan*, ed. Richard Dobson and Fumihiro Maruyama (Tokyo: Center for National University Management and Finance, 2012), 81–84.

authority and devolution of responsibilities to individual academic units and their administrative staff. The decentralization is closely related to autonomy.

AUTONOMY

Nominally, Finland's reformation aims to bolster the autonomy of universities.[34] But what does the concept of autonomy mean? And if the parameters of autonomy change, whose autonomy is at stake or perhaps at risk?

As a principle, autonomy has a long lineage in Western philosophy and assumes varied meanings in different situations. The concept of autonomy courses through the ancient Greek tradition, the humanistic concerns of German theorists from Immanuel Kant to Humboldt, and, on the U.S. side, John Rawls's liberal notions of justice and self-determination.

In Finland, the constitution embraces the principle that "the universities are self-governing."[35] In this sense, law confirms that higher education institutions are a special place. But the idea of autonomy has developed beyond the formal sense of the term and is employed in three ways.

First, intellectual autonomy implies academic freedom. At bottom, it signifies that scholars are at liberty to define their own research interests and pursue them, yet must conduct themselves in an ethical manner. In other words, academic freedom is not an absolute. It comes with responsibilities such as respect for the rights of students and restraints regarding some forms of speech—usually specific types of hate speech and for thwarting sedition. Moreover, intellectual autonomy is more than a matter of individual inquiry and expression. It bridges to collective prerogatives. This kind of autonomy suggests horizontal governance rather than primarily top-down rules and regulations.

Second, administrative autonomy can provide more scope for university senior administrators to steer the course. Institutional autonomy thereby impacts participatory and democratic governance.

Third, for Finland, institutional autonomy is evident in realms like quality assurance. Although government regulates the number of degrees by educational field and decides on the universities that award them, each university, as we have seen, is supposed to define quality and evaluate its own activities.

34. On autonomy in higher education in Finland, I am grateful for several exchanges with Tero Erkkilä, associate professor in the Department of Political and Economic Studies at the University of Helsinki, and Ossi Piironen, then a PhD student at the Finnish Graduate School, University of Helsinki; Piironen, "The Transnational Idea of University Autonomy and the Reform of the Finnish Universities Act," *Higher Education Policy* 26, no. 1 (March 2013): 127–46.

35. Ministry of Justice, Republic of Finland, *The Constitution of Finland* (Helsinki: Ministry of Justice, 2011), http://www.finlex.fi/fi/laki/kaannokset/1999/en19990731.pdf (accessed April 25, 2014).

FINHEEC has audited the procedure and could call for a re-audit. Global governance agencies like the OECD serve as reference points for reforms in these procedures at the national level. It may assess the Finnish system and can provide external reviews. Uniform criteria are promoted by the European Association for Quality Assurance in Higher Education (ENQA).[36]

Institutional autonomy in Finland has meant that the public and government *trust* higher education institutions to be responsible for their own procedure and quality. Survey research casts light on this pattern. The 2012 *European Quality of Life Survey* registers Finns' high trust in public institutions (though not in politicians and political parties).[37] Similarly, *Science Barometer 2013* indicates that more than 70 percent of Finnish respondents have high levels of trust in the country's police, defense forces, and universities and colleges.[38]

In this climate of shared confidence, universities not only have latitude to establish modes of research assessment for their own use but also may decide whether they want to invite external evaluators. Public grants and loans have not been closely tied to the results of an evaluation, as it is with accreditation in the United States. FINHEEC auditors and those of its successor organization, the Finnish Education Evaluation Centre, have focused on a university's processes for meeting the goals of quality assurance.

The Finnish philosophy and practice of institutional autonomy are thus mediated by culture. Trustworthiness, collegiality, and broad participation, including student membership in self-evaluation and audit groups, remain significant features of the Finnish system of higher education. In a discussion of this issue, a representative of the Student Union of the University of Helsinki explained that the culture of the university is to strive for the common good. It is not normal for students to think as customers. In her perspective, an egalitarian ethic manifests in social relations among students themselves and between students and professors.[39]

36. See European Association for Quality Assurance in Higher Education, *Standards and Guidelines for Quality Assurance in the European Higher Education Area* (Helsinki: ENQA, 2009), http://www.aqu.cat/doc/doc_19019963_1.pdf (accessed May 3, 2014).

37. Eurofound, *Third European Quality of Life Survey—Quality of Life in Europe: Trends 2003–2012* (Luxembourg: Publications Office of the European Union, 2013), http:// digitalcommons.ilr.cornell.edu/cgi/viewcontent.cgi?article=1347&context=intl (accessed May 17, 2014); author discussion with Timo Hämäläinen, Sitra Fellow, Finnish Innovation Fund, Helsinki, May 12, 2014.

38. Finnish Society for Scientific Information, *Science Barometer 2013* (Helsinki: Ministry of Education and Culture, 2013), 12–24, http://www.minedu.fi/OPM/Verkkouutiset /2013/11/sciencebaro.html?lang=en (accessed May 17, 2014. (On the variance among countries in public confidence in and skepticism of universities, cf. chapter 1 of this volume.)

39. Author discussion with Anne Rautanen, specialist (higher education policy and the development of teaching), Student Union of the University of Helsinki, Helsinki, April 30, 2014.

Interwoven with these domestic factors, pressures to harmonize with external actors are increasingly felt. In particular, the need to compete for outside funding contributes to a modification in the scope of autonomy, evident in the shift toward EU framework programs and structural funds. Finland itself lacks a strong donor tradition; charitable contributions to universities are not customary or tax-exempt. The country's private foundations and endowments support some students, professorships, and cultural activities (for example, those related to maintaining and developing the traditions of the Swedish-speaking community).[40] External sponsors provide a small but growing part of total university budgets.

Under rapidly changing conditions, the question of financial autonomy centers on university-market relations. Notably, those at the executive helm of a university gain prerogative in managing its funds yet can lose institutional autonomy in relation to the business world. Government has slackened the reins of regulation and helped orient higher education institutions to opportunities in the marketplace. For the state, the justification for this move lies in cost containment and world-class standards. To excel, universities need to mobilize external funds. This route is consistent with EU strategy, which injects market values. And the regional guidelines resemble global narratives, but with contextual nuance.

Ultimately, this comes down to who controls universities as spaces of contestation and reflection. With lightened *direct* government regulation and the expansion of market relations, higher education institutions themselves take initiative for installing regulatory reforms. University audits, for example, are a form of normative accounting. They track the implementation of reforms and are normalized through market practices such as point systems. Known as "benchmark indicators," numbers are employed to gauge quality. The usefulness of knowledge is then taken to mean relevance, impact, and measurable outcomes judged by criteria such as the frequency of citations in level A, B, or C publications.

Used in the MEC funding model beginning in 2015, this system is a means for establishing incentives for greater visibility in international venues, a factor that counts in ranking systems. But who decides what is designated as relevant, and which journals weigh heavily? Does this epistemic validation discourage or marginalize unconventional thinking and challenges to it? And how to reframe the national language question in the face of educational globalization when high ratings are usually given to English-language

---

40. Finland's private funders include Jane and Aatos Erkko, Svenska Kulturfonden, Suomen Kulttuurirahasto, Jenny ja Antti Wihurin Rahasto, Emil Aaltosen Säätiö, Koneen Säätiö, and the Swedish Cultural Foundation. Meanwhile, Parliament supports a research institute, the FIIA; some think tanks are closely connected to political parties; and others, such as Demos Helsinki, seek to maintain more distance from their providers of revenue.

publications rather than to local and regional channels? What then are the long-term implications for the development of a small-language country like Finland and its knowledge structure?

The problem is that incubators for profit-seeking activities can diverge from the university's truth-seeking purposes. Also, the autonomy-*from*-what formulation needs to be revised at universities, where it is more a matter of *for* which and whose purposes. To search for an answer in the Finnish context, we will again look for the historical momentum.

EQUITY

Trends depicted in the preceding discussion have been central to the making of Finland's academic values. In particular, massification, a part of the welfare state agenda, broadened access to higher education throughout the country. With the policy of regionalizing higher learning, opportunities for university education spread across traditional subnational lines demarcating southeast, northeast, east, and Lapland. While cities such as Helsinki, Turku, Tampere, and Joensuu are home to major universities, the more remote locations of Finland introduced courses of study related to their particular milieus, as with Arctic studies at the University of Lapland. Branch campuses, university centers, and research and teaching units lacking their own physical sites have also cropped up in municipalities without full-fledged higher learning institutions—for example, in Pori, Kajaani, Kokkola, Lahti, Mikkeli, and Seinäjoki. The programs and forms of institutional governance of course vary, but a common mission is to translate the principle of education for democratic citizenship into practice, for instance, in collegial bodies. Finland's universities have long wrestled with how to rebalance the guiding ideal of equity and the dynamics of social stratification.

In modernizing the purposes of Finnish universities, three dimensions of equity remain especially challenging: language and ethnicity, gender, and differences among institutions of higher learning. Finland's constitution contains the cornerstones. It not only sanctifies the rights to Finnish and Swedish language and culture but also recognizes the rights of indigenous people to cultivate their own languages and cultures.[41]

In our times, the number of residents who speak Finnish as their first language are a large majority: by 2014, 4.87 million people, or 89 percent, of the population. Swedish speakers constituted only 5.3 percent of Finland's population in the same year, down from 11 percent in 1920.[42] Against this

41. Ministry of Justice, Republic of Finland, *The Constitution of Finland*, 4.

42. Anni Lassila and Aleksi Teivainen, "Swedish Speakers Outnumbered by Foreign Language Speakers," *Helsinki Times*, May 1–7, 2014; Jan Westö, unpublished background paper, April 4, 2014.

backdrop, the most recent reforms at the University of Helsinki stipulate the minimum number of professorships for Swedish-speaking instruction, a board for the coordination of teaching in Swedish, and a provision for a vice rector who speaks Swedish. In addition, it specifies the roles of regional student organizations, four of which are for Swedish speakers and which are to be self-governing for the purposes of supporting their intellectual endeavors and social conditions.[43]

By now, historical forces and legal provisions have quieted the language question, and ethnicity is not a raw issue. While Finland is a rather homogeneous country, it has diverse minorities. According to Statistics Finland, the number of Sami speakers is 1,903.[44] Other Sami people are more proficient in Finnish and also conversant in Sami. Another ethnic group is the Finnish Roma, who have inhabited Finland for more than five hundred years and have long encountered prejudice and discrimination. The 10,000 Roma identify as both Roma and Finns who bear the constitutional right to develop their own language and culture. The Sami groups and Roma not only have suffered inequities but have little representation in the Finnish Parliament. To shed light on this legacy, the University of the Arctic and Oulu University offer Sami studies. The curricula emphasize minority issues: languages, cultures, and history, as well as connections to other indigenous peoples and the natural environment.

In Finland's increasingly multicultural society, home to growing flows of immigrants, Russian and Estonian speakers are among the most numerous newcomers. In addition, it has over 10,000 people whose first language is Somali, English, Arabic, or Kurdish.[45] A crucial factor facing higher education institutions is thus proficiency in the Finnish language and cross-cultural communication. Language instruction entails a cost but can bring social and economic gains, especially given Finland's aging population and pronounced needs in the labor market.

Like the language and ethnicity marker, gender equality is a story of advances and ongoing challenges. A predominant representation of women in higher education degree programs is an overall OECD trend. The Nordic countries in particular have become an emblem for promoting gender equality in both education and politics. Indeed, World Bank data indicate that Finland is among EU and world leaders in tertiary enrollment for women.[46] Forty-eight

43. Universities Act 558/2009 (as amended up to 315/2011), 26 and 34, http://www .finlex.fi/en/laki/kaannokset/2009/en20090558.pdf (accessed May 20, 2014).

44. Reported in Lassila and Teivainen, "Swedish Speakers Outnumbered by Foreign Language Speakers." Presumably, this figure refers to those whose mother tongue is Sami.

45. Ibid.

46. World Bank, *World Development Indicators*, http://databank.worldbank.org/data /views/variableSelection/selectvariables.aspx?source=world-development-indicators (accessed April 10, 2014).

percent of Finnish women and 31 percent of men have earned higher education degrees.[47] And 47 percent of government ministers and 43 percent of
the members of Parliament are women (compared to 17 percent of national
legislators in the United States and 22 percent in England).[48]

Nevertheless, researchers report a "glass ceiling" for women academics at
Finnish universities and document the barriers. Picking up on the work of
feminist scholars, Johanna Kantola asks: Why do women disappear in Finnish
institutions of higher learning?[49] On the basis of a case study of one department at the University of Helsinki, statistical findings, and ample interview
data on the gender division of labor and how gendering operates, she highlights subtle forms of discrimination in competition for jobs, teaching assign-
ments, and the degree of support in PhD supervisory practices. Kantola points
to favoritism for male insiders, silencing women's voices, and other inimical
gendered practices.[50] Needless to say, it is difficult to generalize from her intensive research in a single department or update her ethnographic evidence.
Also, one would not expect official figures published by universities to allow
for the kinds of subtleties that she detected. That said, University of Helsinki
records show that women constituted about half of the total teaching and research staff in recent years but are underrepresented at the senior rank. At the
uppermost tier (level 4), women held 28 percent of the posts in 2013, and 52
percent at the next highest (levels 3 and 2) in the same year.[51]

Another marker of stratification is divergence among universities. While
MEC pledges to provide equitable funding for all universities, they are stratified, their missions are not identical, and they have myriad specializations.
The University of Helsinki remains dominant; it draws about one-quarter of
public funding for all Finnish universities.[52] As a research-intensive and comprehensive university, it has an advantage over the smaller and more focused
universities in attracting additional revenue. Or in view of the scale of Finnish

47. Ibid.

48. Pasi Sahlberg, "Why Gender Equality Matters in School Reform," *Washington Post*,
September 6, 2012; Johanna Kantola, "'Why Do All the Women Disappear?' Gendering
Processes in a Political Science Department," *Gender, Work and Organization* 15, no. 2
(March 2008): 203, notes that women hold 60 percent of government posts.

49. Kantola, "'Why Do All the Women Disappear?' citing Liisa Husu, *Sexism, Support
and Survival: Academic Women and Hidden Discrimination in Finland* (Helsinki: Social
Psychological Studies 6, University of Helsinki, 2001), and Husu, "Women's Work-Related
and Family-Related Discrimination and Support in Academia," in *Gender Realities: Local
and Global*, Advances in Gender Research, vol. 9, ed. Marcia Texler Segal and Vasilikie
Demos (Bingley, UK: Emerald Group Publishing, 2005), 61–99.

50. Kantola, "'Why Do All the Women Disappear?'"

51. *University of Helsinki Annual Report 2013*, http://www.helsinki.fi/annualreport
2013/figures.html (accessed May 20, 2014).

52. Aarrevaara, "Oh Happy Days!—University Reforms in Finland," 86–90.

higher education, one might even think of the entire national system as a single multicampus university, with varied branches and faculties.[53] Bear in mind that all together, Finland's 14 universities enroll 168,000 students (114,000 full-time equivalents).[54]

In this setup, structural conditions induce each university to engage in niche marketing, known as "profiling" in Finland. The 2009 reforms amplified the differentiation among them. The two universities organized as foundations under private law (Aalto and Tampere University of Technology) clearly strive for a competitive edge in generating revenue beyond provisions from the public sector. And Aalto has had initial success in raising private money.

In apportionments from the ministry, output-oriented and performance-based allocations trigger more competition among universities. Consider, for example, the spirit of the following statement by MEC: "Through computational funding state funding is allocated so that the universities that perform above average in quality, impact and profitability benefit the most."[55] With the quality of publications as a factor in the government's funding mechanism, one would expect differences among universities to continue to increase.

How are judgments about research output actually made? Whereas the sheer quantity of publications does not count, a scheme of ordinal numbers of knowledge production by universities is now in place. Informed by Norwegian, Danish, and Australian experiences with classification, Finland's universities have designed their own tools for evaluating the quality of research by discipline. Prompted by a Finnish rectors' conference, and under the umbrella of the Federation of Finnish Learned Societies, more than 200 expert members of 23 panels rated domestic and international publication channels: journals, series of papers, conferences, and book publishers. They considered about 20,000 journals and series and 2,000 publishers. The ratings have three levels: (1) basic, (2) leading, and (3) top. This system of citation analysis is meant to incorporate a Finnish point of view and give publication channels in the two national languages their due. The mandate is to allow for the distinctive national features of Finnish culture, history, and society.

53. Seppo Hölttä, "The Finnish Higher Education System—Governance and Funding," in *University Reform in Finland and Japan*, ed. Aarrevarra and Maruyama, 108. Hölttä credits an OECD review group for likening the Finnish system to one multicampus university.

54. Ministry of Education and Culture, Republic of Finland (Tomi Halonen, Department for Higher Education and Science Strategy and Steering Group), "HE and HE Funding Models in Finland" (Helsinki: MEC, April 30, 2014), unpublished. According to the same source, the polytechnics comprise another 148,000 students (114,000 full-time equivalents) and are funded by both the national government and municipalities.

55. Ministry of Education and Culture, Republic of Finland, "Vahvemmat kannusteet koulutuksen ja tutkimuksen laadun vahvistamiselle" (Stronger Incentives to Strengthen the Quality of Education and Research) (Helsinki: MEC, 2014), 16.

The classifications are supposed to be used at the aggregate levels, not to assess individual researchers, determine allocations for specific universities, or make recruitment decisions.[56] Yet worries about bibliometrics persist. The long-run consequences of these pragmatic compromises over listing publications on creativity, interdisciplinarity, and reflection about really big research questions are uncertain.[57]

This "Publication Forum" exercise in Finland may be viewed as an effort to express a small-country voice in the global debate about quality assurance and to buffer transnational forces. Domestically, it is academics' response to government's call to craft instruments for evaluating institutional performance. It blends the two currents. Yet, arguably, the inconvenient issue is that the quality of scholarly research is uncountable and constrained by numerical proxies for managerial accountability. It is an open question whether these regulatory reforms will discourage risk-taking in setting research agendas and further repurpose universities.

Moreover, this mechanism for classification under the rubric of the 2009 reforms rests on the express premise that universities are autonomous in using different mechanisms for developing their own activities. This steering of knowledge production therefore appears consonant with the Finnish way of governance. The ministry regulates targets, spawns processes, and seeks cooperation and consensus among colleagues at the universities. Academics themselves participate in decision making about the caliber of research. At the same time, this approach also converges with overall EU standards, without exactly mirroring them. Indeed, one would not expect EU metrics to give scope to a distinctive Finnish texture.

The interactions between convergence and divergence charted above are linked to globalization strategies, or, it is worth repeating, generally known as internationalization at Finnish universities. Political authorities at the national and regional levels factor them into formulas for funding universities.

GLOBALIZATION OF EXPORT SERVICES

In Finland and elsewhere, globalizing universities is seen as a means to improve the higher education system and establish a more competitive economy. Finnish expertise in education is valued as an export product.[58] For a

56. Otto Auranen and Janne Pölönen, "Classification of Scientific Publication Channels: Final Report of the Publication Forum Project (2010–2012)," https://www.tsv.fi/julkaisufoorumi/english.html?lanf=en (accessed May 9, 2014).

57. Sami Pihlström, "Academic Publishing and Interdisciplinarity? Finnish Experiences," *Human Affairs* 24, no. 1 (January 2014): 40–47.

58. The government of Finland does not prepare data on the economic value of knowledge exports. In MEC and other official documents, education export services is not treated as a separate item but subsumed under other statistical categories.

country with an oversupply of university graduates, knowledge commerce is a potentially big business. There is growing emphasis on marketing development, cross-border programs of technological skills, school design, teacher training, and capacity-building for administrators. Finland's universities are important players in tendering offers for delivering these services. They focus on selected countries, among others, Saudi Arabia, China, and some in sub-Saharan Africa.[59]

In the transnational knowledge business, Finland treads on its history of involvement in global governance networks, more extensive than can be detailed here. For many years, it has provided development assistance to impoverished areas in the global South and expertise for institutions such as UN specialized agencies and the World Bank. For donors, Finland's renowned schooling is an icon of educational knowhow. So, too, this country's record of investing heavily at home in knowledge and innovation and developing a technologically intensive economy are widely viewed as exemplary.

Global governance organizations have recruited Finnish consultants and advisors for contracts on overseas projects and training missions. Finland has in turn readily engaged clusters of knowledge actors: not only bilateral and multilateral agencies for international cooperation and development but especially purveyors of the overall EU reform agenda for harmonizing quality assurance criteria and standards.

Finland's ministries have given impetus to this drive for competitiveness in the global market for education and research. The funding formula for allocations to universities registers the mobility of students and faculty to and from Finland, master's and PhD degrees awarded to foreign nationals, and internationally competitive research funding. The Finnish government has created parastatal agencies such as FinNode, a mechanism to spark innovation and encourage partnerships with enterprises in the market, and the Centre for International Mobility, which facilitates flows of students across borders. The government also encourages universities to be more commercially active with emerging technologies and increase their knowledge exports.

Incentivized to do so, each university has crafted its own strategies and targets for internationalization. Still, internationalization is relatively new at Finnish universities and at a rather low level. According to Statistics Finland, Finland exports more students than it imports: 10,123 outbound versus 8,990 inbound in 2010; 9,913 versus 9,172 in 2011; and 10,014 versus 9,655 in 2012.[60] Of the degrees conferred in the latter year, 5.1 percent were awarded to

59. Author discussion with Seppo Hölttä, professor in the School of Management, University of Tampere, Helsinki, May 8, 2014.

60. Irma Garam, *Facts and Figures—Summary 3C/2013: International Mobility in Finnish Higher Education in 2012* (Helsinki: Centre for International Mobility, 2013), 3, chart 1, http://www.cimo.fi/services/publications/facts_and_figures_summary_2_2013 (accessed May 20, 2014).

international students: 0.8 percent, at the lower (bachelor's) level; 7.8 percent, higher (master's); and 16.3 percent, PhD.[61]

Since Finland has not until recently charged tuition, financing student exchange programs and operating study-abroad programs beyond the EHEA are expensive activities. Even with tuition fees for incoming non-EU and non-EEA students (about 77 percent of the international students in Finland), the sum applies only for some master's programs. MEC estimates that the costs of educating international students at Finnish universities amount to 12 million euros— $16,482,400—per year.[62] Notwithstanding scholarship programs (in some cases, government disbursements), and although Finland's universities promote study and research abroad, interest in these opportunities has declined.[63]

Nationwide, population flows are also problematic. Finland is experiencing a brain drain, with more higher-degree holders leaving the country than moving into it.[64] Many would-be visitors and potential residents regard Finland's harsh climate, its peoples' reputed social reserve, and their uncommon language as inauspicious: barriers to integrating in its academic culture, society, and work environment.

While these institutional structures and cultural issues certainly matter, regional and global discourses about knowledge economies are equally salient. EU scripts endorsing neoliberal policies have influenced Finland's regulatory reforms; policy tools such as university funding formulas adapt them to the local context.[65] Even with multiple filters, the results are inflections in the language of repurposing education for knowledge societies in the global marketplace. True, the admixtures of global, regional, and national idioms are not expressed in a singular manner. These differences are displayed in myriad ways.

Diverging Ideas

The 2009 Universities Act was greeted by street demonstrations in Helsinki and other cities, unusual in Finland where manifest resistance to government led by coalitions of political parties is generally muted. Demonstrators, mostly

61. Statistics Finland, "University Education—University Students in 2012," appendix, table 5, Saantitapa: http://tilastokeskus.fi/til/yop/2012/02/yop_2012_02_2013-06-19 _tau_005_fi.html (accessed May 20, 2014).

62. Katja Boxberg and Aleksi Teivainen, "Tuition Fee Trial Flops," *Helsinki Times*, April 10–16, 2014.

63. Ministry of Education, "Strategy for the Internationalisation of Higher Education Institutions in Finland 2009–2010" (Ministry of Education, 2009), 14, http://www.okm.fi/export /sites/default/OPM/Julkaisut/2009/liitteet/opm23.pdf?lang=fi (accessed May 18, 2014)

64. Ibid.

65. Åse Gornitzka, "Channel, Filter or Buffer? National Policy Responses to Global Rankings," in *Global University Rankings*, ed. Erkkilä, 75–91, attempts to disentangle diverse factors that shape policymaking.

students, occupied the main building at the University of Helsinki. But the protests were small and of short duration. Objections to university reform took the forms of lobbying, papers prepared by academics, and the presentation of statements, some of them argued with empirical evidence. An oft-heard position was that supporters and opponents of the reforms alike subscribe to the principles of democracy and equitable resource allocation but disagree about policy adjustments.[66]

In Finland, academic activists find representation in trade union movements. Among them, the Finnish Union of Finnish Researchers and Teachers sometimes works with the Finnish Union of University Professors. But members of the university community by and large come together on an ad hoc basis. In the brouhaha over the 2009 reforms, most of the noise came from the social sciences, humanities, and law faculties, with little participation from natural sciences.[67] Opposition to charging tuition and fees drew support from three political parties: the Greens, the Left Alliance, and the Swedish People's Party.

Debates about university reforms festered. Their implementation caused deliberation and consternation. Probing questions were posed: Autonomy relative to what? Mergers toward what end? Proposed tuition fees for whom?

Leaders of higher education institutions welcomed university autonomy on the ground of freedom of maneuver: universities could manage their internal affairs. They could rationalize structures in a country with a bifurcated higher education system of fourteen universities and twenty-four polytechnics serving a small population. Mergers of campuses, faculties, departments, research institutes, and libraries were to spearhead innovation, spark creative energies, and reduce duplication. The argument is that with looser ties to regulatory authorities, universities can gain access to stronger fund-raising channels. To be sure, the unfolding situation in Finland is that universities have to find new ways to cover their costs and deliver a quality education.[68]

Yet critics raised questions about autonomy from the business world, its influence on academic programs, and working conditions for university staff members. Some professors refused to comply with the implementation of reform. They would not submit time management reports, and doctoral students supported by small grants withheld payments of rent for their university office space.[69] These acts of defiance were mostly symbolic; dissent, limited until 2015, when thousands of demonstrators at three Finnish universities simultaneously protested the government's austerity program and plans to cut

66. Author discussion with Rautanen.

67. Ossi Piironen, currently senior researcher, Ministry for Foreign Affairs of Finland, University of Helsinki, email message to the author, July 9, 2013.

68. Author discussion with Kari Raivio, former chancellor and former rector of the University of Helsinki, Helsinki, Finland, May 12, 2014.

69. Piironen, email message to the author.

deeply into education spending. So too the director of the National Library of Finland, an independent institute within the University of Helsinki, balked at instructions to reduce staff by 25 percent on the grounds that cultural heritage is protected by the constitution and MEC's order violated this mandate. In the face of civil disobedience, authorities held that as part of the university, the library cannot avoid staff reductions, though the number could be lowered.

Open disagreement about charging tuition fees surfaced in public debates, including in the media. A number of proponents of university reform favor charging. They contend that Finland already levies fees for other social services, for example, at health care clinics and for day care.[70] Universities in European countries such as Denmark have started to charge tuition fees. And, as mentioned, graduates in Australia and other countries pay retroactively after reaching a certain income threshold.

According to one proposal, the Finnish government would issue a voucher for only one degree; students themselves would pay for higher degrees. Universities would then compete for the vouchers. This competition, it is envisaged, would improve the quality of teaching.[71] But this proposition met with widespread disapproval. There is little sympathy for payer tuition for Finnish citizens partly because it is at odds with a widespread belief that free university education is a right that should not be encumbered by economic hardship. Many people with whom I had discussions recall their own socioeconomic backgrounds in different regions of the country and attest that the welfare policy of free tuition enabled them to earn university degrees and that without it, they would not enjoy their current social well-being. They invoke the story of Finland's transition from an agricultural to an industrialized society in which information technology, knowledge, and education were mainsprings. As a result of this public investment in human resources, Finland, with 0.1 percent of the world's population, now produces 1 percent of global knowledge, measured by the publication of scientific papers.[72]

Contention surrounds tuition fees for students from outside the EU and the EEA. Those who back this initiative say that Finland cannot afford to subsidize them and that many overseas students do not stay and work. On the other hand, it is argued that their home countries pay for pre-university education and that Finland, which admits only top students to its universities, gains by adding net value to the knowledge economy.[73] Another concern is that price discrimination discourages promising international students whom

70. Author discussion with Raivio.

71. A claim recounted by Virtanen in discussion with author.

72. According to Raimo Väyrynen, former president of the Academy of Finland and former director of FIIA, in my discussion with him in Helsinki, May 14, 2014.

73. Author discussion with Teivo Teivainen, professor of world politics, University of Helsinki, Helsinki, Finland, December 9, 2015.

Finland seeks to attract. Moreover, it rouses sentiment in support of the "gateway theory": the adoption of tuition fees for a pool of international students is a step toward imposing them on domestic students.[74] Opponents of charging non-EU students have held that it is an opening wedge for privatizing universities and belies Finnish sensibilities.

An additional misgiving is that welfare policies are underpinned by the root values of social solidarity and equality. In this debate, university reforms ignite deep issues about identity politics and ethics centering on who is an insider and outsider, whether such stark distinctions should even be drawn, and how to secure opportunity for everyone.

Innocence Lost?

Trying to cope with the effects of severe global and regional economic crises, Finland faces an economic and political gap in sustainable welfare. Its levels of economic growth, public debt, youth unemployment, income inequality, and population aging put stress on spending on higher education. A conundrum is how to address the problem of affordability, maintain the country's educational achievements, and update its university system. Overall, the response is to save the Nordic welfare model by modifying it. This entails adjusting the chain of policy instruments, universities, and normative values.

In the Finnish government's steering mechanisms for higher education, the key policy instrument is the university funding formula. Periodically, MEC alters the ratio of "core" and "strategic" funding for higher education institutions: in the most recent formula (for 2013 on), 90 percent and 10 percent, respectively. In the core, scientific publications count for 13 percent; competitive research funding, 9 percent; and internationalization, 6 percent. The 10 percent of the total for strategic development consists of a university's strategic plan, its implementation, national service, and science policy aims.[75] Within these parameters, MEC parleys with universities and engages them in setting targets on issues such as the intake of students. In a small country, it is not difficult to plot trends and project needs, for example, on the basis of demographic data and upcoming retirements in different occupations, and thereby plan.

Since government scaled back its ministerial machinery for direct controls so that higher education institutions are responsible for carrying out negotiated agreements, universities are expected to develop an infrastructure for evaluating their own performance and setting specific performance goals for the next cycle of strategic funding. It is understood that the ministry trusts universities to carry out their end of the bargain.

---

74. Boxberg and Teivainen, "Tuition Fee Trial Flops."

75. Ministry of Education and Culture, Republic of Finland, "HE and HE Funding Models in Finland."

Unlike Anglo-American government agencies, MEC subscribes to a notion of *social accountability*. Bequeathed with taxpayers' money, higher education institutions are believed to be responsible to the public at large. In the Finnish educational community, it is widely held that universities' contributions to society are realized over the long run and not amenable to predominantly short-term measures. For its part, MEC maintains that Parliament, elected by the public, creates the framework in which the ministry is obliged to operate. After an election, a new governing coalition draws up its program, and MEC's mandate is to carry out the provisions and advocate for universities in budgetary politics.[76] Education bills are prepared for Parliament, reviewed in committee, and usually approved without modification. In fact, parliamentarians typically give notice to their regional interests—a "home" university's connections to business and the labor market in a local constituency—and the status associated with higher education rankings, but not the details of applying the university funding formula. The politicians delegate this task to MEC's minister and staff. Although MEC occasionally approaches Parliament concerning legal issues, it exercises discretion in agenda setting for universities. When MEC apportionments are made, each university decides on the internal distribution of funding. The whole process proceeds in regular steps.[77]

Nonetheless, there is an emergent tension. Although Finnish quality assurance is not supposed to enter into funding allocations for individual higher education institutions, MEC's emphasis on performance is ultimately linked to the power of the public purse. Picking up on this tie between quality assurance and money, skeptics contend that the ministry's funding formula straightjackets universities; they have little choice but to comply with its regulatory measures. It is feared this structure will breed institutional conformism. How could public universities refuse to abide by the formula? How could these institutions—two of them supposedly private but mainly in legal terms—forfeit most of their financial support, derived from the state, and absorb drastic reductions in personnel, academic programs, and upkeep? In question is where this steering will lead Finland.

By all indications, a semi-regulated system is evolving.[78] Finland is developing a new *Nordic privatizing welfare model*.[79] Its characteristics are

76. Author discussion with Anita Lehikoinen, permanent secretary, Ministry of Education and Culture, Helsinki, Finland, May 15, 2014.

77. Turo Virtanen, email messages to author, May 28, 2014, June 2, 2014, and December 8, 2015.

78. My formulations in this paragraph owe much to discussions with Heikki Patomäki, professor of world politics at the University of Helsinki, Helsinki, April 9 and 28, 2014, though I alone am responsible for the views expressed here.

79. Author discussion with Lehikoinen; John Kvist and Bent Greve, "Has the Nordic Model Been Transformed?" *Social Policy & Administration* 45, no. 2 (April 2011): 146–60.

considerable state intervention in the economy, generous social provision, corporatism, a shared belief in dialogue among multiple stakeholders, the adoption of new managerial approaches, and a gradual shift toward increased use of market mechanisms in the public sector. In this mix, soft policy instruments are used to simulate markets within public institutions. Symbols such as logos, the language of business, and numerical schemes are in play. More and more, universities are becoming self-regulatory in their market practices. While their styles differ, senior administrators alike fashion pro-market inducements for academics. Normative framing of strategic planning, measurable outcomes, metrics for performance, and rankings are commonplace. Databases such as KOTA and Vipunen are information systems that monitor compliance.

Paralleling internal accommodations to university reforms, the state redeploys the financial resources at its disposal. Notwithstanding the argument that university education and research are a distinctive sphere that benefits society at large, the ratio of public to private spending on higher education is declining. In this *retrenched Nordic social democracy model*, the hierarchy of the market gradually cuts against egalitarianism. At universities, profit-seeking activities, such as in mergers with pharmaceutical companies or at hospitals owned or run by higher education institutions, can depart from the university's truth-seeking purposes and present conflicts of interest.

Let me quickly note that this pattern is consistent with the distributional consequences of certain global governance agencies' policies, such as those of the EU area, the World Bank, the WTO, and some, though not all, large foundations' programs aimed at enhancing well-being.[80] Dealing with those ramifications in detail would however take us afield, and other studies educe compelling data.[81] Suffice it to say that agencies like UNDP and the International Labour Organization (ILO) retain only remnants of their social democracy visions.[82]

80. See chapter 3 and, for empirical evidence on donors' activities, chapter 6.

81. E.g., Murphy, *The United Nations Development Programme*; Jan Klabbers, "Marginalized International Organizations: Three Hypotheses Concerning the ILO," in *China and ILO Fundamental Principles and Rights at Work*, ed. Roger Blanpain (AH Alphen aan den Rijn, Netherlands, and Frederick, MD: Aspen, 2014), 181–96.

82. See chapter 3, 63–64. Here it should be emphasized that the more critically oriented agencies, or voices within them, have been downgraded. For example, dependency analysts drew inspiration from a gifted group of economists assembled by Raúl Prebisch in the UN Economic Commission for Latin America and the Caribbean, which now takes a more conventional tack. The UN Centre on Transnational Corporations was transferred from UN headquarters in New York to Geneva and converted into an office in the United Nations Conference on Trade and Development, whose bite is notably softened. Since the 1970s, other UN specialized agencies have similarly faced opposition to what are deemed welfare policies and subject to pressures to tamp down their advocacy for social protection. Although critical thinkers in international institutions have sought to regroup, they have not, on balance,

Quite innocently, Finns placed their trust in global governance organizations and practices. This innocence was not naïveté. After Finland enlisted in the EU and endorsed the ideals of UN institutions, these groupings underwent large-scale changes: what, in the education realm, the European Union calls a "modernisation agenda" for gaining competitive edge. For all practical purposes, this program is becoming governance by numbers. Standards and quality are increasingly linked to funding formulas and gauged by a slew of metrics.[83] Yet particularly for a small country like Finland, caliber is a matter of who defines the criteria and controls the data.

The haunting question is whether Finland's central values of mutual trust, cooperation, and egalitarianism can be preserved at universities whose scripts increasingly converge with global discourses. Or will they be lost in the repurposing of higher education institutions? Resolving this dilemma is a matter of summoning homespun ways to hone universities' purposes in light of the changing global landscape.

In an industrious country famed for its knack for creative design, people have entrusted much of their social well-being to universities. The hope lies in redesigning strategies to protect the cherished values of cultural heritage and the institutions that convey them to future generations.

---

rebounded within the ambit of neoliberalism. In the scholarly literature, this overall pattern has not been stitched together and warrants further investigation.

83. See Erkkilä, *Global University Rankings*; Kevin Davis et al., eds., *Governance by Indicators: Global Power through Classification and Ranking* (New York: Oxford University Press, 2012); Ossi Piironen, "Transnational Governance by Numbers: Rankings as Mechanisms of Governing" (PhD diss., University of Helsinki, 2016).

CHAPTER SIX

Postcolonial Experience: Uganda

AS WITH THE CASE STUDIES of the United States and Finland, repurposing universities in Uganda betrays the subtleties of history, cultural values, and power relations.[1] While focusing on Uganda in particular, this chapter identifies challenges common to many institutions of higher education in postcolonial countries. It shows ways in which internal and external elements combine, changing institutional norms and practices. The task here is to explore how cross-border structures of knowledge operate. This discussion will examine the intermeshing of vast global networks and university reforms in a country striving to climb the ladder in the world political economy.

The history of higher education in Uganda will be rendered in three periods:

1. Beginning in the nineteenth century, colonialism insinuated narratives in the minds of Ugandans and reeducated them. This system served to weaken their social institutions and sought to efface the wisdom of the people. It bleached local stories embodying cultural inheritance. It brought a different form of hierarchical education, implanting ways of thinking unlike indigenous knowledge. It worked to transform the moral culture.
2. With the rise of anticolonial nationalism, the university symbolized political independence, attained in 1962. Nationalists, Ugandan citizens themselves, assumed policymaking and managerial positions. They maintained a Western-oriented, elitist university culture, which

---

1. For this chapter, I am indebted to Nicholas T. Smith for valuable assistance, advice, and many informative discussions.

they had known as students at home or abroad. But this state-driven education soon encountered tension with the local intelligentsia, shortfalls in resources, and pressure from global governance agencies. Added to these woes, economic turbulence and authoritarian politics devalued the core missions of higher education.

3. And from the 1980s to the present, higher learning in Uganda has fostered market over academic values, stressing efficiency, productivity, and competition. Universities in Uganda have countenanced massification and, in the face of underfunding, transferred a large part of financial responsibility to individual students and their families.

Since the 1980s, Uganda's reform initiatives have varied widely by institution. While enacted as legislation, they are less formal, not as codified and elaborate as in the cases cited in chapters 4 and 5. Yet critically scrutinizing these narratives—how people speak and think about university repurposing—is important to analysis. And Uganda's reckonings with repositioning its universities have generic features.

To be detailed below, the four prongs of Uganda's reform framework are shifts in governance, administrative decentralization, privatization, and global engagement. These overlapping factors constitute central elements in the reformation. While Uganda's university system remains emblematic of national wherewithal, many observers continue to ponder how to overhaul old structures, seen as vestiges of prior eras and ill-suited for current needs, a theme broached at the close of this chapter.

One caveat: This research focuses on Uganda's oldest and best-known university, Makerere, and, to the extent possible, the country's other universities. Had the time and research support been available, I would have spread my net more widely and visited additional nonflagship campuses. However, I was subject to practical constraints that limited the fieldwork. That said, the premier university's experience with repurposing has rippled through Uganda's entire education system.

A Historical Touchstone

Before considering the historical setting, let me interject a personal note. My time in Uganda during the early postcolonial period marks an occasion for comparison to subsequent periods. The reason for serving as a memorist is to create a touchstone for evaluation.

In 1967–68, I was a student in the MA Programme in African Studies at the University of East Africa, Kampala. Two years later, I returned to Uganda as a research associate at MISR and a junior member of the faculty in the Department of Political Science and Public Administration at Makerere University, which was no longer a branch of a regional university. In those heady days,

Makerere won plaudits for its high educational quality. I recall exchanging views with great writers and social scientists: Kenya's celebrated novelist and playwright Ngũgĩ wa Thiong'o, Trinidadian-born and Nobel Prize–winning author V. S. Naipaul, and the Norwegian pioneer of peace studies Johan Galtung, to name a few. The acclaim bestowed on such creative thinkers who wanted to visit or be based at Makerere reflected its eminence. All in all, their home countries spanned the globe, from the global North and South, the West to Eastern Europe. During the Cold War, scholars from near and far worked together, with a shared interest in the postcolonial condition. So, too, students, some of them fleeing conflict zones, came from myriad countries in Africa and other world regions.

To know excellence, we did not feel bound to embrace "objective" measures for nurturing habits of the mind, intellectual curiosity, and love of learning. University rankings had not been invented. A brain race for the upper echelon of higher education institutions was yet to start. Uganda's university had not entered the global fray. Our standards of success were the thrill of intellectual pleasure, a fascination with ideas, the launch of new journals, the vibrant debates that that they triggered, attention from many centers of erudition to Makerere's academic programs, and international conferences that drew all sorts of scholars and practitioners to the campus. The excitement about higher learning was intoxicating. There was mutual intuition based on what could be observed. From this standpoint, I came to believe that knowledge is about quality, not quantity, even in changing times.

I truly enjoyed Makerere's glory years and have not yet recovered from my good fortune. We engaged in stimulating debates about colonialism's lasting imprint, the state's agenda, and how to decolonize knowledge. On a grander scale, these exchanges were about what drives history and how to attain the good life. On these matters of moral reasoning, we vied with other scholars and government officials over vital political issues. Our classes included tutorials: instruction for individuals or small groups of students called upon to parse reading and regularly submit essays. We often gathered in the largest auditorium, in Main Hall, for clashes among giants in the academic and policy communities. There was no dearth of public intellectuals—among others, Tanzanian president Julius Nyerere, Guyanese historian Walter Rodney, and Makerere's head of its political science department, a Kenyan, Ali Mazrui—all of whom could rouse an audience and inspire younger generations of academics and activists. But another fate awaited this university. For reasons outlined below, it spiraled into steep decline, cascading to widespread disenchantment with Uganda's higher education system.

In our times, there is no salvation in romanticizing the past. Rose-tinted memories shade an authenticated telling. One cannot return to the golden age of Makerere's storied history. Local conditions and transnational challenges have reconstituted the university's business. Yet memories of the spirit of creativity for which higher learning in Uganda was lauded can help rejuvenate the knowledge structure. Memory research shows that a better intellectual community is possible in this country and others. Memory is not only history but a method for identifying acts of erasure and modes of recovery. In this sense, the vexing issue is finding appropriate antidotes for resuscitating universities. This rebounding can spring from the path taken by higher education institutions.

Historical Context

THE RUN-UP TO INDEPENDENCE

Taking a long view, education reforms in Uganda emanate from the precolonial and colonial periods, when the market economy accelerated class formation. More differentiation meant greater specialization in the division of labor. There was increasing demand for trained, practiced personnel. Early on, the training embraced indigenous knowledge and life skills.[2] The coming of missionaries and traders, mission schools, seminaries, and madrassas provided literacy and thus social mobility. Soon after Uganda became a British Protectorate in 1894, missionaries introduced brick-and-mortar institutions in which the church and the colonial state produced an educated class to maintain infrastructure: offices, the railway, roads, and so on. Then, in the twentieth century, the roles of upper-level education were to staff the civil service and equip local people to rev up the engines of economic growth.

In most of Africa, university education emerged after political independence. However, North Africa has a different history, South Africa is a special situation, and the metropolitan powers established universities in a minority of colonies, including Uganda.[3] There, the evolution of institutions of higher learning can be traced directly to the launch of Makerere Technical College in 1922. Four years later, many of its technical courses were transferred to Kampala Technical College in the interest of promoting advanced education at Makerere.[4] By the 1930s, the colonial government mounted postsecondary

2. J. C. Ssekamwa, *History and Development of Education in Uganda* (Kampala: Fountain Publishers, 1997).

3. Akilagpa Sawyerr, "Challenges Facing African Universities: Selected Issues," *African Studies Review* 47, no. 1 (April 2004): 4, 56n1. Michael J. Schultheis, "Globalization and Education in Africa," *Chiedza Journal* (forthcoming) notes that Qarawyin University in Fez (Morocco) was founded in 859, Azhar University in Cairo in 975, and the University of Timbuktu (Mali) in the twelfth century, whereas Europe's oldest university, Bologna, dates from 1088. The founding dates of these early universities are hard to pin down because of their incremental growth and in the absence of a formal decree by the sovereign or religious authority.

4. Kenneth Ingham, *The Making of Modern Uganda* (London: George Allen and Unwin, 1958), 163.

courses for the purpose of supplying the labor market with local elites, mostly teachers and bureaucrats.

In 1949, Makerere University College was founded, and its students earned University of London degrees upon graduation. The relationship between Kampala and London, however, ended in 1963, when Makerere, along with Nairobi and Dar es Salaam, became constituent colleges of the University of East Africa. Linking neighboring countries, this transnational university embodied the ideals of cultural and political Pan-Africanism. But powerful forces of nationalism were ascendant.[5] The three colleges separated in 1970, and Makerere became a nominally independent university.

With decolonization, it soon became abundantly clear that a university under a national flag was not tantamount to a system that conveys local norms and beliefs. Symbolized, for example, by the Oxford-Cambridge customs of dining at high table in residence halls (dormitories) and donning gowns (robes) at evening meals, colonial-style hierarchies remained in play. The challenge was to refashion a neocolonial education system and be cognizant of development needs.

In his book *Decolonising the Mind*, Ngũgĩ confronted this quagmire:[6] What should be central to the curriculum at an African university? In which language should African writers express themselves? A metropolitan language with international appeal and greater commercial value or a local mother language, and, if the latter, which one in a multilingual society? Taking an unambiguous stand, he rejected the primacy of English-language narratives and assigned high priority to self-expression in a world context. Mindful of his intended audiences, Ngũgĩ decided to compose his subsequent books in Gĩkũyũ and Kiswahili, followed by translations into English. He sought to use language as a means of empowerment.

Ngũgĩ's discourse on "the quest for relevance" unequivocally embraces locally based internationalism fueled by a passion for learning.[7] From his perspective, this is a matter of the order in which European and other knowledge sets are presented to readers in their own contexts. According to Ngũgĩ, it is important to know where to start: in Africa, democratic and national perspectives should radiate out. But, he vowed, one knowledge set need not eclipse another.

In this respect, Ngũgĩ's reasoning intersects with that of disparate Western philosophers, such as Bloom and Nussbaum, who agree that to the extent that

---

5. For details, see James H. Mittelman, *Ideology and Politics in Uganda: From Obote to Amin* (Ithaca: Cornell University Press, 1975).

6. Ngũgĩ wa Thiong'o, *Decolonising the Mind: The Politics of Language in African Literature* (London: James Currey, 1986; Nairobi: Heinemann Kenya, 1986). This collection of essays set off a surge of postcolonial writings on epistemological exclusions linked to material dispossession.

7. Ibid., 87–109.

education challenges the pressures of conformity and stimulates the imagination, it is "relevant" for one's professional and personal lives. Addressing the purposes of a university, Ngũgĩ likewise punctuated the point that educational institutions should stimulate an appetite for knowledge: *"The aim is to instil in the student a critical love of literature, which will both encourage its pursuit in later years, and ensure that such a pursuit is engaged in fruitfully."*[8] To what extent have Ugandan universities fulfilled this aspiration enunciated by Ngũgĩ, himself a graduate of Makerere University College?

THE EARLY POSTCOLONIAL PERIOD

Many academics in Uganda shared Ngũgĩ's hopes for indigenizing learning. Yet, with the onset of decolonization, there was not a detailed agenda for Makerere, then Uganda's only university. It was generally seen as a core institution in nation-building. Its specific roles in producing knowledge and a learned citizenry had yet to be defined. At this stage, the exigencies of development took precedence over the high objectives of university education.

After the 1960s, the "first generation" of African researchers returned home from studying abroad, mostly in America and Europe, and sought to steer the university.[9] Ugandans moved through the pipeline to assume posts on the faculty and in the administration, offices formerly headed by expatriates. Increasingly, the university was deemed instrumental to fostering national identity and a feeling of togetherness. The work of Ugandan artists and young writers were a crucial part of this reformation. The curriculum included new courses in development studies. Controversies in historiography addressed the question of agency. If colonial history featured colonizers as the makers of history, how to rewrite these scripts so that Africans come to the fore? But which ones—political leaders, soldiers, classes, ethnic groups, women, religious communities, or others? In addition, the data available for research questions and public policy were patchy. Official figures were lacking. Academics had to adduce reliable information for analysis.

The "developmental university" supported the goals of the state.[10] Makerere's initial purposes and practices yoked to governmental projects.

8. Ibid., 99, emphasis in original.
9. Thandika Mkandawire, "The Challenge of the Third Generation of African Academics," *CODESRIA Bulletin*, no. 3 (1995): 9.
10. On the "developmental university," see Mahmood Mamdani, "University Crisis and Reform: A Reflection on the African Experience," *Review of African Political Economy* 20, no. 58 (November 1993): 7–20; Thandika Mkandawire, "Running While Others Walk: Knowledge and the Challenge of Africa's Development," London School of Economics and Political Science Inaugural Lecture, Chair of African Development, April 27, 2010, http://eprints.lse.ac.uk/55395/1/Mkandawire_Running_while_others_walk_LSE_African _Initiative_2010.pdf (accessed November 6, 2014); Nico Cloete, Peter Maassen, and

The university became ancillary to the state. Makerere's role was to produce functionaries for public service plus assorted professionals to minister the economy. For its part, the state provided almost all the funding for the university. At first, academics on the left, center, and right accepted this tacit bargain. It was the fruit of national independence. Yet the sequel proved less than satisfying.

Scholars wanted to safeguard intellectual autonomy. The intelligentsia sought to secure its own space for debate, creativity, and academic freedom. After all, universities must be sanctuaries for critical reflection, though not removed from societal conditions. But Makerere's leeway relative to the political sphere was tenuous. And the parameters narrowed. The university had to depend on the state for revenue, and governmental authorities sought to strengthen their legal and managerial control over academe. They adopted the 1970 Makerere Act, followed by the 1971 Universities and Other Tertiary Institutions Act, which ensured that government would be in charge of the university. This bill was passed without the involvement of university stakeholders.[11] In keeping with changing political and economic conditions, these acts were later updated. I will revisit the legislation shortly.

THE TRANSITION FROM A STATIST
TO A MIXED MODEL

Although Makerere had served as a prestigious "national institution" and had endeavored to regenerate local knowledge, it suffered from declining financial support. Nationalist elites had their own political and economic interests. They were also subject to pressures from other local stakeholders and converging global currents.

At this juncture, the rise of neoliberal ideas in the United States and Britain quickly spread to other parts of the world, including East Africa. Global governance institutions propagated this new reform agenda. In chapter 3, we looked at the World Bank, one of the global agencies that prescribed a neoliberal policy framework. The bank's experts on Africa recommended best practices for education in Uganda, centering on deregulation, liberalization, and privatization. Through its coordinating role, technical advice, loan programs conditioned on a standard recipe of reforms, measures for categories that it had designed, and its interpretations of them, this Washington-based institution became a compass for Uganda's higher education policies.[12]

Teboho Moja, "Higher Education and Different Notions of Development," *IIE Networker* (Spring 2013): 21–23.

11. Nakanyike B. Musisi and Nansozi K. Muwanga, *Makerere University in Transition, 1993–2000: Opportunities & Challenges* (Oxford: James Currey, 2003), 13.

12. Samoff and Carrol, *From Manpower Planning to the Knowledge Era*, 28–31.

Ugandan critics have been less than sanguine about the World Bank's impact, castigating its procedures as not only a key element in the global financial architecture but also a social technology.[13]

By dint of the nexus of the interests of Uganda's ruling elite and the World Bank's priorities, support for higher education lagged relative to funding for its primary and secondary schools. In the 1980s, the bank advocated that reductions in higher education financing would increase efficiency and enable government to reallocate resources for training that would better suit labor-market needs. According to David Court of the World Bank and the Rockefeller Foundation, five years of financial reforms at Makerere in the 1990s changed the policy by which students had not been charged tuition fees—they were state sponsored—to one in which 70 percent of them paid.[14] A sharp per capita, though not absolute, drop in government sponsorship for university students was accompanied by a shift to a market orientation in the management of Makerere. Court observed: "The strategic plan and package of reforms which Makerere is applying are not unlike ideas which have been disseminated by the World Bank. . . . Makerere has made the ideas her own and applied them in her own way."[15] In his praise for Makerere's achievements, Court averred that Makerere's "quiet revolution" "sets an example for the rest of the continent."[16] Among the reasons for this imputed success are university leadership and its "unambiguous sense of ownership of the reform process."[17] But what are the grounds for finding that local stakeholders at the university authored the reform process and stood behind it?

Court omits academics' myriad views of the changing purposes of the postcolonial university. University personnel certainly are not a monolith. For example, Mahmood Mamdani, director of MISR, regards Court's analysis as flawed and one-sided. Mamdani argues convincingly: "It was an ingenious way of translating external constraint into internal agency."[18] While his insight about the false equation of external and internal initiative is poignant, the telling issue is how global and national forces intermingle and create buy-in. To clinch Mamdani's point, one could extend its import by showing how, for the most part, material structures and ideas became mutually contained. At bottom, this is a story of accommodation among elites and their shared

13. See, for example, Yash Tandon, *Ending Aid Dependence* (Nairobi: Fahamu Books, 2008).

14. David Court, "Financing Higher Education in Africa: Makerere, the Quiet Revolution" (Washington, DC: World Bank, 1999), i.

15. Ibid., 11.

16. Ibid., 4.

17. Ibid., i.

18. Mahmood Mamdani, *Scholars in the Marketplace: The Dilemmas of Liberal Reform at Makerere University, 1989-2005* (Dakar: Council for the Development of Social Science Research, 2007), 200.

intersubjective framework. As we shall see, it is also about the responses that the reformist agenda elicited from varied actors.

In these interactions, the World Bank's thrust was hardly singular. Let me cite one among the other progenitors of education reforms in Uganda. Like the bank, the WTO embraced the position that education as a public good is an antiquated notion that must be put to rest if it fails to deliver cost-effective and competitive returns. This global governance agency regards universities as service providers. It is supposed to facilitate their cross-border activities and remove restrictions on these flows. As a member of the WTO, Uganda is obligated to adhere to its agreements and protocols. In other words, Uganda is expected to guarantee market access for providers from other countries. The difficulty, as some Ugandans see it, is that "we are asked to accept the view that education is a commodity to be traded in the open market."[19] They face unregulated market forces that bring incoming education commodities.[20] How then is a poor country with a weak private sector and a relatively small, though growing, middle class to apply its own regulations, say, those issued by a national accrediting agency, for the sake of upgrading standards and improving quality?

Academics at Makerere chafed at the erosion of intellectual autonomy. Leaving aside for now instances of blatant disregard for academic freedom, especially marked from 1971 to 1986, traumatic years of political and economic turmoil, intellectual autonomy was transposed into matters of administrative and financial autonomy.[21] In this shift, the university's senior administrators were supposed to take more responsibility for bringing in funding. The state gradually handed over a large share of this burden to them. Yet powerful globalizing forces pared down local officials' own autonomy. If they impinged on competing institutions' unrestricted access to the marketplace, their actions would violate WTO agreements. This is not to excuse local authorities' incursions into academic freedom on the ground of honoring an international accord. But the crux of the matter is what lies behind the rulers' egregious actions. It goes to the structural power that shapes their convictions and policies.

19. National Council for Higher Education, Uganda, "Management and Leadership Training Project: Phase One, African Higher Education in a Globalizing World" (Kampala: NCHE, 2011), 28.

20. A. B. K. Kasozi, "The Development of a Strategic Plan for Higher Education in Uganda 2001–5: The Interplay of Internal and External Forces in Higher Education Policy Formation in a Southern Country," 6, http://heglobal.international.gbtesting.net/media /4251/development%20of%20a%20strategic%20plan%20for%20higher%20education .pdf (accessed November 4, 2014).

21. See Mamadou Diouf and Mahmood Mamdani, eds., *Academic Freedom and Democratic Struggle* (Dakar: Council for the Development of Economic and Social Research in Africa, 1994).

In this phase of Uganda's history, the intended and unintended consequences of market-based reforms reflect a circuit of falling or stagnant unit cost (the real expense that universities incur for educating a student). To pick up the slack and cover high rates of inflation and other needs, such as technological advancement, the university increased the intake of privately sponsored students. Female access to education improved. More students from underrepresented regions of the country could be admitted, though progress on this front, especially for the Northern Region, was uneven, and the imposition of tuition fees further disadvantaged poor and needy families. Government scholarships still favored students who attended the better secondary schools.

At university, computer use and enrollments in science and technology and in commerce and business studies mushroomed. However, only 11 percent of the faculty had earned PhDs. Qualifications and staffing shortages were persistent problems.[22] While teaching loads became heavier, meager salaries for academics could not sustain them and their families. Moonlighting became a commonplace. Morale plummeted. The university hired more part-time personnel for teaching. Funding for basic research dried up. Budget for books and scholarly journals was paltry. Lecture rooms, libraries, laboratories, recreation facilities, and administrative offices were overly crowded. Students rioted and challenged the higher administration. To help assuage them and meet demand, some colleges at Makerere have run classes twenty-four hours per day.[23]

The market model heightened competition and sparked conflicts between Makerere's central administration and its academic units as well as among the units. The struggles were primarily over money, as in the clash between Makerere University and its Business School initially concerning who would control lucrative MBA programs.[24] Public lectures, which large numbers of faculty and students had eagerly attended, became few and infrequent. Academics could not find time to be present for these events. They were too busy making money, trying to stay afloat financially.[25] So, too, Makerere's tradition of tutorials became a relic of a bygone era. With new rounds of reforms, academic quality suffered.

22. National Council for Higher Education, Uganda, "Management and Leadership Training Project," 3.

23. Author discussion with Damalie Naggita-Musoke, professor and dean, School of Law, Makerere University, Kampala, May 17, 2013; author discussion with Sylvia Tamale, professor and former dean, School of Law, Makerere University, Kampala, May 17, 2013.

24. A. B. K. Kasozi, *Financing Uganda's Public Universities: An Obstacle to Serving the Public Good* (Kampala: Fountain Publishers, 2009), 38.

25. Author discussion with Apolo R. Nsibambi, former chancellor of Makerere University, former minister of education, and former prime minister, Kampala, May 31, 2013.

Socioeconomic Context

Next, I want to supplement the overview of Uganda's route to the twentieth century by locating its higher education institutions in their socioeconomic setting. This section will pave the way for mapping specific reform initiatives in the 2000s and their impact. It provides comparative context.

For perspective on the order of magnitude of these changes, let's return to the touchstone established at the outset of this chapter. When I arrived in Uganda in 1967, its population was circa nine million people. The sole university, the University of East Africa, in Kampala, had an enrollment of some 3,000 students. By early 2013, these numbers ballooned to a populace of 37,578,876; 35,761 were enrolled on Makerere's Kampala campus.[26] In the second decade of the 2000s, the student body at all Ugandan universities, other higher degree–granting institutions, and affiliated colleges such as Makerere University Business School, which eventually merged with the National College of Business Studies, totaled 140,096.[27] The number of registered universities proliferated from one public institution in the 1960s to 29 in 2013, plus unlicensed degree and certificate programs. Of the 29, 5 are public; 24, private. More are in the making.

Although state spending on universities relative to GDP has fluctuated, it has, overall, decreased in real if not absolute terms. According to the World Bank, the government of Uganda allocated 3.16 percent of GDP to the entire education sector in 1971; 3.43 percent in 1985; 5.1 percent in 1988; and then 3.28 percent in 2012.[28] On the face of it, this would seem to suggest not only oscillation but a modest increase since 1971, especially if one allows for economic growth in Uganda. The small variation in percentage is, however, nearly nil in aggregate terms. Factors that mitigate the slight percent gain

26. National Council for Higher Education, Uganda, "The State of Higher Education and Training in Uganda 2010: A Report on Higher Education and Delivery" (Kampala: NCHE, 2011), 47, 89; Uganda Bureau of Statistics, *Statistics: Population*, last modified February 20, 2012, http://www.ubos.org/?st=pagerelations2&id=17&p=related%20pages %202:Population (accessed March 20, 2013); Makerere University, "Annual Report 2013" (2014), 8, http://www.muwrp.org/wp-content/files/Makerere-University-Annual-Report -2014x.pdf (accessed October 8, 2014); World Bank, World Development Indicators, last modified September 24, 2014, http://databank.worldbank.org/data/views/variableSelection /selectvariables.aspx?source=world-development-indicators (accessed October 8, 2014).

27. Republic of Uganda, Ministry of Education and Sports, Statistics Section, Education Planning and Policy Analysis Department, "Uganda Education Statistical Abstract" (Kampala: MoES, 2011), 86, http://www.education.go.ug/files/downloads/Education %20Abstract%202011.pdf (accessed October 8, 2014).

28. World Bank, World Development Indicators, last modified August 1, 2013, http:// databank.worldbank.org/data/views/variableselection/selectvariables.aspx?source=world -development-indicators (accessed August 16, 2013). These figures are for primary, secondary, and tertiary education.

are adjustment for the rate of inflation (on average, 8.4 percent per year from 2002 to 2013) and rising demand for university education, reflected in large hikes in enrollments.[29] Whereas the government had served as the principal sponsor for students in the initial postcolonial period, the inception of private universities in the late 1980s and early 1990s and the introduction of fee-paying students at public universities in the 1997–98 academic year reconstituted the revenue structure. Table 6.1 and figure 6.1 capture these developments at Makerere University.

These graphics demonstrate that fee-based students' share of generating funds for Uganda's flagship university shot up from 0 percent to 59 percent between the 1993–94 and 2005–6 academic years. My impression is that if current data were available, they would show even more of an upward swing. Put in perspective, this pattern reflects major alterations in state-university-market relations. A reason for the shifts is a changing conception of public space. The state's responsibility to society for the general good is increasingly assigned to individual Ugandans and their families. The social compact for the well-being of citizens is metamorphosing in both attitudinal and material ways.

The Ministry of Education and Sports (MoES) frankly recognizes the consequences of the move to private payers: "Public funding to higher education has been declining over time, i.e. (Government contribution of $2,532 in 1970 to $639 in 1985 per student and allocation less than 15% of the ministry budget)."[30] More so from a comparative perspective: Uganda lagged behind its East African counterparts in financing upper-level education. State support for public universities in Uganda averaged 0.35 percent of GDP in the 1997–98 to 2009–10 period. In comparison, Kenya and Tanzania spent almost 1 percent during the same years.[31] The MoES views this pressure on public universities as resulting in "poor quality of service delivery."[32] From its market-friendly standpoint, the central purpose of universities is to be an efficient provider of educational services.

The bite is acutely felt on the ground in Uganda, especially if one is mindful that after independence in 1962, admission to Uganda's university was initially without tuition fees. Now, the cost of tuition fees outpaces GDP per capita in Uganda. Working on this research with me, Nicholas T. Smith sampled

29. The rate of inflation, measured by the consumer price index, is taken from the World Bank, World Development Indicators, last modified November 6, 2014, http://databank.worldbank.org/data/views/reports/tableview.aspx?isshared=true (accessed November 24, 2014).

30. Republic of Uganda, Ministry of Education and Sports, "Revised Education Sector Plan 2007–2015" (Kampala: MoES, 2008), 20.

31. Kasozi, *Financing Uganda's Public Universities*, 33.

32. Ibid.

Table 6.1. Public and Private (Student) Contributions to Funding Makerere University, 1993–2005/2006

Year	Government Students	Total Government Funding	% Government of Total Funding	Private Students	Total Private Students	% Private of Total Funding	Total Funding from Both Sources	Total Students	Annual Growth Rate	Makerere Unit Income Per Student
1993/94	6,643	10,713,005,331	100%	701		0%	10,713,005,331	7,344	5.0%	
1994/95	6,494	17,660,738,900	100%	1,412		0%	17,660,738,900	7,906	7.7%	
1995/96	7,089	20,328,433,000	83%	2,280	4,080,059,201	17%	24,408,492,201	9,369	18.5%	2,605,240
1996/97	6,710	19,255,308,734	72%	7,902	7,561,493,114	28%	26,816,801,848	14,612	56.0%	1,835,259
1997/98	6,890	19,500,000,000	69%	7,477	8,799,261,213	31%	28,299,261,213	14,367	-1.7%	1,969,740
1998/99	6,545	22,541,938,000	62%	9,497	13,663,196,178	38%	36,205,134,178	16,042	11.7%	2,256,897
1999/00	6,103	22,990,000,000	60%	14,265	15,080,261,764	40%	38,070,261,764	20,368	27.0%	1,869,121
2000/01	6,133	22,060,000,000	56%	19,112	17,406,254,325	44%	39,466,254,325	25,245	23.9%	1,563,330
2001/02	7,712	26,650,000,000	58%	22,650	19,030,439,000	42%	45,680,439,000	30,226	19.7%	1,511,296
2002/03	7,932	26,260,000,000	47%	22,276	29,438,099,000	53%	55,698,099,000	30,208	-0.1%	1,843,819
2003/04	7,772	26,289,000,000	45%	19,454	31,981,937,218	55%	58,270,937,218	27,932	-7.5%	2,086,171
2004/05	6,799	28,874,000,000	43%	23,906	38,579,239,386	57%	67,453,239,386	30,705	9.9%	2,196,816
2005/06	6,948	38,472,472,000	41%	23,789	56,181,463,787	59%	94,653,935,787	30,827	0.4%	3,070,488

Source: National Council for Higher Education, Uganda, "The State of Higher Education and Training in Uganda 2010: A Report on Higher Education Delivery and Institutions" (Kampala: NCHE, 2010), 32, http://unche.or.ug/ (accessed April 17, 2014), citing A. B. K. Kasozi, *Financing Uganda's Public Universities: An Obstacle to Serving the Public Good* (Kampala: Fountain Publishers, 2009), 164.

Note: Donor funding from external agencies is not included in this table. Contributions are in Ugandan shillings.

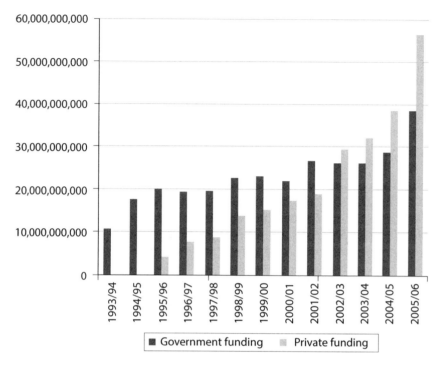

Figure 6.1. Comparison of Government and Private Funding for Makerere University.
Source: National Council for Higher Education, Uganda, "The State of Higher Education and Training in Uganda 2010: A Report on Higher Education Delivery and Institutions" (Kampala: NCHE, 2010), 31, http://unche.or.ug/ (accessed April 17, 2014).

Note: The left column signifies total government funding; right column, revenues derived from private students. Both columns are in Ugandan shillings.

14 private and public universities in Uganda in 2013.[33] He found that at these institutions, the average annual cost for tuition for undergraduate diplomas and bachelor's degree programs in March 2013 came to $620 per year.[34] Compared to the steep price of higher education in some affluent countries, this figure may seem affordable. However, it must be seen in light of Uganda's GDP

33. The sample of undergraduate costs is for the following institutions: International Health Sciences University, Ugandan Christian University-Mukono, Mbarara University of Science and Technology, Makerere University, Mountains of the Moon University, Makerere University Business School, Kyambogo University, Bugema University, Kampala International University, Busoga University, Bishop Stuart University, Busitema University, Ndejje University, and Kabale University. The figures for the fee structures are drawn from the universities' own websites.

34. In this computation, the $620 cost of tuition does not include fees. The data on fees at Uganda's universities are inconsistent and fragmentary. And some official documents issued in Uganda use the terms "tuition" and "fees" interchangeably.

per capita of $572 in 2013.[35] In this case, the price of higher education relative to income levels is much greater than that in the bulk of the more prosperous countries.[36]

Bear in mind that international or, for that matter, domestic comparisons can be fraught if the data fail to adjust for financial-aid grants, effectively reducing the "sticker" (nominal) price for tuition fees. In the United States, GDP per capita was $53,143 in the 2009–13 period; according to the College Board, the net tuition fees, on average, were $12,460 at private colleges and $3,120 for in-state students at public four-year colleges in 2013. And in Finland, with a GDP per capita of $47,231 during the same time span, tuition fees did not exist.[37] Back to Uganda, then: $620 average annual cost for undergraduate tuition at the 14 universities sampled is 8.4 percent greater than its GDP per capita, though it is difficult to obtain solid data for financial-aid grants excluding loans that require repayment. But one can thus surmise that the hardship borne by Ugandan students for the actual outlay on higher education in relation to their means is a multiple of that in wealthy countries, where, as I have recounted, debates about the costs of universities and the return on them are raging. In addition, this dimension of societal well-being must be construed to encompass varied levels of inequality and relative poverty.

The issue therefore becomes which students from what segments of Ugandan society experience the most difficulty qualifying and paying for university. We have already alluded to regional inequality as a factor in opportunities for higher education. While the North and rural areas generally are more impoverished than other parts of the country, it is not surprising that for Uganda as a whole, less fortunate families have marked disadvantages in placing their children at universities and supporting their education.[38]

In this connection, in Uganda in 2013, 38.01 percent of the population lived under the poverty line of $1.25 per day.[39] In 164th place among 187 countries on UNDP's Human Development Index, Uganda's 2013 gross national income is rated in the bottom quintile at .484 and below the sub-Saharan

35. World Bank, World Development Indicators, last modified November 6, 2104, http://data.worldbank.org/indicator/NY.GDP.PCAP.CD (accessed November 20, 2014).

36. As illustrated in chapters 4 and 5.

37. World Bank, World Development Indicators, last modified November 6, 2104, http://data.worldbank.org/indicator/NY.GDP.PCAP.CD (accessed November 20, 2014); David Leonhardt, "How Government Exaggerates College's Cost," *New York Times*, July 29, 2014; the Finnish case, as discussed in chapter 5.

38. Bidemi Carrol, *Private Monies, Public Universities: Implications for Access and University Behavior: A Study of Makerere University* (Stanford: Stanford University School of Education, 2005).

39. United Nations Development Programme, Human Development Report 2014, *Sustaining Human Progress: Reducing Vulnerabilities and Building Resilience*, http://hdr.undp.org/en/countries/profiles/UGA (accessed July 31, 2014).

average of .502.[40] However, these human-development indicators must be adjusted when gender-based inequalities are taken into account. On its Gender Inequalities Index, the UNDP assigns a weight of .529 to Uganda, putting it in the 115th spot among 149 countries in 2013. At the same time, it has made strides. For example, women hold 35 percent of Uganda's parliamentary seats,[41] though it should be said that this measure is not a sufficient gauge of women's influence in government.

Certainly, access to higher education is a key dimension of empowerment and economic activity. Historically, women in Uganda have lacked preuniversity educational opportunities. Beginning in the 1940s, Makerere University College admitted only a handful of female students.[42] Their numbers increased to 73 in 1968.[43] Makerere mainly prepared them for specific roles and "traditional" jobs as typists, receptionists, caterers, and the like.[44] Over the last twenty-five years, the public universities have adopted steps such as bonus points for female applicants so as to boost the percentage of women in the student body. The universities have also mounted gender studies programs. Yet as researchers in these programs highlight, structural barriers and disparities in representation are deeply entrenched. At Ugandan universities in 2010, women constituted 44 percent of student enrollment. But they are still concentrated in certain faculties and underrepresented in other fields of study, particularly in technical areas.[45]

Ultimately, these dimensions of the social fabric are linked to the stark reality that Uganda's scholars and students are entangled in an unsteady structure of higher education. It is unsteady partly because of a lack of political mettle at the top. The ruling elite is heretofore unwilling to provide requisite funding for the universities. So, too, dominant transnational paradigms of higher education reform are promoting policies wherein more students gain access to higher education but public authorities diminish the state's per capita contribution to the budget. Priorities have been established. The rules

40. Ibid., http://hdr.undp.org/sites/all/themes/hdr_theme/country-notes/UGA.pdf (accessed July 31, 2014).

41. Ibid.

42. Nakanyike B. Musisi, "Colonial and Missionary Education: Women and Domesticity in Uganda, 1900–1945," in *African Encounters with Domesticity*, ed. Karen Tranberg Hansen (New Brunswick, NJ: Rutgers University Press, 1992), 172–94. By comparison, Yale and Princeton became coeducational in 1969; Harvard proceeded in stages from the early 1970s and merged with Radcliffe College in 1999, though Harvard Business School started to enroll women in 1963.

43. Joy C. Kwesiga, *Women's Access to Higher Education in Africa: Uganda's Experience* (Kampala: Fountain Publishers, 2002), 207.

44. Ibid., 21.

45. National Council for Higher Education, Uganda, "Management and Leadership Training Project," 15.

and regulations of global governance, as applied in Uganda, are hewed in ways that I will spell out. Meantime, chronic revenue shortfalls are a brute fact of academic life in this country. Education leaders have accordingly sought to ameliorate the condition. Bricoleurs, identified below, have adopted a battery of remedial measures, trial-and-error strategies. The bricolage consists of a set of regulatory reforms.

The Architecture of Reform

GOVERNANCE

Let's back up a bit in the historical journey. From the 1960s to the mid-1980s, Milton Obote, first as prime minister and twice as president, and Idi Amin, a general who became president as a result of a military coup, wielded political violence with abandon and dampened the climate for higher education. These heads of state led brutal authoritarian regimes known for corruption and repression. When Yoweri Museveni, a former student leader at the University of Dar es Salaam, took over as president of Uganda in 1986, academics there looked to fundamental changes in education policy. They wanted greater control over their institutions, sustainable financing for them, and genuine respect for academic freedom. To what degree have these expectations been met? What kinds of reforms followed?

The Museveni government's initiatives of the late 1980s and 1990s reached an inflection point when it adopted the Universities and Other Tertiary Institutions Act, 2001, sanctioning regulatory authority and signaling policies to come.[46] Although this act has subsequently been amended, it still provides the basic legal and institutional framework for Ugandan universities. As such, it is a linchpin for planning national development.[47]

The 2001 legislation established the National Council for Higher Education (NCHE) to advise the minister responsible for accreditation of universities, monitor and evaluate them, and ensure national standards. The president of Uganda appoints the NCHE chairperson, and the minister names its executive director. It is mainly funded by Parliament and receives grants, gifts, and fees, some of them levied on students. The procedure for setting up new universities is by application to the NCHE, which makes its recommendations on licensing to the minister. Then the president, if satisfied, confers a charter. Noticeably, the 2001 act says little about the language of instruction or the status of Kiswahili in a country where many languages are spoken—an important

---

46. Republic of Uganda, Universities and Other Tertiary Institutions Act, 2001, Supplement No. 6 to *Uganda Gazette* 94, no. 19 (April 6, 2001).

47. A government agency, the National Planning Authority, is charged with coordinating and managing this process.

issue in neighboring Tanzania. It only stipulates that an official language in Uganda (English) and "any other language" shall be a medium of instruction at universities.[48]

In short, this legislation details how authority is exercised, ways to build capacity, and the modalities for implementing policy. It set the tone for reforming universities in the early 2000s. By law, authority would primarily be a matter of central control. The president, minister, and their appointees were to steer Uganda's knowledge governance structure.

A challenge facing higher education leadership was to determine the role of academic deans in governance. Generally, they lack management training, are given incentives to adopt corporate practices, and embrace business enterprise models. Vital to effective university governance, decanal authority was and is subject to cross-pressure from officials who allocate resources, colleagues who insist on maintaining academic values, and students demanding a better education.

Problems with public finance management, including leakage of cash flows, failures to provide instructional materials, and deficiencies in addressing the economic aspects of instructors' classroom absenteeism and tardiness worsened chronic underfunding of universities. In the face of spikes in enrollment and cramped facilities, the difficulty was how to cope with a government allocation for tertiary institutions that averaged only 11 percent of Uganda's education budget circa 2007 and was trending downward.[49] In the eyes of numerous academics, the conditions for upholding university ideals had become precarious.

Intellectual freedom, in particular, was a matter of concern. Have constraints on it eased since the fall of Obote's and Amin's autocratic regimes and after scholars from across the continent issued the 1990 "Kampala Declaration on Intellectual Freedom and Social Responsibility"?[50] This statement spotlights the political and social crises besetting universities in Africa and the intelligentsia's obligation to champion high standards of ethical conduct. Sections B and C of the declaration are devoted to the academic community's right to carry out their intellectual pursuits at autonomous institutions of higher education.[51] These passages emphasize that to the extent that independent inquiry and the democratic means of self-government at African universities are

48. Republic of Uganda, Universities and Other Tertiary Institutions Act, 2001, 81. Parliament voted in 2005 to adopt Kiswahili as a second official national language, but measures to promote it in higher education have been slowly enacted.

49. Makerere University, "Strategic Plan: 2008/2009–2018/2019" (Kampala: Makerere University, 2008), 9.

50. Reprinted in Diouf and Mamdani, *Academic Freedom and Democratic Struggle*, 349–53.

51. Ibid., 351.

POSTCOLONIAL EXPERIENCE: UGANDA [185]

impeded, academic freedom is at risk. The declaration is oft cited as a lodestar for academic freedom struggles, with reverberations across Africa.

Undeterred by such rights claims, the Ugandan government adopted the 2013 Public Order Bill, restricting political debate and the freedom of assembly. It closed media houses, banned news outlets, and clamped down on civil society rallies and political opponents. Opposition leaders were arrested for calling for walk-to-work protests over fuel hikes, the escalating cost of living more generally, and public graft. University students participated in these uprisings and mounted a strike in the face of a doubling of tuition fees.[52] Public universities experienced a flurry of protests by non-teaching staff who wanted pay hikes, faculty demanding salary increments, and students contesting the resultant closure of Makerere. Following a long- running standoff between management and faculty, joined by students, over payment of $13.5 million allowance in arrears, Museveni shut down Makerere in 2016.

Even with this turmoil, higher education institutions in Uganda are not encountering the extent of flat-out repression, detentions, and threats that stained the 1970s and 1980s. Academic freedom was more directly and forcefully violated during these times. On the whole, Uganda's scholars now engage in wide-ranging debates and attempt to push the boundaries of dissent. Though sometimes veiled rather than muzzled, criticism and deliberation are tolerated. Universities continue to provide space, albeit circumscribed, for clear thinking. However, coercion takes many forms.

Structural conditions fetter academic freedom in subtle ways. Universities' economic marginalization hinders open inquiry. In particular, the drying up of funds for basic research limits the scope of intellectual pursuits. It is hard to tell how many academics keep their heads down and voices muffled because they figure that self-policing is the prudent course in the low-pay, high-workload system in which they are ensconced. Others have the courage of their convictions, speak up, and act on principle in keeping with the core values of universities as affirmed in their mission statements and strategic plans.

Makerere's avowed values include "academic independence" and "institutional autonomy," alongside "allegiance to the institution" and "customer responsiveness."[53] This purposing makes one think hard about the intersection of knowledge and business. In practice, which priorities win out? The emphasis suggests a shifting balance, partly linked to attitudes, some of them the product of a legacy of strife in the country.

52. Adam Branch and Zachariah Mampilly, *Africa Uprising: Popular Protest and Political Change* (London: Zed Books, 2015), 130–32.

53. Makerere University, "Repositioning Makerere to Meet Emerging Development Challenges," Strategic Framework: 2007/08–2017/18 (2007), http://pdd.mak.ac.ug/sites/default/files/archive/Makerere%20University%20Strategic%20Framework%20Revised%20after%20FPDC.pdf (accessed September 11, 2014).

In postconflict Uganda, the trust needed, including with political officials, to reinvigorate the university system is in short supply. Survey research
shows that the general public regards education as the top priority for increased government spending.[54] Too, recurrent student riots over the state of
higher education are a patent sign of mistrust of power holders. Authorities
have greeted student unrest over proximate wellness issues with a combination of concessions and crackdowns, including the use of tear gas, arrests,
and jail. The sensibilities of striking students continue to jibe with faculty
members' discontent, culminating in their strikes over depressed salaries,
small and delayed pensions, and the overall climate for research and higher
learning.

Quite clearly, underlying problems of rights and responsibility have not
faded away. Academic freedom is fragile. Autonomy in the sense of independence of mind is constrained by underfunding and controlling political and
administrative structures.

DECENTRALIZATION

Paradoxically, centralized control led to administrative decentralization.
Center-driven university initiatives featured the delegation of elements of executive authority to midlevel management in individual academic units. This
is in line with the best practices of world universities. In a way, decentralization
is an instrument used by those at the helm for achieving cost-effectiveness.[55]
While holding the purse, the central administration transfers much of the job
of generating revenue onto colleges, schools, and departments.

Decentralization at Ugandan universities coincided with a devolution of
governance tasks in the country as a whole. Although one can trace this history to earlier times, the Museveni regime accentuated the pattern. It is evident, for example, with regard to local government and public budgeting.[56] It
is consonant with a neoliberal framework and World Bank policy that encourages citizens to look to private means and local government for services and to
provide resources for it. By shifting responsibilities for financing development
to firms and the localities, it suits the national political elites.

54. Afrobarometer, "Let the People Have Say," Afrobarometer Round 6, Survey
in Uganda, 2015, 51, http://afrobarometer.org/sites/default/files/publications/Summary
%20of%20results/uga_r6_sor_en.pdf (accessed February 10, 2016).

55. See Elizabeth Popp Berman, "Thinking Like an Economist: On Expertise and
the U.S. Policy Process," Occasional Papers of the School of Social Sciences, Institute for
Advanced Study, Princeton, No. 52, http://www.sss.ias.edu/files/papers/paper52.pdf (accessed September 12, 2014).

56. Gina M. S. Lambright, *Decentralization in Uganda: Explaining Successes and
Failures in Local Governance* (Boulder, CO: First Forum Press, 2011).

At Makerere, a turning point was the conversion to a college system. A committee headed by Edward Kirumira, with support from the Norwegian Agency for Development Cooperation (NORAD) to facilitate its aims, drafted a report, approved by University Council in 2005. It called for a three-level structure: central administration, colleges, and departments. It also contained provisions for mergers, resource reallocation, and implementation. In this system, there would be no deans. But some units were ill-disposed to couple with others—to enter "forced marriages," as a Makerere professor quipped.

A new reform committee, chaired by Barnabas Nawangwe, a former dean of the Faculty of Technology, and partly funded by the Swedish International Development Cooperation Agency, planned full implementation, with allowance for amendments, of the proposed restructuring by 2013. The deanships would be retained for the purposes of coordinating and managing departments and operate in conjunction with department heads. Deans, though, would not handle finances, which were to be vested in colleges and their principals. The colleges in turn endorsed the reforms, provided that they would increase authority and safeguards for financial devolution.[57]

Yet worries about the consequences, some unintended, of this decentralization linger. A major concern is that it is excessive and lacks adept coordination. Specifically, the central government must give public universities permission to raise tuition fees, which are below cost. While academic units receive revenue drawn from private students' fees, only 2,000 students of the 13,000 admitted to Makerere each year are government sponsored.[58] As a result, student enrollment and competition among academic units mount. Each unit is attempting to mobilize resources. In a country with small private markets and few big companies, colleges and departments compete for tuition fees and strive to become more marketable. Concretely, this means that the Department of Philosophy, for instance, introduces a course on the philosophy of tourism, a degree program in secretarial studies is offered, classes that prepare students for careers as consultants are initiated, and so on.

Meanwhile, academic units contest the delivery of funds from the center. Their representatives claim that money is not transferred in a timely way and that the units lack direct access to the university's chief financial officers. The units within and among universities hunt for personnel. Poaching professors is a common practice. Public and private universities vie with one another. While the financial incentives vary, they jockey for dividends.

The competition for talent and salary crisscrosses with opportunities at think tanks. One of these, the Economic Policy and Research Centre, is

57. Author discussion with Edward Kirumira, professor of sociology and principal, College of Humanities and Social Sciences, Makerere University, Kampala, May 21, 2013.

58. Author discussion with John Ddumba-Ssentamu, professor of economics and vice chancellor, Makerere University, Kampala, June 6, 2013.

housed at Makerere. The center's work is oriented to development policy. It is headed by the minister responsible for finance and planning and Makerere's vice chancellor (the principal academic and administrative officer at British and other Commonwealth universities). The government of Uganda and a host of donors, including Canada's International Research Centre, the Bill & Melinda Gates Foundation, the William and Flora Hewlett Foundation, and the Netherlands Directorate-General for International Development, furnish funding. The Economic Policy and Research Centre also partners with the Brookings Institution's Africa Growth Initiative. Another tank, Advocates for Development and Environment, publishes policy briefs, reports, and papers, and encourages dialogue among stakeholders. Support comes from several donors: among them, the Ford and MacArthur foundations, the International Institute for Environment and Development, and the Netherlands embassy in Kampala. The Uganda Development Policy Management Forum and other think tanks similarly seek to analyze and influence policy. On the whole, think tanks in Uganda are small and partly, if not heavily, sponsored by donors.

On the university side of the knowledge structure, senior administrators increasingly fret about budgetary deficiencies. Makerere's leaders maintain that the formation of colleges imposes additional costs, including salaries for principals, their staff, offices, equipment, and "top-up allowances."[59] In this arrangement, the persistent problem is that both higher-ranking and college-level administrators can succumb to managerialism—groupthink and a technocratic mind-set.

Not surprisingly, some academics are loath to relinquish old ways. Forestry economists, for instance, are reluctant to teach first-year economics to students in other fields of study. For various stakeholders, the structural issue is that autonomy in academe takes on more economic meaning.[60] Self-determination becomes a matter of survival skills and self-financing. The fiscal dimension entails underwriting a large part of the university's business, including base salaries and research costs. In Uganda, there is little national support for this work. Individual academics are left to source some or all of it as well as supplement their low income, which can lead to compromises in bidding for outside contracts. The risk lies in transposing academic freedom into the freedom to accumulate capital.

59. Ibid.; "The State of Makerere University Ten Years after the Universities and Other Tertiary Institutions Act (UOTIA)," workshop organized by the Makerere Institute of Social Research and the Human Rights and Peace Centre, MISR Public Policy Report No. 2 (August 23, 2011), 9–11.

60. Author discussion with Samuel Kyamanywa, professor of agricultural entomology and acting principal, College of Agricultural and Environmental Sciences, Makerere University, Kampala, June 5, 2013.

Under the circumstances, there is brain drain of two types: full, entailing an exodus from the university; and partial, wherein a portion of time is contracted out.[61] In fact, the consultancy industry in Uganda is flourishing. It does not fall squarely under formal regulatory authority, save blatant forms of corruption. In effect, the practices of intellectual engagement have changed. When research is commissioned, the terms of reference are given; the problems to be addressed, predetermined. Academic peer review is infrequently practiced. The investigator can be beholden to the benefactor. Research findings are merchandised. Critical inquiry is diminished. The rules of knowledge production and exchange are reformed.

PRIVATIZATION

In the face of rising student activism and faculty dissatisfaction with the state of the university, Ugandan officials have opted for privatization as a means to meet mounting challenges. Its main facets are threefold: opening more private universities and increasing enrollment at public institutions of higher learning; augmenting demand-driven, vocationally oriented programs; and outsourcing educational services.

The founding of a private higher education institution, the Islamic University, in 1988, and the admission of fee-paying students at Makerere in the early 1990s were turning points in a system in which the state had been the only provider of university education. The origins of Uganda's Islamic University can be traced to 1974, when President Amin met King Faisal of Saudi Arabia at an Organization of Islamic Cooperation summit conference in Lahore. The two heads of state agreed to launch an Islamic university in Anglophone Africa. Uganda's next president, Museveni, embraced this project. Backed by the organization's financing, the Islamic University set up a campus in Mbale, Uganda, and later formed a multibranch system. The enlargement came to include Kibuli near Kampala's central business district, Kabojja exclusively for women, and Arua, which attracts students from the South Sudan and the eastern Congo. The university has sought to address a specific legacy of colonial education: an imbalance wherein Christian missionaries built schools, Muslims went to madrassas, and few of the latter entered Makerere.[62]

In the years following the establishment of the Islamic University, the number of private universities and the intake of students at registered public

61. Author discussion with Njuguna Ng'ethe, associate research professor, Institute for Development Studies, College of Humanities and Social Sciences, University of Nairobi, Nairobi, May 27, 2013.

62. Author discussion with Abdul Karim Nasser Ssesanga, professor of management and administration of education, Islamic University in Uganda, Kampala Campus, Kampala, May 24, 2013.

universities grew appreciably; and the expansion of primary and secondary education continued to heighten demand for admission to institutions of higher education. Moreover, national economic growth, however uneven, boosted the pool of applicants.

These pressures, the level of funding, and the volume of self-sponsored students altered the caliber of higher education. Supposedly, the budget gap could be addressed by bringing in additional tuition and fees. The return of a portion of earned revenue to academic units was expected to provide incentive for moving in this direction. This strategy effectively lessened the scope of the public sector in higher education.

By 2005/2006, the share of private fee-paying students at Uganda's public universities reached 80.2 percent of the total.[63] The percentage of privately financed students of course varies by institution. At Makerere, the apex of the system, it came to 70 percent in 2013. Although Makerere remains a nominally public university, it is effectively becoming a private academy.[64]

New evening courses, weekend classes, and distance-learning programs proliferated. Admitting more students to universities with inadequate facilities magnified the discrepancy between supply and demand. Overcrowding and understaffing are increasingly acute problems. The official figure for part-time faculty is 47.5 percent, which the National Planning Authority regards as "inconsistent with what is required to maintain high quality education and training standards."[65]

To tap other revenue streams, academic institutions have signed contracts with outside firms for facilities previously subsidized by central authority: bookstores, guest houses, printing shops, and so on. They are now in the hands of private entrepreneurs. While their net returns can be quantified on balance sheets, there are also qualitative differences in the knowledge structure itself, which encompasses fundamental, though not necessarily all, university services. The ethos of higher learning is rapidly evolving in tune with globalizing forces.

REPOSITIONING IN THE GLOBAL
KNOWLEDGE STRUCTURE

While there is scant evidence of an overall national policy for the globalization of higher education, its rudiments can be detected. Ugandan universities have doubtlessly recognized the need to design a globalization strategy. Academics have appreciated the importance of a proactive stance lest their universities be

63. Republic of Uganda, "National Development Plan (2010/11–2014/15)" (Kampala: Government Printer, 2010), 215.
64. Author discussion with Moses A. Golola, professor and acting executive director, National Council for Higher Education, Uganda, Kampala, May 31, 2013.
65. Republic of Uganda, "National Development Plan (2010/11–2014/15)," 215.

takers rather than makers of global knowledge. But how to capture opportunities and reposition themselves?

With Makerere transitioning to the 2010s, its acting vice chancellor empaneled a team chaired by Robert Ikoja-Odongo to take stock of the impact of globalization on the university and make recommendations.[66] Its report identifies opportunities: namely, forms of regional cooperation in higher education, information technologies, and Uganda's intellectual diaspora. It notes that globalizing trends also present threats, especially the digital divide, the brain drain, and large costs for physical infrastructure including adequate connectivity and fiber optic cable. Given that globalization has this double edge, the challenge is to reap its net payoffs. High on the list of proposals for redialing into globalization are building the capacity of faculty and staff, rehabilitating facilities for the diffusion of knowledge, investing in academic research, and opening to "relevant" partnerships so long as Uganda avoids "becoming a front desk for international institutions."[67] According to team leader Ikoja-Odongo, some of these recommendations were ultimately "adopted via the University Strategic Plan, some through annual work plans and some through projects e.g. buildings, connectivity and increasing private funding."[68]

Efforts had long been underway to realize opportunities identified in the Ikoja-Odongo report: regional cooperation, information technologies, and links to the intellectual diaspora. There are numerous cross-border projects for collaboration and knowledge-sharing, research ventures, software development e-networks involving universities elsewhere in the global South, and appeals to diasporic communities for funneling their skills, expertise, and capital to the home country. Although Ugandan universities already have basic ingredients of a globalization strategy in place, the report emphasizes the need for others and for better coordination.

Makerere maintains active exchange agreements with several universities: among them, Bergen, Uppsala, Lund, Humboldt, North Carolina, North Dakota State, Rutgers, and Michigan State. To operate these programs, a small International Affairs office with a modest budget is tasked with processing applications, looking after health insurance and local clinics, arranging secure accommodations and transportation to and from the campus, advising

66. Robert Ikoja-Odongo, "Makerere University: Strategy for Addressing Implications of Globalisation in Higher Education: Uganda Paper" (unpublished, circa 2010). The preliminary challenge for Ikoja-Odongo's team was to consider how to diagnose the contents of globalization. In this connection, see Isaac Kamola, "The African University as 'Global University,'" *PS: Political Science and Politics* 47, no. 3 (July 2014): 604–7.

67. Ikoja-Odongo, "Makerere University," 12.

68. Robert Ikoja-Odongo, vice chancellor of Soroti University of Science and Technology and former principal of the College of Computing and Information Sciences at Makerere University, email message to author, July 23, 2013.

students, facilitating joint supervision of their projects, creating databases, preparing memoranda of understanding, and developing new ties. Amid heated competition among public and private universities in Uganda and neighboring countries, the number of international students (graduate and undergraduates) at Makerere reached 1,899 in 2011.[69]

NCHE data indicate that all Ugandan universities enrolled 15,932 international students in 2011, most of them at private universities, led by Kampala International University, with a sizable contingent from Kenya.[70] The Trade and Tourism Ministry's Market and Education Service project has sought to augment export earnings generated by international students above the $32 million level realized in 2004.[71] Whereas India, the United Kingdom, and other countries have operated programs and campuses in Uganda, its private universities, particularly Kampala International University, have maintained campuses in Nairobi and Dar es Salaam and represent potential sources of revenue.

These ventures beg questions about quality control and certification. A semi-autonomous body, the NCHE not only accredits institutions and programs but also denies it, as it has at the privates. For instance, the NCHE disqualified PhD degrees awarded by Kampala International University in 2011 and 2012, ruled that they must be revised, and closed small programs. But as a regulatory authority for accreditation, NCHE lacks staff and budgetary support. Besides its state allocation and student fees, the NCHE draws on donors, such as the Rockefeller Foundation, Ford Foundation, Carnegie Corporation, and the government of the Netherlands. They fund specific projects but not basic operating expenses.

A small agency, NCHE networks with accreditors in Kenya and Tanzania, and establishes benchmarks, informed by other regulatory bodies' prototypes.[72]

69. National Council for Higher Education, Uganda, "The State of Higher Education and Training in Uganda 2011: A Report on Higher Education Delivery and Institutions" (Kampala: NCHE, 2013), 38, http://www.unche.or.ug/publications/state-of-he/state -of-higher-education.html (accessed October 8, 2014); author discussion with Martha Muwanguzi, senior administrative assistant, International Affairs, Makerere University, Kampala, June 6, 2013.

70. National Council for Higher Education, Uganda, "The State of Higher Education and Training in Uganda 2010," 47, http://www.unche.or.ug/wp-content/uploads/2014/04 /The-State-of-Higher-Education-2010.pdf (accessed September 30, 2014).

71. The data on export earnings from higher education are spotty and do not distinguish between onshore and offshore (e.g., branch campuses in Kenya) revenue. See Josephine Maseruka, "Uganda to Earn $60m from Foreign Students Annually," *New Vision* (Kampala), September 27, 2010, http://www.newvision.co.ug/D/8/13/733349 (accessed November 7, 2014); Observatory on Borderless Higher Education, *Uganda: Moving Beyond Price to Recruit International Students*, Borderless Report (April 2012), http://www .obhe.ac.uk/newsletters/borderless_report_april_2012/uganda_moving_beyond_price _recruit_international_students (accessed November 7, 2014).

72. Author discussion with Golola.

It looks to a plethora of reference points. International quality assurance groupings and initiatives that share common ground include the UNESCO-World Bank Global Initiative on Quality Assurance Capacity, the Africa Quality Assurance Network hosted by the Association of African Universities, the Europe-Africa Quality Connect project, the Africa Union Commission's African Higher Education Harmonization Strategy, the Africa Quality Rating Mechanism, and the Inter-University Council for East Africa. They provide guidelines and identify best practices. A consultant who studied their content and prescriptions reports "clear evidence of convergence" among them and finds that "diversity and harmonization are not mutually exclusive" across and within regions.[73]

Yes, there is *"converging diversity"* in setting global and regional standards.[74] But hierarchic relations lie behind the narratives. A set of discursive practices is evident in touting institutions' profiles. The dream is to gain global recognition, to be a world-class university. Better rankings are a means to convince government and donors to support universities and a way to attract students. Higher education institutions prize the rewards in this global race for the top.

As for African universities in general, none of them appeared among the 100 leaders in the 2014–15 *Times Higher Education* University Rankings. The University of Cape Town placed 124th and two other South African universities made the top 300.[75] According to the 2014 Webometrics Ranking for Africa, produced by the Spanish Research Council, South Africa led the region with 9 of the 15 upper spots.[76] Cape Town was number one, followed by Cairo University, the American University in Cairo, the University of Nairobi, Mansoura University, and Alexandria at 2, 8, 9, 10, and 15, respectively.[77] Webometrics rated Makerere 13th in Africa; 1,134th worldwide.[78]

In Uganda, rankings are posted on university websites and reflected in the popular media, for example, in the newspaper *New Vision*.[79] These results sparked varied reactions. In an increasingly status-conscious society, the

73. Peter J. Wells, "The DNA of a Converging Diversity: Regional Approaches to Quality Assurance in Higher Education" (Washington, DC: Council for Higher Education Accreditation, 2014), 21.

74. Ibid., emphasis added.

75. The Times Higher Education University Rankings 2014–2015; Goolam Mohamedbhai, "Should South African Universities Be Globally Ranked?" *Inside Higher Education*, November 5, 2012, http://www.timeshighereducation.co.uk/world-university-rankings/# (accessed October 8, 2014).

76. Webometrics, Ranking Web of Universities 2014, http://www.webometrics.info/en (accessed October 8, 2014).

77. Ibid.

78. Ibid.

79. Chris Kiwawulo, "Makerere Ranks High in Sciences," *New Vision*, January 4, 2013, http://www.newvision.co.ug/news/638627-makerere-ranks-high-in-sciences.html (accessed January 4, 2013).

National Planning Authority recognizes that global university rankings carry a lot of weight and are a way for Ugandan universities to elevate their standards.[80] But the NCHE has not promulgated rankings on the ground that they create unhealthy tension and make distinctions that can be divisive. Its acting executive director, Moses Golola, held that global rankings resemble IQ tests in that they fail to take into account differences in culture and background.[81] In his view, ranking systems attempt to measure aspects of performance that cannot be measured. And, he says, Ugandans are not well versed in the techniques for manipulating rankings.[82] He comes down on the side of the debate that argues that the numbers system is flawed because savvy institutions game it and that standards must be internally generated, not primarily externally driven.

More philosophically, this skepticism resonates with suspicion of underestimating the capricious and incalculable, the characteristics of academic life that proponents of utilitarian views of usable knowledge do not entertain. To some observers, however, the principles and values that the longstanding purposes of a university cultivate are useless; these ideals seem old-fashioned. In today's climate, the fight is over how to nurture humanistic sensibilities in a context where applied knowledge is needed without reducing a university to a technocracy. Undoubtedly, the practical challenges are crucial. The dilemma lies in reconciling a lack of resources for adequately staffing and maintaining universities with surging student enrollments, which higher education institutions cannot attenuate lest they lose revenue. And student numbers are likely to continue to increase exponentially. Yet levels of funding for instruction and research are decidedly incommensurate with this trend. Coupling of budgetary constraints and an unsupportive political environment thus hampers educational development.

In this context, local educators rely on donors to fill the gap in public support for research. In 2010–11, for instance, the NCHE was able to fund only three research proposals out of fifty-seven submitted.[83] Meanwhile, African intellectuals seek "autonomous spaces for interacting with each other in 'a commonwealth of scholars.'"[84] But how to carve out autonomous discourses and drive the agenda when donor agencies are sponsoring most of the research at public universities? The bulk of allocations are for applied work; little, for basic research. Donors, mainly philanthropies in the global North and development agencies, offer financing for centers of excellence, some of them

80. Author discussion with Abel J. J. Rwendeire, deputy chairperson, National Planning Authority, and former minister of state for higher education, Kampala, May 23, 2013.

81. Author discussion with Golola.

82. Ibid.

83. National Council for Higher Education, Uganda, "The State of Higher Education and Training in Uganda 2010," 20.

84. See Mkandawire, "Running While Others Walk," 33.

networking initiatives, in thematic areas such as technology and innovation, water, and health. These partnerships share best practices, hold workshops, mount training sessions, and tender consultancy contracts. The difficulty is that they can breed dependence. And the infusions of loans and grants fluctuate and eventually peter out. Patrons typically suffer fatigue and reformulate their priorities. For clients, the challenge is to nip off funds in the short run while generating renewable resources for the long term. What then is the actual experience in this regard?

A collective effort by seven U.S.-based foundations, the Partnership for Higher Education in Africa (PHEA), provided $440 million over ten years to institutions of higher education and scholars in nine African countries.[85] Trailing the two largest recipients, South Africa and Nigeria, Uganda captured 10 percent of the disbursements.[86] Makerere alone received more than $42 million. Concluded in 2010, the PHEA delivered tangible benefits, including expanded Internet connectivity, better library facilities, and help for marginalized groups' access to the university. The PHEA grant makers also invested in the Next Generation of Academics initiative for training early career scholars as a way to address the problem of faculty regeneration and challenges facing women in the higher education system. The mechanisms included postgraduate programs and curriculum development. Correlatively, other learning grants are for the next generation.

PHEA's consultant hired to gauge its accomplishments and limitations found that it succeeded in establishing consensus among foundations with different institutional cultures, building infrastructure at African universities, and maintaining a long-running coalition, though without a clear exit strategy.[87] But she should have trolled for information on the ground from local stakeholders. The interviewees for her study are foundation officials, staff, and their associates in the United States and their overseas offices.[88] In the absence of empirical evidence gathered in Africa, one is left to ponder the role of grantees in planning and shaping PHEA-sponsored programs.

85. The cohort consisted of Carnegie Corporation of New York, the Ford Foundation, the John D. and Catherine T. MacArthur Foundation, the Rockefeller Foundation, the William and Flora Hewlett Foundation, the Andrew W. Mellon Foundation, and the Kresge Foundation.

86. Suzanne Grant Lewis, Jonathan Friedman, and John Schoneboom, *Accomplishments of the Partnership for Higher Education in Africa, 2000–2010: Report on a Decade of Collaborative Foundation Investment* (New York: PHEA, 2010), 1.

87. Susan Parker, *Lessons from a Ten-Year Funder Collaborative: A Case Study of the Partnership for Higher Education in Africa* (New York: PHEA, 2010). Also see Megan Lindow, *Weaving Success: Voices of Change in African Higher Education* (New York: Institute of International Education, 2011), a study published with support from PHEA.

88. Parker, *Lessons from a Ten-Year Funder Collaborative*, 43–44, where a list of interviewees appears.

Is there ownership of projects at the universities that received the grants? While it is hard to discern the exact points where control lies, structural power between the needy and their international patrons is nevertheless integral to this hierarchical relationship. It is asymmetrical. Deals are struck between unequal parties. As a report published by PHEA's secretariat attests, this partnership has influenced the agendas and perspectives of other donors, African governments, and individual and corporate funders.[89] By its own account, PHEA leveraged its efforts with several purveyors of reforms, such as the EU, NORAD, and the World Bank.[90] And in the education sector, donors, mostly northern governmental institutions, have formed an umbrella organization—Uganda's Education Funding Agencies Group.[91] The impact of donors on higher education policy is reflected in their shared priorities, for instance, converging views on advancing programs dedicated to the next generation of scholars. While various funders have established grants under the-next-generation rubric, it remains to be seen what they have in mind: who among a populace is deemed to constitute this generation, the extent to which particular subgroups will be represented, how these learners will be equipped to discover new knowledge, and with which paradigms.

After PHEA ended and the World Bank invited U.S. private foundations to the table, the bank presented its agenda for building infrastructure and expanding the role of markets in African universities.[92] In Uganda, its emphasis is on an institutionalized process of consensus formation, not content per se. This is a transaction between patron and client. The effects may be seen in the ways that procedures, such as for training administrators and evaluation, are carried out rather than in prescriptions for the particulars of what is taught in the classroom. Still, the availability of funding for certain fields of study instead of others is a form of indirect influence. As Court's report, sponsored by the World Bank and Rockefeller Foundation, says, this matter comes down to ownership. When ideas are perceived as imposed by external actors, they can spark resistance and rejection.[93] While some local actors' thinking about

89. Grant Lewis, Friedman, and Schoneboom, *Accomplishments of the Partnership for Higher Education*, 6.

90. Ibid., 6–7.

91. Its members are the World Bank Group, the EU, Development Co-operation of Ireland, Netherlands, Japan, Germany, the World Food Programme, United Nations Children's Fund, Britain's Department for International Development, African Development Bank, and USAID; Kasozi, "The Development of a Strategic Plan for Higher Education in Uganda 2001–5," 4, 17.

92. Author telephone discussion with New York foundation program director, January 3, 2011; author discussion with former New York foundation program officer, also advisor in the Ministry of Planning and National Development, the Republic of Kenya, Nairobi, May 28, 2013.

93. Court, "Financing Higher Education in Africa," 11.

loans converges with World Bank ideas, the subtle issue is the ways in which the bank's measures are built into conditions for loans and technical advice. In this regard, Samoff and Carrol find that "conditionality can disguise ownership" of a reform package.[94] And when implemented, these programs take on the trappings of a national university.

Makerere's self-representations of its regulatory framework, for example, are emblazoned on its logo adorned with crested cranes, the national bird. The sprightly image of these birds in full plumage and standing on one leg, symbolizing that the country is not sitting still but moving forward, is powerful. This pennant looks and feels Ugandan. The branding is seemingly local though consonant with a global trend for universities to advertise their comely labels more noticeably than ever.

In the evolving amalgam of donor-university relations, leveraging influence is more effective than imposing policies. Donor agencies use ownership discourse as a way to lessen their responsibility for the success or failure of regulatory reforms.

Correspondingly, since Ugandan universities are subject to the WTO agreements to which the Kampala government is a signatory, an agency like the NCHE can exercise but limited regulatory authority. It is constrained in its efforts to restrict market access because private providers from overseas gain easy entrée for establishing branch campuses, degree programs and certificates, and distance learning, all subject to light national control over these services. Local universities thus come into direct competition with the pressures of the global marketplace. Aware of the need to abate these forces, the NCHE notes that Uganda is deficient in understanding the linkages: "educators, students, and the general public are seriously lacking in awareness on the forces which are impacting on the design of higher education courses and programmes."[95] In this connection, the academic curriculum is deemed to be narrowing, with less scope for liberal approaches to learning and more space for vocational training suited to employers' needs and expectations of universities.[96] With stretched financial resources, more emphasis on technical and business skills comes at the expense of literary and other humanistic knowledge.

A Stocktaking: Whither Purposes?

Can higher education in Uganda bounce back and regain its footing? Since the early postcolonial period, when its lead university was renowned for innovative research and its accomplished graduates, institutions of higher learning

94. Samoff and Carrol, *From Manpower Planning to the Knowledge Era*, 34.

95. National Council for Higher Education, Uganda, "Management and Leadership Training Project," 42.

96. Ibid., 39–40.

in Uganda have responded to a rapidly altered global environment by aligning with new demands and pivoting toward a business model. Emphasis is given to growing enrollment, raising funds, and connecting more thoroughly to a global meshwork of knowledge.

With these changes, Uganda's universities have scored successes. Signs of their revival are an improved research culture, advances in technology, and wider appreciation of the importance of PhD training. For example, despite budget shortages, Makerere's University Senate and Council, followed by the NCHE, approved MISR's interdisciplinary PhD in social sciences. Launched in 2012, it has garnered financial support for its critically oriented programs in political economy and cultural, historical, and political studies. Geared to prepare younger civic-minded Africans for engaging globalizing forces, this initiative is run by Ugandans and primarily staffed by them.

The universities' achievements also include expanding access to higher education in terms of both numbers and representation of the general population. But less-privileged applicants who have not had the same opportunities, particularly in marginalized regions, are disproportionately admitted as private payers. And while the percentage of women in the student body, faculty, and administration has increased, gender equity by discipline, rank, and pay remains problematic.

Meanwhile, repurposing universities is fraught with tensions over core values. As higher education in Uganda becomes more attuned to global governance agencies' policies for promoting free markets, local universities and regulatory authorities such as the NCHE encounter conflicting interests. For instance, in 2013, Buckingham University, a private British university, suspended accreditation for some of its courses at Victoria University in Kampala. The controversy centered on Uganda's proposed legislation regarding homosexuality. Buckingham registered concern about freedom of speech in this area. When it called for a statement on gay rights, Ugandan authorities held that this provision was not part of the original memorandum of understanding. Additionally, the Ugandan side maintained that university regulations accord with national laws, not British standards.[97] In Uganda, penal courts do not abide homosexuality. Ugandan officials at Victoria University pointed out that students are not asked about their sexual preferences. The Ugandans refused their British associates' demand on the ground that Africa should say no to impositions from outside providers. Buckingham then terminated its affiliation with Victoria. Soon thereafter, the Ruparelia Group, a private company headed by a Ugandan-born entrepreneur, took over ownership of Victoria University.

97. Author discussions with Golola, Nsibambi, and Ssesanga.

More broadly, the contention is about whose and which values shape higher education in this postcolonial country. In fact, Uganda does not have a general policy in regard to international partners or donors. Each university in Uganda, as well as its several units and individual researchers, has the prerogative of collaborating with them so long as the arrangements are in keeping with national legislation and norms. While the pressure for fund-raising becomes more acute, donors emphasize their expectations regarding the importance of measurable impacts of the allocations. The cogent question becomes what kinds of impact and knowledge are stressed. And whose research questions are valued and devalued? The matter comes down to who sets the academic agenda.

In the give-and-take among actors, Ugandan policymakers are determined to refurbish universities. The country has prepared a multitude of national development plans, institutional strategies, and visionary documents projecting targets all the way to 2040.[98] These visioning exercises can represent either genuine commitment or empty gestures. Although the former is of course desirable, the latter obtains in the absence of a predictable funding formula for bolstering the production and dissemination of knowledge, professed to be key components of development.

True, strengthening universities requires more than money. Yet without a feasible financing framework backed by public support, universities are left to improvise. The result is what I have called educational bricolage. Makeshift arrangements are the order of the day. Planning units keep designing road maps; however, higher education institutions, try as they may, are struggling to follow them.

Repurposed universities in Uganda are therefore in a quandary. Sustained support for undertaking original research, training PhD students, and developing faculty talent is still in short supply. Higher education institutions are diminished to the extent that they become instruments of money culture and default on their academic missions of democratic education, critical self-reflection, and freedom to pursue intellectual curiosity. Personally, I believe that universities fundamentally stand for loving ideas and inquiring what it means to share the human condition.

The particularity of a sense of purpose looms large in a postcolonial setting that had prided itself on an illustrious university. After a period of deterioration, fast economic growth in the 2010s has failed to erase its grave consequences. Now, local protagonists are attempting to expand policy space. They strive to steer the higher education system and, at the same time, navigate a globally competitive environment. There is no dearth of innovative ideas and

98. Republic of Uganda, National Planning Authority, *Uganda Vision 2040* (Kampala: National Planning Authority, 2013).

policies. Concrete initiatives include efforts to retrieve lost narratives; incorporate indigenous knowledge in university curricula in areas such as sustainable use of natural resources, technology, architecture, medicine, and art; and establish a Pan-African University with regional campuses that emphasize research. More extensive collaboration among stakeholders in the university and the local community is another priority. And detailed proposals for viable funding frameworks are on the table.[99]

Amid this fluidity are but two certainties. To work, the strategy must be organic to recipients, not merely donors. If higher education innovations are imported without local support systems, they are likely to be denied as when the human body rejects a heart transplant. The changes must be integrated in, or emerge from, the existing social organism. Second, their realization will require intellectual imagination and political grit. Toward this end, a higher education system must surmount contextually specific challenges. As a practical matter, policymakers must come to grips with particular mechanisms and processes of university repurposing—funding formulas, centralized and decentralized budgeting, ranking systems, quality assurance protocols, and the like, highlighted in these pages—as they alight in their own settings.

That said, common trends are prevalent in the postcolonial, neoliberal, and social democratic prototypes of university reform.[100] It is sufficient to note three of them. First, state disinvestment in higher education is driving university executives to act more entrepreneurially and adopt aims that better serve market-driven actors. Second, universities are increasingly seen as not only recipients of funds but also sources of revenue—for example, from their medical centers, faculty-generated companies, and export services—for the local and national economy. Third, the academy's lax pace in adjusting to fast-moving globalizing forces is partly attributable to factors other than the tradition of shared governance, however eroded on many campuses. Part of the difficulty, it must be forthrightly said, lies with the professoriate. There is a defense of faculty privilege, and, for some in our ranks, prioritizing scholasticism over teaching, a trust that we must deserve. Instead of being just self-protective, scholars ought to adopt a self-critical stance. While it is right to fault political officials, bureaucrats, and corporate executives, we should also look at ourselves, the extent to which we merit our privileged position, and whether our performance is commensurate with our obligations. We certainly have shortcomings and should not be let off the hook. Our calling requires introducing better pedagogies that pique intellectual curiosity, instill capacity

99. Apropos the latter, see Kasozi, *Financing Uganda's Public Universities*, especially 200–215.

100. Ken Conca, professor of international relations in the School of International Service, American University, email message to author, January 23, 2016, provided incisive comments that helped me pull together the themes in this passage.

for creative risk-taking, and enkindle critical sensibility. A central mission is to encourage students to face the question anew of the duties and responsibilities that democratic citizens should bear in a turbulent world.

Now, the task in the final part of this book is to assess the directions in which higher education is headed and propose corrective steps. What follows is investigative, perhaps provocative, yet meant to be constructive.

PART III

Outcomes

CHAPTER SEVEN

Polymorphism

A CENTRAL THESIS OF THIS BOOK is that the primary purposes of universities are retreating and that new ones are advancing. This chapter searches for what is replacing the old. And it addresses the question of why would the latter be treated as but an important intellectual legacy.

Seismic shifts constituting globalization bring insecurity to knowledge institutions. They have shaken the university, which is a peculiar enterprise in that scientific inquiry produces uncertainty. The quest for truth or, as postmodernists would have it, truths can destabilize existing certainties. Inasmuch as research is supposed to both substantiate and undermine extant knowledge, universities are self-critical of what they produce.

After all, by raising penetrating questions, Socrates's dialogues sowed doubt. Answers to his questions advanced understanding but were not expected to be definitive. Einstein shared this sentiment. As the story goes, when one of his students asked if the final exam in physics posed the same questions as the previous year, he said, yes, but this year's answers are different. Too, answers may generate additional questions. We thereby discover what is not yet known and new avenues for investigation. The point of it all is to seek to illuminate, clarify, and focus—a process that can disturb conventional thinking.

While looking for predictability in life, most people grapple with increasing uncertainty about the future.[1] This is partly due to the extent to which technological innovations have accelerated social and market relations. Not only the speed but the volatility and instability are remarkable, as in the global economy and the natural world.

---

1. Ulrich Beck, *World Risk Society* (Cambridge: Polity Press, 1999), 2, maintains that in a "world risk society," the very idea of security is no longer viable. According to Beck, *The Cosmopolitan Vision*, trans. Ciaran Cronin (2004; Cambridge: Polity Press, 2006), there is an erosion of securities, hitherto considered calculable by expert knowledge but increasingly incalculable.

[205]

Have globalizing forces and changes in national political economies meant that universities' first principles have gone the way of the dinosaur? Doubtless, for many students and their families facing formidable practical pressures, some professors' ideal of learning for its own sake, enriching the mind, and developing moral reasoning seems secondary, if not quaint and misguided. To the extent that this orientation finds traction at a time when the contemporary university seeks to be "relevant," it is shared by only a minority of faculty. The charge for educators is to apply their skills to the "real world" rather than wrestle with deep questions about what accounts for the presumptive realities seen by the naked eye. Emphasis is increasingly given to the here-and-now rather than to fathoming non-observable underpinnings of perceptions, at least those not seen through standard methods. That is to say, the payoff supposedly lies in useful knowledge even if it entails sacrificing fundamental inquiry.

The danger in favoring immediate returns from academic programs and personnel lies in throwing universities off-kilter in relation to their primary purposes. The metamorphoses result from the power of material interests, of which Dewey had emphatically forewarned; fierce competition within countries and across borders; and changing beliefs about the roles of the public and private spheres. As we shall see in this chapter, university repurposing is evolving toward polymorphism. In the transition from the historic to the nouveau, multiple missions coexist. At polymorphous institutions, they pile up and recur. While some are receding, others are crystallizing. Both the means by which this happens and the ends are the crux of the issue.

Context

At the outset of this book, I noted the paradox that universities are becoming more alike and more different. The evidence in part 2 shows how this convergence and divergence are interconnected, forming polymorphism. Context is crucial to this development because structural accounts tell only part of the story; fine-grained analysis reveals messy entanglements, sprawling histories, and multiple ethnographies. The general pattern takes shape along a broad spectrum.

To consolidate where the three country studies have taken us: the cases of neoliberal, social democratic, and postcolonial universities detail the experiences of institutions of higher learning in the United States, self-evidently a large country with a heterogeneous population; and in two small ones, Finland, which has a relatively homogeneous populace, and Uganda, where there is a welter of ethnic and linguistic communities. While the two exemplars in the global North are in the upper tier of affluence by world standards, Uganda is on the poverty-ridden end of the scale. Although these cases may not cover the whole gamut in the world, I believe they offer a good indication of a wide swath of it.

The commonality among these situations is striking. Universities in the three instances evolved in countries that experienced civil war and international wars. In all of them, higher education institutions, or their forebearer schools, originated during the colonial period. They were initially influenced by religious traditions: Puritanism in New England, the Lutheran Church in Finland, and the Anglican faith in Uganda more so than Catholicism and Islam, also practiced there. As they became primarily secular, the universities adopted European models with their lineages of Humboldt's and Newman's intuition.

Each educational system has had to address its national question. Historically, nationalism has been a matter of constructing a national identity and involved building workable educational institutions. Up to today, this also concerns the representation of minority populations: mainly racial and ethnic groups in the United States, Swedish speakers in Finland, and peoples marginalized by the politicization of ethnicity and race in Uganda.[2] The three cases considered here are further characterized by continuing challenges of stratification in class and gender. As potential engines of social mobility and national power, universities are pivotal to these issues.

The stories of universities' regulatory reforms are differentiated on axes that run vertically and horizontally. Verticality plumbs the history of higher education in the three countries. In the colonial period, the metropolitan powers implanted their own systems. The imprint in the United States was initially from England; in Finland, Sweden and Russia; and Uganda, England. The timing of this imposition reflects the churning of history in both the metropoles and their dependencies. The rhythm of history changed at political independence in 1776, 1917, and 1962, respectively, when these countries began to fashion their own institutions of higher education.

In addition to tempo, vertical depth reaches political culture, the particularities of ways of life. These are meanings and habits accumulated over the generations, providing social cohesion to varying degrees and in different ways. Chapters 4, 5, and 6 point to the widespread notion of individualism in the United States, the idea of *sisu* (perseverance) in Finland, and the amalgam of inherited solidarities rooted in local communities and religion along with the imaginaries of national integration in Uganda. Also the result of historical dynamics such as conflicts and memories of them, the levels of trust and mistrust in the civic cultures of these countries similarly range in the ways shown in part 2 of this book. Surely every country has its myths that can bind a society and make a significant impact on educational policy.

The lateral dimensions of reforms in the case-study chapters encompass broadly similar themes of managerialism, competitiveness, decentralization, privatization, and globalization. But these are not identical and subthemes

2. All cases are of course complex and bear their own subtleties. Branch and Mampilly, *Africa Uprising*, 115–18, depict three national questions in Uganda: the Northern question, the Buganda (heartland region) question, and the Asian question, each one a legacy of colonialism and the ways that postcolonial governments have treated it.

emerge. Different kinds of privatization, for example, are context specific. The funding vehicles and financing arrangements are customized by locale and according to the overall availability of resources. Tuition fees and student debt relative to GDP in the three counties are widely apart: the per student burden is the least in Finland because of its rather egalitarian distributional policies, greatest in Uganda with its lower national income, and in between in the United States due to the large size of the economy in relation to the high cost of education.

Convergence and divergence are therefore not mutually exclusive. Rather than being pitted in opposition, they are interwoven. Polymorphism signifies that convergent and divergent trends combine. This complexity is increasingly in flux, evinces intriguing ambiguities, and offers clues for detecting new possibilities.

What began as simple narratives about the purposes of universities has morphed into a mosaic of purposes in ways that I will spell out. The means are displacing the ends of higher education. Short-term tactics and strategies are becoming long-run goals. To arrive at this point, first to the narratives.

Rerouted Narratives

In our times, the narratives about universities as institutions devoted to the life of the mind and for the joy of discovery often seem facile, backward-looking, or just plain romanticism. It is frequently said that institutions of higher education must refocus on the actualities of preparing students for roles as knowledge workers in a hard-driving, fast-paced global marketplace. Resultant reforms are intended responses to these conditions and accompanied by new narratives. These scripts showcase the world-class dream.

Bricoleurs dream up comforting stories about ways to make this story come true. Discourse brokers are tasked with facilitating the process. They are webmasters, public relations specialists, assistant deans of communications and outreach, marketing managers from advertising firms, graphic designers, and consultants. These narrators convert keywords into common talk, parlance already underlined in this book: strategic planning, best practices, benchmarking, branding, visibility, productivity indices, quality assurance systems, and measurable outcomes. I have remarked that the catchwords are generated by material structures and symbolic meanings that are reshaping universities. Resources are allocated for disseminating messages and logos: pictorial images, as exemplified by crested cranes in full plumage in the Uganda case, or likable coinages used in commercial printing and electronic communications to merchandise an identity. Awards for student achievement and fund-raising campaigns display these placards. Logo makers have shifted the underlying motif from truth and beauty to technology-savvy entrepreneurship. In these signature statements, business metaphors are normalized and, as marketing is intended to do, used as a form of narrative entrapment.

The relationship between the university and students—"customers"—is cast in retail terms. Universities increasingly represent themselves as providers of utility, distancing their functions from Flexner's vision of useless knowledge. Critics of this move say that the contemporary narratives signal a shift in the pantheon of university values. Complaints about shibboleths, mantras, vacuous terminology, and corporate clichés are often heard. The charge is that they saturate the mind and displace serious intellectual engagement. Marina Warner, a British cultural historian and novelist, writes: "As universities are beaten into the shapes dictated by business, so language is suborned to its ends. We have all heard the robotic idiom of management as if a button had activated a digitally generated voice. Like Newspeak in *Nineteen Eighty-Four*, business-speak is an instance of magical naming, superimposing the imagery of the market on the idea of a university."[3] Her fury is directed at the grip of market ideology and, as she puts it, the "gagging" effects of reforms enacted by its enthusiasts.

Market ideology at universities is not just about academic values becoming money values. More is at stake. Money itself is not the problem. Rather, the purpose of money is the hovering issue: this is a matter of financing higher education—what the money is supposed to do.

When university personnel monetize costs and benefits as inputs and outputs of knowledge institutions, they lose sight of what the public is really paying for. Whatever the other pressures, scholars bear a responsibility for empowering better-informed citizens, enriching popular culture, and throwing light on matters of policy. Community engagement in turn offers opportunities to raise unfamiliar, even troublesome, questions. But academics often feel inhibited from participating in the national dialogue because of the way in which money influences their work environment. Donors can sway the mission of a university. Patrons want a return for their money, gauged by impact. Some of them insist that their bidding gets done. The outcomes may or may not coincide with the lasting outcomes that the academy has long held dear. In this situation, market power permeates knowledge production and distribution.

A crucial link in this chain is competitiveness. This theme is explicit in mission statements and strategic plans, and implicit in exercises such as national and global rankings. In the U.S. case, it is a vital feature of claims about American exceptionalism and incorporated in speeches by leading politicians. However, not all university managers or former administrators subscribe to this part of the narrative. For instance, Cole of Columbia University takes issue with a preoccupation with national competitiveness:

3. Marina Warner, "Learning My Lesson," *London Review of Books* 37, no. 6 (March 19, 2015), http://www.lrb.co.uk/v37/n06/marina-warner/learning-my-lesson (accessed August 27, 2015).

I am not interested in an international Olympic games of academic winners and losers. Nor am I interested in counting gold medals or Nobel Prizes held by Americans with the objective of feeding ethnocentric pride. . . . I believe the evidence shows that competition is beneficial for the growth of knowledge, and that the growth of knowledge is good for the larger society. . . . By and large, the growth of fundamental knowledge (as well as goal-oriented knowledge) has led to innovations that have improved the health, the social well-being, and the economic welfare of the citizens of the world.[4]

Cole adds that the growth of knowledge and the improvement of universities in different countries can be mutually beneficial: "the better the universities in other nations become, the more likely it is that their scholars, scientists, and engineers will become collaborators with Americans."[5] Like Cole, other authors of university narratives express their preference for breaking out of the national cage and developing a worldly scenario. Such ascendant narratives embellish cosmopolitanism. They aim for universality in their outlooks and programming.

The question then becomes what kind of cosmopolitanism. Is it a West-centered cosmopolitanism from above? Is it a subtle way of saying that global knowledge governance dominated by the West is best for universities aspiring to be world class? A concern is that while initiatives such as MOOCs coming from Stanford, MIT, and other elite universities offer new opportunities, they simultaneously crimp indigenous forms of knowledge generation and dissemination. This criticism of cosmopolitanism from above draws attention to structural inequalities underpinning the win-win scenario projected by knowledge agents at top research universities in the West. The point is that although mutual gains may be realized, some knowledge institutions benefit at the expense of others.

All told then, polymorphous narratives are fluid and contested. They represent efforts to address varied publics with different needs, expectations, and potential contributions. Under prevailing conditions, the evolving moral purposes of universities fluctuate and are uncertain.

Moral Purposes

Faced with mounting demands, university managers must look after the stature of their institution but risk addling the moral purpose of the university. At stake is the viability of a learned community intent on teaching and

---

4. Cole, *The Great American University*, 469.
5. Ibid.

research and for the general human good. While Humboldt's and Newman's visions were to stimulate craving for knowledge and engagement with big questions, great thinkers in China, India, the Middle East, and other parts of the world have also addressed broad civilizational concerns. In his aversion for abandoning these goals, Einstein, ever a humanist, frowned on not only overly specialized inquiry but, I believe, narrow professionalization lacking appreciation for a wide range of knowledge. Something of a polymath himself, Einstein showed great respect for intellectuals with expertise in their specific field *and* the ability to skip among and within disciplines.

To be concrete, I recall my own experience in university administration. The economics department highly recommended a job candidate and asked for approval. His curriculum vitae and letters of recommendation indicated that he was an astute econometrician fresh out of graduate school and already with stellar publications. In my office, he laid out his research itinerary in technical terms and demonstrated superb communications skills. But when I said that if hired, he would be asked to teach an introductory course in economics, including readings drawn from the classical school—Smith, Ricardo, and Marx— the candidate demurred. He could not enter a conversation about this body of literature. Moving on in the interview, I found him to be adept at explicating statistical data but unable to connect spokes to a hub of knowledge beyond his subdiscipline of econometrics. I felt obliged to ask my colleagues on the search committee and the department chair to revisit our priorities in hiring.

At issue are the overall concerns of the academy. They are imperiled when the new management ethos is breaking up common space. While trumpeting the importance of multidisciplinarity, university managers are converting a social activity carried out by colleagues comprising an institution committed, in principle, to exchanging ideas into a form of atomistic individualism. Scholars are expected to raise capital and maximize the number of their publications in top presses and prestigious peer-reviewed journals. Publication in major venues can yield impressive scores in terms of an individual scholar's impact, thereby marking productivity and boosting a university's position in rankings. Effectively, these measures are used to cull faculty and turn over personnel at a rapid clip. A type of creative destruction, it fosters innovation but also shakes trust, frays the moral fabric of the university, and reduces incentive to invest in building interpersonal relations. The sense of community dwindles.

It is worth pausing to reflect on what has happened. History shows that moral corruption is a slippery slope that can become more slippery. In many fields, external funding is available for purportedly impartial research that corresponds to the desires of sponsors. Prominent academics are paid for their expertise and awarded grants and travel money so as to support corporate agendas. Industry consultants are funded to weigh in on matters of public policy. They testify at hearings of legislatures, lobby, and provide evidence in defense of or against particular products. Some of these "authorities" have become powerful players on the national and world stages. The issue of consultancy arrangements has come to light in debates over bioengineered foods in billion-dollar industrial wars involving companies like Monsanto and organic firms such as yogurt makers.[6] Corporations want their investment to yield results, and researchers, while bound by the ethics of academic integrity, are motivated to secure the resources that enable them to generate publications. Usually, conflicts of interest do not arise. But in some cases of commercial and government-financed research, investigators cater to the interests of their patrons. Or the lure of sponsorship slants an academic's findings and the results cannot be corroborated.

The inability to replicate findings in a large number of experiments has stirred disagreement about the importance of reproducibility and falsification. This pivots on which and whose epistemological standards are applied. Positivists believe in the scientific method wherein research is carried out by testing hypotheses and subjecting the findings to empirical validation. On top of this, positivists insist that data and normative values are separable and that the results of experiments are subject to replication.

But there is more than one paradigm for the conduct of inquiry. Postpositivists dispute the tenets of "scientism"—the belief that empirical verification proves or disproves a proposition and is therefore the route to explanation. They claim that data are linked to a system of knowledge production and are value laden. According to them, data points are not fixed but vary in time and context. Furthermore, it is argued, the complexity of morality and social structures is mutable, spawning ever-changing kinds of research questions and explanations for empirical phenomena.

Ethical questions are rife among sociologists who query the fact-finding process in ethnography. They have spotlighted researchers' alleged ethical violations, including misrepresenting sources or even imagining situations.[7] In addition, reviewers and editors are faulted for failing to do their due diligence with regard to the accuracy of field notes, events, and dates. The matter becomes one of not only individual moral choice but how social knowledge is produced.

At this juncture, historical studies and the humanities enter into understanding behavior. Aesthetic experiences such as encountering a work of art can

6. The propriety of academic scientists' financial links to industry and commercial pursuits, as with genetically modified crops and pharmaceuticals, is a longstanding controversy, often vetted in the media and by former university administrators. For example, Eric Lipton, "Emails Reveal Ties in a Food War," *New York Times*, September 6, 2015; Bok, *Universities in the Marketplace*; Rhodes, *The Creation of the Future*.

7. E.g., sociologist and ethnographer Alice Goffman's *On the Run: Fugitive Life in an American City* (Chicago: University of Chicago Press, 2014), a compelling book about drugs, criminals, and policing in Philadelphia, fired up fierce debate about research conduct, how evidence is generated, and how to assess it.

push social researchers to ask important questions. Artwork offers credible conceptions and opens worlds of understanding. In all, philosophical commitments concerning the nature of knowledge and ways to conduct scientific investigation undergird scholarly discourses about the reliability of academic research.

Allowing for different intellectual traditions, universities have sought to codify standards for research, monitor compliance, and curb breaches. However, ambiguities are shot through these labyrinthine regulations. To take one instance, institutional review boards were set up to protect human subjects from harm caused by research, as in certain experiments on vulnerable populations (children, economically disadvantaged minorities, mentally disabled people, and prisoners). Authorities have provided these boards with a growing number of protocols to guard against abuses of ethical conduct. But in the implementation, regulatory instruments can have the unintended consequence of undermining researchers' free expression and academic freedom.[8]

Some of the underlying problem is associated with the rush to publish. Peer-reviewed publications are weighed heavily by university administrators in thrall to ranking-driven agendas, mostly emphasizing research over other scholarly responsibilities. This tendency correlates with unethical practices involving flawed data and skewed observations, especially in disciplines in which positive outcomes rather than negative findings are deemed most fruitful and therefore more likely to be published. Fabricated results have caused serial retractions from journals and prompted debate about what's behind it. Much of this gathering controversy centers on reward systems. While dissent from mainstream paradigms is often designated as publication in so-called "B" or "C" journals, illustrated as the risk in the Finnish case, success in publication in orthodox "A" journals can bring career advancement, recognition, and extra compensation.

Merit pay systems often value the quantity of scholarly papers placed in leading outlets and the amount of external funding brought to the university. At some universities, administrators confer bonuses for this kind of success. They hand out hefty pay envelopes to faculty and staff deemed high achievers. This manner of compensation may be defended on the ground that it is the very same system of remuneration used by trustees to reward CEO performance. And if this practice is ethically justifiable for one employee and perhaps her topmost deputies, then it must be so for others. Arguably, however, the potential hazards are patronage and increasing inequality within an avowedly collegial atmosphere. More egalitarian measures, such as a step system of salary increases for advancement, are in force at some universities with active unions or faculty and staff associations. But with neoliberal reforms and the weakening of trade unions, these arrangements too seem to be languishing.

8. As discussed in Cole, *Toward a More Perfect University*, kindle locations 5211–25, 5198–5211.

As is, managerialism builds more loyalty than legitimacy. While the importance of public spiritedness is acknowledged, the knowledge structure can constrain intellectual diversity. More and more, the existing system of management encroaches on intellectual autonomy. As the case-study chapters show, intellectual autonomy is repurposed as administrative autonomy, which, in turn, is repurposed as financial autonomy. As often as not, the bestowal of autonomy is the contraction of autonomy. The meaning of autonomy withers. Its content is no longer predicated on the basic moral precepts of the university. Inscribed in mission statements and on the plaques prominently displayed on campuses and websites, lofty phrases about the pursuit of wisdom and appreciation of beauty are salutary reminders. At best, these epigrams represent what knowledge institutions are supposed to be for. At worst, they are window dressing for the transformation of universities. For all practical purposes, they betray what is ornamental and less operationally meaningful.

Data-driven management is becoming more than just a means. As generally implemented, this ethic signals a departure from a commitment to democratic decision making, critical thinking, and academic freedom. It embodies a restrictive conceptualization of higher education and works to reduce complex organizations to numeric values.

To fix the problems of the twenty-first-century university, one need not reject big data or digitalization. It would be shortsighted to underestimate the genuine contributions and potential. These tools bring improvement in the form of better teaching, access to troves of information for research, more accountability, and attention to streamlining procedures. However, one should not jump too quickly on this bandwagon without clarity about the purposes they serve.

It is worrisome that means are quickly gaining global traction and being decoupled from what higher education is fundamentally about. Then again, likely the pursuit of ends is never-ending. It entails a perpetual search for human fulfillment.[9] Surely, on this journey, there are ways of expanding the moral imagination.

Multiple Purposes

Universities are neither solely blending into isomorphism nor only separating into more varieties. Intermingling in a polymorphous state of affairs, their purposes can hardly be grasped in terms of a one-size, two-size, or any number of sizes fits-all notion.

Drawing on his long experience as president of Harvard, Bok finds nuance in the dynamics of multiple missions of higher education. He charts the

9. I have benefited from David D. Corey, "Liberal Education: Its Conditions and Ends," *Perspectives on Political Science* 43, no. 4 (December 2013): 195–200.

proliferation of the aims of the American university from grooming young men for leadership positions, preparing students for useful occupations, and emphasizing research to cultivating the minds of undergraduates through a broad liberal education while also producing scholarly works in the humanistic sciences. Bok notes that newer purposes have been added to the old: service to local business, government, neighborhoods, and overseas universities, plus economic development, as in Silicon Valley and with start-up companies and venture capital funds.[10] He grapples with the question of whether the expansion of purposes leads to compatibility or incompatibility in institutional mission. Are universities developing in a coherent manner?

According to Bok, multiple missions often complement one another. Professors who advise government or intergovernmental agencies may derive lessons from their hands-on experience and introduce them in the classroom. Liberal arts faculty can help relate applied work to redeeming questions. Yet the university's sundry goals may also be at odds with one another. For example, an emphasis on practical training can sideline the humanities and diminish basic research. Weighing these considerations, Bok contends that university leaders bear responsibility for maintaining "a proper balance" among the purposes of higher education institutions.[11] He recognizes the need for difficult choices, especially in situations of retrenchment when trade-offs must be made. "Mission creep"—incorporating more functions, faculties, and facilities—is costly, and universities should not strive to be all things to all people. Myriad aims can be at cross-purposes with one another and result in friction.[12]

While Bok provides an astute analysis of the perils of multiple purposes, it is worth unpicking his formulation about "a proper balance." His proposition is problematic precisely because the doers and the knowers quarrel about the right balance. Similarly, the particularizers and the conceptualizers, as well as devotees to the disciplines and to interdisciplinarity, multidisciplinarity, and transdisciplinarity, want to strike different balances. And some faculty members insist that shared governance implies that resolving these contentious issues is a scholarly responsibility decided by open debate and in consultation with administrators responsible for reallocating money across units to focus on the university's highest priorities.

That said, Bok's reflections suggest that there is not a magic number of purposes. There is no logical reason why few are better than many. More is not a greater or lesser good. But just the same, institutions of higher learning must have first priorities for guiding decisions on programming and allocations. The purposes of knowledge institutions should not all be put on the same

10. Bok, *Higher Education in America*, 28–31.
11. Ibid., 31–33.
12. Ibid., 36–37, 69.

plane. Some win out over others. With a plurality of purposes, the question becomes which ideals are primary. And which ones are secondary, superfluous, or harmful to the sense of community, which is at the heart of the university, understood as a collegium based on commonalities and mutual trust? Making this determination is crucial lest there be institutional drift wherein a university's mission is a potpourri of goals. In this regard, after his retirement from the University of California, Kerr noted the tendency of institutional mission to be a wide spectrum resulting in a large "shopping list" of ideas about what the university should seek to accomplish.[13]

In the triad of core purposes, one mission should not be hoisted above the other two. Rather, the principal missions interact with one another. At different times in particular settings, such as during the McCarthy period in the United States when flagrant transgressions of academic freedom threatened the soul of the university, one element in the troika took on greater salience. In the McCarthy era, the defense of academic freedom enabled democratic education and critical thinking. Proper teaching and research could not be carried out without releasing the shackles on academic freedom. The latter is not merely a means for pedagogical ends or knowledge-seeking, for, in other contexts, democratic decision making and a critical disposition are requisites for maintaining academic freedom. The central missions of the university therefore interconnect not in a circular manner but as historically specific conditions warrant. The challenge is to use the interplay among core missions as a creative tension for innovation and not allow them to be pitted against one another.[14]

In navigating this terrain, an eclectic mix may represent a temporary fix, but its hallmark is an uneasy coexistence among competing purposes. Meanwhile, a rational-choice, means-ends calculation provides little help sorting out the historical and philosophical quandaries that underpin pressing day-to-day judgments. Without a firm grasp of foremost purposes, improvising with a repertoire of policy instruments can beget a jumble. Missions just pile up, absent any real way to make them fit together. Educational bricolage lacks coherence because the bits and pieces of reformist reforms fail to come to terms with the structural challenges in knowledge production and dissemination.

If universities' missions are therefore not readily additive in a linear fashion, it is important to distinguish between their transient and transcendent purposes. With institutional adaptation, educational reformers have layered series of transient purposes atop transcendent ones. The supplements keep

13. Clark Kerr with Marian L. Gade and Maureen Kawaoka, *Higher Education Cannot Escape History: Issues for the Twenty-First Century* (Albany: State University of New York Press, 1994), 167.
14. I am grateful to Conca, email message, for raising this point.

universities astride currents of events, but they may quickly become passé. It could be said that rapid alteration in missions is desirable, but where is the compass to orient an institution on this course?

Valuing engagement in the broad world context in which universities are situated, I cling to the view that iconic purposes merit priority. To this point, I think back to when young American men received draft numbers, were subject to the vagaries of conscription, and faced the prospects of a government order to fight in the Vietnam War or imprisonment for refusal. On what basis would I, a student at the time, decide whether to heed my duty as a citizen of the state or follow the dictates of conscience? While most of my professors lectured in their respective fields of specialization without also using their expertise to illuminate spiraling issues of social justice—life-and-death matters—public debates on campus squarely addressed them. In a memorable forum, an eloquent political scientist who believed that saying no to the policies of a democratic state is the road to nefarious forms of government, conceivably fascism or anarchy, dueled with a Catholic priest and acclaimed poet, Father Daniel Berrigan, who, like Antigone in Sophocles's classic Greek tragedy, claimed that there is a higher, religious authority that one must follow. This exchange homed in on whether one is obligated to comply with the call of the state, right or wrong, or honor other moral scruples. The conflicting positions on how to choose reach directly to critical dialogue about just war, passionately rendered by theorists of democracy and ethicists, and provide perspective on great issues of the day. This excursion into moral philosophy guided my thinking more meaningfully than all my ostensibly applied studies in graduate school. The issues at stake in this soul-searching speak to our times as well. Universities have organized many forums on social injustice, such as on contentions by Black Lives Matter, an international movement ignited by killings at the hands of law enforcement officers of African Americans in 2013. This movement wages campaigns to protest continuing violence under the aegis of the state and as a result of systemic racism.

Events on American campuses in the 2000s evince parallels between contemporary social justice movements, Black Lives Matter among them, and antecedent organizations like the Black Panthers.[15] Without underestimat-

15. Founded in 1966 and active until the early 1980s, the Black Panther Party advocated self-defense against the U.S. government in predominantly African American neighborhoods for the sake of protecting residents from police brutality. It placed women in leadership roles (though gender bias in its ranks continued), established community programs such as free breakfasts for children and health clinics, and sought to optimize use of the media and visual imagery. The Black Panthers ultimately split as a result of internal discord and infiltration by Federal Bureau of Investigation operations, known as the Counterintelligence Program.

ing important differences, it can be said that the societal issues that sparked these national and international movements—institutional racism and tensions between the police and minority communities—remain. Present-day controversies over how to make amends for U.S. universities' profiteering from the slave trade—and, for some, even justification of it—are emblematic of live history.[16]

No question, universities must engage burning issues of the day. But they inevitably change: today's relevance often lapses into fleeting instances. While seeking to keep abreast of the flow of events, higher education institutions are elevating select missions in the hierarchies of purposes.[17] Pulling them together, the evidence shows that four ingredients constitute a new form of utilitarianism. First, it prioritizes useful knowledge and problem-solving skills, increasingly at the expense of basic knowledge. Second, this repurposing is associated with market values. From the beginnings of higher education in my case-study countries, the older approaches to utilitarianism trained personnel for the clergy and the state, prepared graduates for certain occupations, and provided a cultivated lifestyle for the children of the elite. Gradually but especially in the past half century, the utilities of purpose have expanded to include the determinate values of competition, metrics, performance, and self-regulation. Third, the new utilitarianism puts unbending faith in the promise of technological development as a path to vitalizing higher education. Finally, adherence to a version of globalization that favors an educational-services export model is on the rise.

I have argued that although university leaders pay homage to the university's long-established purposes, these principles are paling in the face of the values du jour. The newer ones are supplanting their antecedents in good part because gilded players are dominant and others try to keep pace with them. One university president, Michael Crow, and his coauthor, William Dabars, refer to this phenomenon as "Berkeley and Harvard envy." They reason that aspirations to catch up with the top tier are inculcated into academics.[18] Exercises such as benchmarking and institutional rankings result in emulation. The web of governance agencies mapped in chapter 3 induces imitating standard-bearers. Universities have abetted this mimetic trend. It is playing out as fundamentally more than modest accommodation.

In ordering universities' purposes, the plot has become the subplot and vice versa. It is not an exaggeration to say that the last half century has experienced a paradigm shift in purposing universities. This transformation revolves around a preponderant worldview about higher education and elicits disparate reactions. Different perspectives are brought to bear.

16. See chapters 4 and 8.
17. This ascent is traced in chapters 4, 5, and 6.
18. Crow and Dabars, *Designing the New American University*, 122.

Responses

Faced with monumental changes in higher education, many educators regard them as unstoppable, in fact advantageous, and celebrate them.[19] Particularly in times of budgetary stress, supporters of neoliberal reforms look to philanthropies, among them corporate funders, for revenue streams. University managers encourage academic entrepreneurs to become skilled in technology management, compete for awards, and strive for recognition. In an entrepreneurial culture, self-promotion becomes normal comportment. By contrast, this trait is exceptional in work cultures in countries where a degree of modesty and humility are customary.

A second response to the tumult in academe is to romanticize the intellectual life of the past. Nostalgists indulge their memories and want to re-create earlier incarnations of the university. Yearning for a previous era, their idealism feeds into critiques of the shifts in higher education. Yet it is a lament for a pristine historical period before the rise of neoliberalism at universities of lore. This imaginary is frozen in time. One still has to confront the problem of how to cope with present-day conditions and go forward into the future.

Third, others push back against neoliberal policies. Resistance against the erosion of academic values and the rise of market values is evident in Britain. In 2012, scores of eminent intellectuals formed the Coalition for the Defence of British Universities to safeguard academic freedom and, as historian and former British Academy president Keith Thomas put it, to combat the distortion of "the very purpose of the university."[20] Its founding members also include presidents of other learned academies and the Royal Society of London, Nobel laureates, past university principals and vice chancellors, members of the House of Lords, and ex–cabinet ministers. In addition, protests against the government's reforms and the general direction in the British education system have featured the occupation of buildings, including at the London School of Economics and Political Science, inspired by similar occurrences at the University of Amsterdam and elsewhere. Students demanded an end to the focus on measurable outputs, a restoration of funding for humanities courses, and more scope in university governance. In various countries, student activists have sought to stanch harsh practices such as predatory lending for higher education. A student debtors' movement, the Student Debt Campaign, in the United States has advocated collective disobedience as a counterweight to the debt trap.[21]

19. In outlining responses, I am borrowing from Adam Habib, "Managing Higher Education Institutions in Contemporary South Africa: Advancing Progressive Agendas in a Neo-Liberal and Technicist World," *CODESRIA Bulletin*, nos. 3 and 4 (2011): 5–9.

20. http://cdbu.org.uk/ (accessed September 15, 2015); Shiv Malik, "Coalition of Thinkers Vow to Fight Marketisation of Universities," *Guardian* (London), November 8, 2012.

21. Andrew Ross, *Creditocracy and the Case for Debt Refusal* (New York: OR Books, 2014).

Finally, some university executives, faculty, and students want to engage the forces steering higher education within the confines of conditions as they actually are, not just as they would have them, with a view to altering the parameters and achieving structural reform.[22] They provide actionable plans that would lead to elemental change. This entails focusing on feasible means without confusing them with social and educational ends. Yet the means—the regard for democratic procedures and the willingness to trust friends and strangers—cannot be cleanly separated from ends. It is not merely that one is more important than the other.

In light of all the pressure on higher education, a major task is to conduct the business of the university as a way to facilitate realizing its trinity of primary purposes. These intangibles are cornerstones for building strong institutions that do a better job of teaching students, contributing to the growth of new knowledge, and probing public issues, partly by raising disquieting questions and adapting to changing conditions. As I will argue in closing this book, corrective steps and additional, carefully honed objectives are possible. An appreciation for what should remain the same and what constitutes plausible alternatives to the world-class dream will be key to shaping the future of the university.

22. Habib, "Managing Higher Education," recounts attempts to engage systemic forces so as to transform the balance of power at South African universities.

CHAPTER EIGHT

Plausible Alternatives

THE ONUS OF THIS BOOK is to diagnose universities' changing priorities and practices at a time of rising educational globalization. This evokes the most fundamental question about institutions of higher education: What are they really for? [1] Unfortunately, rather than engaging in open dialogue on this issue, the scholarly community is largely following decisions made ex ante about knowledge institutions and their relationship to power. I have argued that the academy is in the main undertaking problem-solving exercises on how to fulfill the dream of becoming world-class institutions. These dynamics have fueled oft-caustic debates over the performance of universities and a lot of foreboding about the future of higher learning. Seen through a global lens, they are stifling a broader discussion about what is happening to the soul of universities and where they are going.

More than metaphor, the dream of the world-class university for all is a galvanizing narrative objectified as regulatory reforms. It imparts a core rationale for educational globalization. Dispensed by national, regional, and global governance agencies, this ideology is forged by power brokers and embraced by power holders. [2]

In the American setting and reaching beyond, the contemporary writer Ta-Nehisi Coates provides a worldly account of the power of dreams and how he escaped it. [3] Telling his story of growing up with racial violence on the streets of Baltimore, he recounts the American dream of opportunity for all, a free and just society. This dream has captured the minds of the general public. But, according to Coates, it is belied by white supremacy and pervasive fear in the

---

1. In this chapter, special thanks to Yoonbin Ha, Patrick Thaddeus Jackson, and Manuel Reinert for helping to sharpen my arguments.

2. As documented in chapter 3.

3. Ta-Nehisi Coates, *Between the World and Me* (New York: Spiegel and Grau/Random House, 2015).

black community stemming from enslavement and obfuscated by notions of "personal responsibility" for salving societal inequalities: the script that pins the blame for hand-to-mouth existence and widespread crime on individual choice and poor moral judgment.

The breach between the dream and freedom from this illusion became apparent during his intellectual journey as a student at Howard University. Coates describes Howard as "the Mecca," a crossroads of cultures, a place where self-reflection and the power of knowing displaced comforting dreams. In hewing a path for the future, he emphasizes the importance of struggling for memory of heritage and wisdom, but stops short of proposing concrete steps. Coates's insights nonetheless help in understanding shifts in higher education in two respects: his portrayal, placed in context, of narrative entrapment in a dream world and how universities may enable the mind to break free from the grip of misapprehension.

Cumulatively, a trove of social science research backs up Coates's chronicle of the gulf between standard narratives and tangible experience. Studies of racial and ethnic politics in an era of large-scale migration, multiracialism, and generational change depict growing divides among classes and racial groups, spawning debates about whether common discourses about transformation are warranted or serve as binding myths.[4]

This issue of representations, driving forces, and transformative steps is where this concluding chapter is headed. To frame the discussion of plausible alternatives, I want to catch some of the most important points from the preceding chapters. I will then suggest course corrections and address the practical matter of translating the "ought" into the "can." The objective here is to imagine afresh possibilities for strengthening university systems.

A Basis for Corrective Steps

This cross-regional study of the neoliberal, social democratic, and postcolonial models shows that in each country case considered here, universities originated under the yoke of imperial rule: British and Russian empires featuring internal domination by local elites. The educational systems examined in the three case studies initially developed particular forms of hybridity: in the United States, mainly English and German; in Finland, Swedish and Russian; and in Uganda, indigenous and British. Over time, the authorities tailored ideas about higher education to national conditions. Throughout these

---

4. Ira Katznelson, *City Trenches: Urban Politics and the Patterning of Class in the United States* (Chicago: University of Chicago Press, 1982); Jennifer Hochschild, *Facing Up to the American Dream: Race, Class, and the Soul of the Nation* (Princeton: Princeton University Press, 1995); Robert Vitalis, *White World Order, Black Power Politics: The Birth of American International Relations* (Ithaca: Cornell University Press, 2015).

histories, paradigms for structuring higher education and creating knowledge have traveled. Globalizing technologies make them even more mobile.

In the last half century, universities have gained significance as core actors on the global stage because they generate "soft power" and can infuse governance agencies with intellectual strength. The capacity for training skilled professionals equipped to collect and evaluate information positions higher education institutions as an important resource for enhancing national security. Universities are also expected to boost economic development, technological innovation, national competitiveness, and export-service earnings. In the post-1960s phase of globalization, they have designed their own foreign policies, linking to counterpart institutions in other countries, importing overseas students, and negotiating deals for franchise campuses, shared courses, technology transfers, and management contracts. In short, universities are scaling up and thrusting out in the world arena.

Meanwhile, states, markets, and the public demand that universities better serve societal needs and improve their effectiveness. Although universities' responses to this pressure vary, as they must in their distinctive historical and cultural milieus, the overall pattern is the repurposing of higher education.

Knowledge institutions are straying from their prime academic purposes and opting for ancillary goals and rhetorical conventions, which, if used promiscuously, become platitudes. I have contended that universities' missions of developing habits of the mind, rousing intellectual curiosity, and fostering a love of learning are on the wane. In that a new form of utilitarianism is overtaking them, there is an inversion of priorities. At repurposed universities, the norms underpinning metrics trump venerated values. These norms are instrumental to the market and for the state but not necessarily integral to the high ends of knowledge generation and dissemination. The emergent set is "useful" and "relevant" rather than "useless," as is much basic research, at least until some of its irrelevancies are applied and discovered to be relevant. Hence, the interplay of different clusters of missions, the longstanding and newer ones, is largely unintended and may be contradictory.

The evidence in this book indicates that the current trends are unsustainable. Simultaneously accommodating heightened standards for the academy's performance, massification, state disinvestment, and private sources of revenue and endowment earnings subject to the vagaries of market cycles is a nonviable proposition. It transposes universities into something other than institutions entrusted to enable students to cherish the joys of the quest for new knowledge. The space dedicated to reflecting on civilizational values and advancing principled criticism so as to prepare successor cohorts of active, democratic citizens for the future world is narrowing. Increasing managerial control, substituting a contingent workforce for tenure-line faculty, upping the number of full-time administrators relative to instructional personnel and researchers, compensating executives at a level that undermines faculty trust in them, exacting heavy debt payments from students and their families, and allowing susceptibility to outsize influence from philanthropies, some of them corporate funders, and global governance agencies are not in the public interest. Given all the demands placed on universities, these are systemic binds, not merely the malfeasance of particular institutions.

If systems of higher education stay on their present course, the outcomes will be grim for all but a batch of well-resourced universities. These elite institutions, mostly in the global North, have advantages that set them apart in the educational divide. But even if the harbingers for universities are ominous, the landscape is not without auspicious possibilities.

Something bigger than ad hoc change is called for. Commendable as it may be, bricolage is not enough. Put simply, tweaking the situation is insufficient. When money culture is front and center, and when a serious commitment to high educational ideals dwindles, structural rather than reformist reforms are needed.[5] While the two are to some extent intertwined, the reforms for refurbishing universities must be systemic.

My suggestions for ways forward are therefore for *systems* of higher education rather than for individual institutions. Unlike recommendations for reforms within set parameters, the proposals advanced below entail systemic change. And to avoid misapprehension, I should emphasize that these are not meant to be policy "solutions." Policy-driven proposals themselves raise prior issues about what is the problem, who frames it, and how to diagnose it. Moreover, what is a solution? Is it supposed to be a panacea? A recipe? A blueprint? A manual with how-to-do-it instructions?

If the answers to these questions about understanding the problem are unclear, there cannot be solutions. And without an appreciation of what lies behind it—interests and power as they relate to class, racial, ethnic, gender, national, and other forms of cultural identity—solutions will be illusory. Hence, throughout this book, I have sought to bring to light the stakes and consequences of particular ways of framing the problem in differing contexts. Clearly, then, it would be foolish to look for an across-the-board solution for all universities at all times and in all places.

5. While imaginative recommendations for reformist reforms are valuable, the goals differ from the scope of remedies advanced here. For example, a carefully thought-out set of guidelines prepared by William G. Bowen and Michael S. McPherson, *Lesson Plan: An Agenda for Change in American Higher Education* (Princeton: Princeton University Press, 2016), 104–5, aims to increase efficiency in the delivery of higher education and rests on metrics to evaluate outcomes. Interested in improved educational attainment (degree completion in a timely way) at an affordable cost, the authors forthrightly offer a caveat: "Deeper measures of outcomes as enhanced creativity, improved critical thinking, better social skills, and civic contributions are too complex for this short book and for the state of measurement capabilities—though they are hardly unimportant" (106).

Although I don't have a simple, easy solution, I have great faith in the possibilities for changing course and finding workable alternatives. I take comfort in the belief that institutional adaptation can flow from the foregoing explanations of how universities are being reconfigured and the forces at work in this great transformation.

Structural Reforms

Below, I offer a multipronged approach to ways that university systems can advance, and map the contours of the journey. Although each proposed step is not a remedy by itself, my claim is that a combination of them would have a bootstrap effect on higher education. Taken together, they could well be a starting point for recalibrating universities' purposes.

Tame the Narrative: Master discourses of educational reform that bear the cachet of Wall Street and the tech industry are drowning out other stories of higher learning. Coinages used in strategic planning by corporations and promulgated by global governance agencies have become commonplace in a competitive arena. Universities race for a top rank but are not performing in their own event.

The narrative of world-class excellence bundles competiveness and metrics, and occupies the academic habitus, the structured dispositions and values learned by faculty and graduate students.[6] The mind-set is wrought by this discourse. But the metrics are too easy, a tempting way to pin performance on concrete criteria without considering intangibles such as sowing curiosity about what it means to share the human condition and build or lose trust.

If the practice of measurable outcomes fails to accommodate other kinds of outcomes, the challenge is to produce alternative measures and counternarratives.[7] Representatives of the rankings industry and the academic community are developing initiatives to pilot smarter counting such as the EU's U-Multirank, which features methodological departures from standard higher education comparisons.[8] And leaving aside the issue of methodology, other intellectuals are striving for elemental shifts and trying to find counterpoints, language appropriate for achieving a better academic world.[9]

6. On the concept of habitus, see Pierre Bourdieu, *The Logic of Practice* (Cambridge: Polity Press, 1990), 66–67.

7. As discussed in the European context in Erkkilä, *Global University Rankings*.

8. See chapter 3, 72. Alternative rankings, including *Universitas 21*, mentioned earlier in this book, are now available. Hazelkorn, *Rankings and the Reshaping of Higher Education* (2nd ed., 2015) details the growing market for global university rankings and draws attention to new systems, their capabilities, and their pitfalls.

9. As in postcolonial discourses about decolonizing the university. See Ngũgĩ, *Decolonising the Mind*, and the discussion in chapter 6 of this volume.

In this unsteady state, the humanistic realm of study is in danger of being whisked away; the liberal arts, depreciated. A utilitarianism of present-day, data-driven concerns—"just-in-time education"—is displacing emphasis on the classics. And the power of numbers is not about to disappear. But it should be harnessed and not allowed to serve as a set of determining factors in making decisions at universities.

Scores, as in global rankings, and algorithms are formulas based on inputs, including unstated assumptions and discretionary categories that filter in and exclude certain data. They are used to represent complex social phenomena but with little or no auditing, oversight, or controls in place. These numeric systems tend to be opaque, partly the work of private companies and treated as proprietary knowledge. This modeling may skew outputs and significantly influence the lives and careers of students and faculty. Inasmuch as proprietary information is kept secret, the modalities ought to be accompanied by stipulations warning about a lack of accountability and assurance of the right to challenge their use as well as the underlying logic. The riposte is to enact regulatory reforms that seek out algorithmic transparency. Beyond disclosure of information, a system of algorithmic accountability would provide understanding of automated decision making and its consequences.[10]

To me, technology has the potential to serve as a key tool in righting imbalances between data-oriented and classical fields of study. I remain sanguine because at best, technology eases the relationship between mind-expanding learning and the constraints of time and space. So long as educators discern how to complement technology in different subject areas, it can empower them to share knowledge and enhance student-centered pedagogy. For instance, live, interactive classrooms bring together medical schools in Europe and Africa and feature instruction on up-to-date surgical procedures. Surely, the differences that connectivity is making to poor countries in the global South are remarkable. The Open Access Movement expands flows of information, ideas, and research findings. In these exchanges, however, protecting regional accents in indigenous ways of thinking and coming to terms with the coloniality of knowledge are unsettled issues. While obstacles to bridging the digital divide remain formidable, the creative possibilities of technological change are unbounded. Technologies can help amend a reigning narrative by virtue of their capacities for storage, retrieval, and delivery of inflections on it, and also facilitate crafting alternatives.

At worst, however, the misuse of educational technology begets big data to the detriment of small data: empiricism based on ethnographies, granular

10. Marc Rotenberg, Julia Horwitz, and Jeramie Scott, eds., *Privacy in the Modern Age: The Search for Solutions* (New York: The New Press, 2015); Nicholas Diakopoulous, "Accountability in Algorithmic Decision Making," *Communications of the ACM* 59, no. 2 (February 2016): 56–62; Marc Rotenberg, "Bias by Computer," *New York Times*, August 11, 2016.

material, description, and culturally specific information. While technology generates and processes an abundance of information, the tools may or may not be used to produce knowledge. Creative insights involve showing relationships, rearranging them, and deriving meanings. This is crucial for gaining perspective on the predominant narrative of world-class higher education and the purposes of knowledge institutions.

Taming the narrative means that each university must author its own story about how to strike balances in knowledge production and diffusion and set epistemological standards for gauging steps toward attainment. This process calls for strong *mission differentiation* rather than mimetic repurposing. Given the power of the narrative, it is important to tell different stories.

The principle of differentiated missions applies within and among higher education systems. It implies sufficient institutional autonomy with accountability at several levels: a rubric of self-governance, including checks and balances among administrators, faculty, staff, students, and trustees. A democratic ethos anchors internally derived standards and accountability procedures such as peer review for tenure and promotion and program review. This takes societal trust in higher education. Social accountability is about the level of confidence in a national political culture and in the soul of the university, an issue addressed below.

Relink the Global and the Local: High-quality university systems are striving to meet targets in their strategic plans, but they cannot be all things to all people. As they go global, many educational systems are disengaging from the local communities where they are situated.[11] Negotiating limited resources, multiple tasks, and weighty workloads, university personnel must calculate trade-offs in their involvement in globalizing and localizing activities. Given infatuation with world-class standing, investing time and money in exploring the particularity of a home culture is usually the more compromised element. Yet there is a cost to this often unintentional swing away from locality.

In myriad smaller as well as large cities, the cultural resources are plentiful. Performances by musicians and dance troupes, art galleries, and museums are robust spaces for stimulating the imagination. Learning about diasporas offers great opportunities for grasping the global. Immigrants' stories about identity present firsthand experience in how social differences are treated. Their telling

11. This is not to overlook community building by some universities. Notably, certain privates in the United States such as the University of Pennsylvania, the University of Chicago, and Johns Hopkins University are investing in surrounding neighborhoods, including blighted and crime-ridden ones, features that detract from efforts to recruit students. Universities with sufficient means also sponsor engaged research by students and faculty in nearby areas as well as overseas. Cornell, for example, funds a team project on participatory-action initiatives to achieve flood resilience in upstate New York, community health in Ecuador, and land use in a biosphere reserve in India.

provides insights into how a host society works. By listening to these voices, the home community can better understand its own sense of terroir: its particularity, customs, gastronomy. But in the face of disturbances brought by global flows, certain publics are intent on safeguarding their perceived authenticity, a collective self-image that may turn into an emotionally charged issue. And this provides occasions for university faculty and students to step up and interpret narratives of terroir as manifested locally. It allows institutions of higher education to put their missions of teaching and research to work for the public good. The operative choice is the level of support for local initiatives.

This matter also hinges on the degree to which a university system is structured in a bottom-up and top-down manner. Which approach gains precedence? In the majority of cases, revenue is directed to building education in a hierarchical manner. This is the flagship concept in which a small number of institutions are in leadership positions.[12] Core funding from government has mainly gravitated to these favored, highly selective, research-intensive institutions. Sometimes their allocations are channeled through intermediary bodies such as research councils and national academies, which apportion money on a competitive basis. Yet the allotments are concentrated in already stronger units. Private, local concerns and overseas donors typically award grants to the same prominent institutions. Not surprisingly, the flagship model has its advocates at elite institutions. In the words of the vice chancellor of the highly regarded University of Cape Town: "the selected research universities should be funded at a level that enables them to succeed in a globally competitive environment—and this clearly cannot be afforded by all."[13]

Coordinating bodies, such as the AAU and the African Research Universities Alliance, for research universities link leading institutions in their respective contexts and across borders. The AAU is comprised of 62 members in the United States; the Alliance, 15 from eight African countries. These elite organizations and their counterparts in other world regions are exclusive networks with membership largely by invitation only.[14] While cognizant of

12. John Aubrey Douglass, "Profiling the Flagship University Model: An Exploratory Proposal for Changing the Paradigm from Ranking to Relevancy," Center for Studies in Higher Education Research & Occasional Paper Series 5.14 (April 2014), http://cshe .berkeley.edu/sites/default/files/shared/publications/docs/ROPS.CSHE_.5.14.Douglass .FlagshipUniversities.4.24.2014.pdf (accessed October 13, 2015). For an elaboration of the notion of the flagship model and proposals for modifying it, see Douglass, ed., *The New Flagship University: Changing the Paradigm from Global Ranking to National Relevancy* (Houndmills: Palgrave Macmillan, 2016).

13. Max Price, "The Future of the University," *Financial Times*, October 7, 2014.

14. Among the other coordinating bodies of top research universities are the Association of Pacific Rim Universities, the Group of Eight in Australia, the League of European Research Universities, and the Russell Group in the UK. Their activities and requirements for membership of course vary.

their responsibilities and interests in uplifting the systems of higher education in which they are lodged, these groupings nevertheless reflect or accentuate hierarchical relations within countries and in global society. They provide privilege, prestige, and access to research-related activities: fellowships, joint-degree programs, conferences, and collective advocacy for financial support.

The alternative to concentrating excellence and resources in a subset of universities is to establish a horizontal system of knowledge institutions with a geographical spread and by field of specialization. While vertical systems and economies of scale have facilitated technological and scientific breakthroughs, the horizontal strategy for achieving excellence favors equity over world-class hierarchies. For proponents of this approach, such as Hazelkorn, the best strategy for advancing higher education is to develop "world-class systems rather than world-class universities."[15] She notes that the neoliberal model of world-class universities uses free-market mechanisms as policy instruments for the purpose of vertical differentiation. In contrast, the social-democratic paradigm aims at superlative quality by distributing funding for research centers and for faculties with different competencies around a country, though it is not without its hierarchies. Australia and Norway lean toward a regionalization strategy as a way to bolster equity, and the Scottish Parliament adopted a bill in 2013 to develop a dense network of regional institutions for "further education" (short-term degrees provided at colleges, with provisions for mobility to universities).[16] Scotland is configuring single-university and multi-university regions with new mergers and in which flagship institutions can form. With regionalization, the overall aim is to build a world-class system of higher education.[17] In postcolonial settings, the picture is more mixed; the goals, diffuse, though, as we have seen, some countries in the global South aim to catapult their universities into the top 100 or 200 on global ranking charts. There, the general tendency is to move from the statist, elitist form in place at political independence toward market-oriented verticality.

Commit to "Cultures of Creativity": Inasmuch as creativity begets excellence, universities have long sought to determine from where creative ideas stem and how to foster imaginative thinking, original insights, and audacious visions.[18] Courses in neuroscience, creative writing, and the creative arts,

15. Hazelkorn, *Rankings and the Reshaping of Higher Education* (1st ed., 2011), 206.

16. Scotland, Parliament, "Scotland Post-16 Education Bill [As Passed]" (June 26, 2013), http://www.scottish.parliament.uk/S4_Bills/Post-16%20Education%20Bill/b18bs4 -aspassed.pdf (accessed February 22, 2016).

17. Hazelkorn, *Rankings and the Reshaping of Higher Education* (1st ed., 2011), 185–86.

18. A raft of distinguished scholars, including Max Weber, *The Protestant Ethic and the Spirit of Capitalism*, trans. Talcott Parsons (New York: Scribner's, 1958) and C. Wright Mills, *The Sociological Imagination* (New York: Oxford University Press, 1959), have

among others, are dedicated to this aspect of learning. Similarly, governments and corporations seek to stimulate innovation: for instance, Finland's Innovation Fund is a public investment platform for tapping creativity. Meshing with these endeavors, innovation policy and Internet creativity are rising fields of study in the academy. While they largely concern applications of research, the more onerous challenge is the process of kindling creative impulses behind both tangible and intangible results.

The Nobel Prizes, awarded for creativity, offer a glimpse into this process. At its 2001 Centennial Exhibition, "Cultures of Creativity," the Nobel Museum in Stockholm remembered the winners of this citation. The exhibition focused on what drives creativity and how to promote it. It recalled that Alfred Nobel, a nineteenth-century industrial baron and inventor, funded the prizes from the riches of his factories, which produced explosives, some of them for military uses. Yet late in life, he became involved in the peace movement. This tension in his ideas and experience reflects the destructive and constructive elements of creativity, the light and dark sides of creativity.[19]

The Centennial Exhibition searched for the roots of creativity in the biographies and inventions of Nobel laureates, recognized for their ingenuity in a wide range of fields, including the natural sciences, literature, and peace.[20] For the sake of brevity, some illustrations will suffice. One trait of creative people such as the physicist Marie Curie, who, together with her husband, Pierre, made breakthrough discoveries about the basic principles of matter, is that they tilt against the mainstream and cut against convention. For the poet, novelist, and dissident Boris Pasternak, creativity meant dissolving boundaries and remolding images of the world. He chronicled his journey through Soviet times and recounted how he found motivation and determination to write reflectively in an atmosphere of persecution. The prominent chemist Linus Pauling, after mulling a problem for years, suddenly found answers. He drew not only from his subconscious but also from taking firm stances on public issues, such as in his opposition to nuclear weapons testing. Dag Hammarskjöld, a poet and UN secretary-general, derived creative ideas from an inner realm of spirituality, nature, and self-discipline. For him, it was the tranquility of aesthetics that conferred voice. Martin Luther King Jr., at the Nobel Prize ceremonies in 1964, spoke about the power of resistance and the "creative turmoil of genuine civilization struggling to be born."[21] And playwright-poet Wole Soyinka attributed his creative energy to Yoruba mythology, the melding

---

pursued the theme of sparking creativity. Efforts to cast new light on it are imperative not least because of the younger generation's turn to technological intensity in creative ways.

19. Ulf Larsson, ed., *Cultures of Creativity: Birth of a 21ˢᵗ Century Museum* (Sagamore Beach, MA: Science History Publications, 2006), 14–15.

20. This paragraph draws on ibid., passim.

21. Ibid., 147.

of cultures in Nigeria, and the years he spent imprisoned during the country's civil war.

After lingering at this exhibition for several hours, trying to connect the biographies of masterminds, I could not define an archetype of a creative individual; the experience had yet to gel for me. I continued to ponder the keys to creativity.

However vast the variation among fertile intellects, it is nevertheless possible to etch generative features of inspiration. Among them, the environment for creativity is vital. Not only physical spaces but also epistemic networks are salient for enabling productivity. Paradoxically, a climate of educational freedom to reformulate given truths is crucial. And suffering, a contingent rather than a necessary condition, may catalyze creative power. Consider the South African Nobelists whose intellectual formation came during the apartheid era: Max Theiler received the Prize in physiology or medicine, as it is called, 1951; Albert Lutuli, peace, 1960; Alan Cormack, medicine, 1979; Alan Klug, chemistry, 1982; Desmond Tutu, peace, 1984; Nadine Gordimer, literature, 1991; F. W. de Klerk and Nelson Mandela, peace, 1993; Sydney Brenner, physiology or medicine, 2002; and J. M. Coetzee, literature, 2003. A cauldron of violence, the white redoubt, spawned many other great writers, artists, and physicians from both the privileged and the most marginalized segments of society. They include Christiaan Barnard, André Brink, Athol Fugard, William Kentridge, Miriam Makeba, and Hugh Masekela. In what may appear to be fields removed from distressing social conditions, like physiology and medicine, the atmosphere of repression drove some individuals to seek the pleasure of scientific discovery. Their creativity emerged on the fringes of world order during a period of immense pain and instability.

While apartheid South Africa is a special case, educators today have opportunities to integrate the arts from multiple instances of unspeakable repression and fragility in their academic programs through videos, teleconferencing, and study abroad. Arts integration on other subjects and in all courses, from anthropology to zoology, offers creative stimulus. It spurs research creativity for students and faculty alike.

For some people, creativity means living apart from cultural prohibitions and taking risks in disturbing rule-bound casts of mind. It may entail betraying silences, learning how to listen to diverse voices, and allowing quirky thinking, feisty intellects, and new ways to see things. Working with students, faculty should intensify efforts to nourish the qualities associated with creativity: a feeling of wonderment, the power of observation, resolute determination to hunt for clues to the unknown, a willingness to dare to fail in the face of skepticism and even derision, and the courage to unplug from commonsense wisdom that breeds conformity.

All told, a mix of elements comprises creativity, more pronounced in some cases than others: versatility, playfulness, and the kind of athletic stamina developed from watching the ball. A mental workout requires striking the ball cleanly and with zip, staying balanced, and anticipating the next move. It concentrates the mind.

Create Incentives for Public Intellectuals: In 1987, an American historian, Russell Jacoby, published *The Last Intellectuals*, a book that depicted the waning of intellectual life outside academe and the retreat of academic intellectuals behind esoteric concerns and jargon.[22] For Jacoby, they have constructed an inaccessible scholasticism to which society pays little heed. And Nicholas Dirks, a former chancellor of the University of California at Berkeley, is among the scholars who chimed in by arguing that pervasive anti-intellectualism in the United States is an inauspicious atmosphere for inquiry in pivotal fields like philosophy and literature that can elevate a nuanced public discourse.[23] Today, the decline of public intellectuals is apparent, with few exceptions, in many parts of the world. It is hard to find the caliber of an intelligentsia that marked the eras of Bertrand Russell in Britain; C.L.R. James and Frantz Fanon in the Caribbean; Raymond Aron, Simone de Beauvoir, and Jean-Paul Sartre in France; William F. Buckley and Edward Said in the United States; and others who uplifted popular debate. There are relatively few successors.

Sharing a fascination with ideas, intellectuals of different persuasions dispense knowledge in the public arena. As soon as intellectuals publish and speak to audiences, their actions are not neutral but consequential and correlate with power in one of two ways. Some intellectuals align with power and generate research that serves it. They attempt to strengthen existing arrangements and make them work more efficiently within given parameters. These are Weber's rational individuals in science and technology. Unlike professional experts, other intellectuals think critically and, like Machiavelli, seek to reveal how power operates. Those whom Gramsci called organic intellectuals aim to uncover the mechanisms of power and alliances to it. Similarly, in his Reith Lectures, broadcast on BBC, Said stressed that the intellectual's vocation is to articulate a view, a message, or give voice to people who have been silenced and marginalized. According to Said, the intellectual's role "has an edge to it, and cannot be played without a sense of being someone whose place it is publicly to raise embarrassing questions, to confront orthodoxy and dogma (rather than to produce them), to be someone who cannot easily be co-opted by governments or corporations, and whose raison d'être is to represent all those people and issues that are routinely forgotten or swept under

22. Russell Jacoby, *The Last Intellectuals: American Culture in the Age of Academe* (New York: Basic Books, 1987).
23. Nicholas B. Dirks, *Autobiography of an Archive: A Scholar's Passage to India* (New York: Columbia University Press, 2015). This discussion harks back to Richard Hofstadter, *Anti-intellectualism in American Life* (New York: Knopf, 1963).

the rug."[24] In fine, his argument is that the intellectual represents a particular location in a hierarchy and a perspective and conveys it to the public.

By the same token, since public intellectuals themselves are stratified by gender, race, and ethnicity, their ideas flow from different angles. The intersections of views and positions in a hierarchical social structure are matters of standpoint, though not mechanically. This point refocuses attention on the historical issue of the exclusion of the voices of women, working classes, underprivileged minorities, and other groups from representations of the public sphere.[25] And since Said's death in 2003, social media, personal blogs, and other modes of communication have offered new possibilities for transmitting the types of counternarratives that he had in mind. Advanced technologies allow new spaces for intellectuals to reach multiple publics and counterpublics.[26] The Internet facilitates work by younger intellectuals who animate public debate through websites and magazines such as *Jacobin*, *n+1*, and *The Point*, where ideas, some about policy alternatives, are exchanged.[27] There is the near public: students, faculty, administrators, and alumni. And there are national, regional, and global publics arrayed along different axes, such as the moneyed and the poor, the politically cognizant and the apathetic yet potentially active strata.

The relationship between intellectuals and these publics is a thorny issue. The question is whether an intellectual is beholden to the institution with which she is affiliated and the implications of being associated with its reputation. Sartre spoke to this point when he declined the 1964 Nobel Prize in literature on the ground it would put him in a compromising position. He stated that assent to such a public honor would connect his personal work and commitments to the awarding institution. The stature and respectability of Sartre as the Nobel Prize winner, he said, would not be the same as for Sartre the writer. Moreover, since the conferment of past prizes did not, in his opinion, represent equally writers of all ideologies and nations, he felt that his acceptance of the Nobel might be unjustly interpreted. For these reasons, Sartre

24. Edward W. Said, *Representations of the Intellectual*, 1993 Reith Lectures (New York: Pantheon, 1994), 11.

25. Habermas, *The Structural Transformation of the Public Sphere*, provoked interventions on the exclusion of "the Other" from this space as well as from a gendered public sphere and a virtual public sphere.

26. Pioneering work by sociologists explores the issue of multiple publics. See Craig Calhoun, "Introduction: Habermas and the Public Sphere," in *Habermas and the Public Sphere*, ed. Craig Calhoun (Cambridge, MA: MIT Press, 1992), 1–50; Michael Burawoy, "For Public Sociology," *American Sociological Review* 70, no. 1 (March 2005): 4–28; Michael Kennedy, *Globalizing Knowledge: Intellectuals, Universities, and Publics in Transformation* (Stanford: Stanford University Press, 2014), 140–53.

27. Evan R. Goldstein, "The New Intellectuals," *Chronicle Review* (November 18, 2016): B4–8.

decided that he would not allow himself to be institutionalized.[28] Shunning the Nobel and other prestigious prizes signifies a refusal to trade in creative talent for individual advancement and fame. Likely, this act is meant to affirm honorees' intellectual freedom and assert that a public audience, not a committee of patrons, is the best judge of creative endeavors.

Like Sartre, though rarely with the same lofty accolades, some contemporary freelance intellectuals are thriving, enjoy certain autonomy, and manage to earn a living. To be mundane, most intellectuals, however, need a steady job and the benefits that come with it, including medical insurance, an employer's contributions to a retirement account, and coverage for disability. Yet the dilemma is whether this reliance leads to sacrificing a degree of independence of the mind or even principles. This loss may happen in gradual and subtle ways, more of a slide than one sudden deluge. It may be that intellectuals are hemmed in, with academic freedom attenuated by structural constraints linked to market values and political dynamics specific to a particular context. These assorted factors are hindering more civic engagement by university-based intellectuals.

There is cost to society if scholars fail to enrich public discourse and inject nuanced ideas into popular debate. Academics can be faulted for the tendency to turn inward toward their own hyperprofessional and collectively self-referential concerns. They are being crowded out of the public square by others, some of them social critics—playwrights, musicians, comedians, and digital virtuosos—who also convey sophisticated ideas that bear consequence.

For higher education institutions, the antidote to scholars' reticence is to reward efforts to introduce knowledge and research findings into the public arena. By working more closely with the community, such as in the school system, universities can gain trust. Such initiatives ought to count toward career advancement. Universities could include tangible incentives for public scholarship in procedures for hiring, tenure, promotion, and performance reviews. Finnish universities are one example of a higher education system where the authorities have adopted a formula for allocating funds to institutions partly on the basis of what it calls "third mission," that is, knowledge transfer and societal service. Individual universities then exercise discretion in distributing these resources. In this instance and others, increasing incentives has a price and requires money. The conundrum is how to mobilize additional revenue to invest in innovations.

Challenge Austerity Programs: Educational leaders must play a key role in closing the gap between aspirations and financing. They need to be clear

28. http://www.nobelprize.org/nobel_prizes/literature/laureates/1964/press.html (accessed October 21, 2015). The Nobel Laureates to turn down this honor include Le Doc Tho because Vietnam had not yet genuinely realized peace, three Germans forced by the Nazi authorities to refuse the award, and Pasternak owing to Soviet coercion.

in signaling that money, above all, is a means, an instrument, not an end, in knowledge governance for fulfilling societal responsibilities. It is to be used purposefully. In other words, money is a steering mechanism for realizing universities' fundamental purposes.[29]

Reductions in state funding challenge both public and private universities. When austerity is imposed on the public sector, it ramifies to all except perhaps the richest private universities. It creates the risks of shortchanging students, incurring debt overhang, and relying more heavily on influential donors. In lieu of this route, there are distinct possibilities for arriving at new intersections of public and private spheres and bolstering university finances.

One option is reallocations from the state budget, say, from military spending or mass incarceration, to education. Second, a more progressive policy on income tax that raises the ante for the wealthy and closes loopholes would provide revenue that authorities could channel to higher education. Third, a small tax, a fraction of 1 percent, on financial transactions at the national, regional, or global levels could be used for making increments to university budgets affordable.[30] Fourth, income-contingent repayment, already in force in Australia and Britain, involves a graduation tax levied on students when they enter the workforce.[31] Fifth, cuts in executive salaries and the number of administrators at universities would not only recoup funds but also lend more credibility to anti-austerity initiatives. But to date the agreement and political will required for implementation are lacking. Given this impasse, some players have moved ahead on other initiatives.

In the face of mounting economic pressure and stress on social spending due to rapidly aging populations, a number of countries and regions within them have maintained policies of free or low university tuition. They finance no or nominal tuition fees in a variety of ways. The following exemplars allow us to avoid wishful thinking and consider how these policies actually work and why not promote them elsewhere.

Norway offers free university tuition at public universities, though individual programs, courses, and private higher education institutions may charge. Oslo directs some of the proceeds from its oil resources and from steep tax rates to the educational sector. In Sweden, universities provide free tuition

29. As stated in Ben Jongbloed, "Funding Higher Education: A View across Europe," European Platform Higher Education Modernisation, MODERN Report (2010), 10, https://www.utwente.nl/bms/cheps/publications/Publications%202010/MODERN_Funding_Report.pdf (accessed October 24, 2015).

30. In 1972, Nobel Prize–winning economist James Tobin advanced the idea of introducing a financial transactions tax on all payments from one currency to another and channeling the cash to aid developing countries. Subsequently, variations on this proposal have been put forward.

31. See chapter 4, 133, on a similar financing framework being developed in the United States.

for its citizens and students from EU and European Economic Area member countries, though no longer for those from elsewhere. The funding for higher education—85 percent of it in 2013—mostly comes from the public purse.[32] Swedes generally see education as both an individual benefit and a public good. Aside from political parties' and trade unions' arguments for supporting the welfare state, advocates of no tuition fees maintain that university graduates will eventually pay more taxes than those without university degrees. The Swedish state is said to gain financially from subsidizing universities.

Scotland has held firm on its policy of free university education for Scots and students from the rest of the EU.[33] However, ever since England imposed tuition fees in 1998 and raised the cap to £9,000 (US$12,810 at the current exchange rate) in 2012, Scotland has charged students from the other parts of the UK—England, Northern Ireland, and Wales.[34] And non-EU international students pay. Whereas core public funding provided more than 80 percent of revenue for Scottish universities in the late 1970s, higher education institutions now raise almost half their budgets themselves. It is derived from private sources, EU and UK research grants, contract research, international tuition fees, consultancies, and other services.[35] In addition, by sharing knowledge and through research pooling, Scottish universities concentrate resources and develop centers of excellence in particular fields.[36]

Six continental European countries levy tuition fee levels below €500 (US$612); in eight others, the average is around €750 (US$919), according to a 2010 report and currency conversions at that time.[37] Germany, for instance, since reunification in 1990, has adopted a policy of free tuition at its public universities, including for international students.[38] While pruning expenditure on higher education, including in staffing, the national government and

32. Swedish Higher Education Authority, "Funding" (2013), http://english.uka.se /highereducationsystem/funding.4.4149f55713bbd917563800011054.html (accessed October 30, 2015).

33. It is free for undergraduates at universities and colleges, but MA students pay tuition fees.

34. So as not to become the UK low-cost alternative. Neil Kemp and William Lawton, "A Strategic Analysis of the Scottish Higher Education Sector's Distinctive Assets," British Council Scotland (April 2013), https://scotland.britishcouncil.org/sites/default/files /scotland-report-a-strategic-analysis-of-the-scottish-higher-education-sectors-distinctive -assets.pdf (accessed February 22, 2016).

35. Ibid.; Jamie McIvor, "Analysis: University Tuition Fees in Scotland," BBC, July 11, 2013, http://www.bbc.com/news/uk-scotland-23279868 (accessed October 30, 2015).

36. Kemp and Lawton, "A Strategic Analysis of the Scottish Higher Education Sector's Distinctive Assets"; Manuel Reinert, telephone discussion with Kate Walker, UK Education Advisor at the British Council Scotland, January 11, 2016, as forwarded to author.

37. Jongbloed, "Funding Higher Education."

38. Fewer than 5 percent of students in Germany enroll in private institutions of higher education.

sixteen states within Germany jointly finance public universities and negotiate the appropriations. Individual states then have substantial discretion in allocating the funds. German taxpayers cover the bulk of costs, and revenue is also garnered from fees for some online degree programs and modest administrative charges that students pay.[39]

The debate over barring tuition fees is rife among the Social Democrats, Greens, Christian Democratic and Christian Social Union, and other parties, the coalitions among them varying by state. Proponents of zero tuition submit that it is a way to attract more skilled workers, especially important in a country with a low fertility rate. Many international students remain after graduation, and highly educated people help bring international research funding. Backers of this position also hold that Germany has long endorsed the principle that universal access to education is a cultural human right and that a belief in solidarity is deeply ingrained in the German welfare state. The introduction of costs borne by students and their families, it is argued, would place a greater burden on less affluent members of society. On the other side of this swirling debate, advocates of tuition fees contend that they motivate students to complete degrees in the standard period, enabling them to enter the job market at a younger age. They claim that tuition fees would thereby give graduates more of a competitive edge and lower the cost of education borne by the state.[40]

To cite other counties with no tuition, one can look to Latin America. At present, Argentina offers free tuition for all Argentine undergraduates; Brazil, students who pass qualifying exams and enroll in federal (public) universities; Chile, undergraduates with income below the fifth decile of poverty; Nicaragua, all who pass the qualifying exams; and Uruguay, undergraduates attending the University of the Republic.[41] These policies are controversial, rife with ongoing debates. While the disagreements vary by country, the Chilean case illustrates this contention over tuition-free higher education.

39. Hans-Ulrich Küpper, "Management Mechanisms and Financing of Higher Education in Germany," *Higher Education Management and Policy* 15, no. 6 (May 2003): 71–89; Lydia Hartwig, "Funding Systems and Their Effects on Higher Education Systems Country Study—Germany," *OECD Report* (November 2006); Barbara Kehm, "How Germany Managed to Abolish University Tuition Fees," *The Conversation* (October 13, 2014), http://theconversation.com/how-germany-managed-to-abolish-university-tuition-fees-32529 (accessed October 30, 2015).

40. Jens Schulz, "Tuition Fees in Germany: Much Ado about Nothing?" American Institute for Contemporary German Studies, http://www.aicgs.org/issue/tuition-fees-in-germany/ (accessed October 30, 2015).

41. Conversation with J. Salvador Peralta (Baltimore, February 25, 2017), associate professor and chair, Department of Political Science, University of West Georgia, and his email (February 27 and 28, 2017) to the author. Sources for these provisions are available from the author.

Santiago passed its 2014 tax reform law with an increase in corporate taxes partly to fund universities' missions and to support free education at public and private universities beginning in 2016.[42] Backers of these measures believe that they will go a long way toward addressing deep inequalities in Chilean society, accelerating social mobility, and restructuring the higher education system.[43] To this point, Maria Teresa Marshall, executive director of Chile's Council of Rectors, submits that the market has governed higher education, but "it cannot be like that anymore because education is a civil right."[44] Yet detractors of the reform hold that it will impede the country's economic growth. Chilean opponents of free tuition say that they want to improve market-driven education; however, they face mass protests over charging students as well as over widespread corruption in the higher education system.[45] Still, a serious concern lingers: that is, free higher education is generous to its users, a group usually dominated by the children of the well-off, many of them white and with privileged backgrounds. It is said to be iniquitous for taxpayers at lower-income levels who do not realize as much benefit from this policy and, in some cases, are unable to pay for books and the cost of living at university.

Like Chilean critics of free tuition, Bowen and McPherson, presidents emeriti of Princeton University and Macalester College, respectively, similarly offer strong arguments against free and low tuition in the United States.[46] They claim that eliminating or significantly reducing tuition payments would disproportionately help economically better-off students, more so than disadvantaged populations. According to Bowen and McPherson, this policy would be unrealistic for three reasons: shared financing among individuals and their families, government, and philanthropies has always been the American way; those who stand to benefit economically should bear at least a portion of the cost of university; and that without tuition, students lack incentive to complete degrees in a timely manner. But the authors should engage counterarguments: among them, some countries, whose universities also draw, to varying degrees, on a mix of revenue streams, have changed course

42. Republic of Chile, Ministry of Education, Ley N° 20.845, 2015, "De inclusión escolar que regula la admisión de los y las estudiantes, elimina el financiamiento compartido y prohíbe el lucro en establecimientos educacionales que reciben aportes del Estado," https://www.leychile.cl/Navegar?idNorma=1078172 (accessed November 4, 2015).

43. Rosalba O'Brien, "Chile Passes Landmark Tax Reform into Law," Reuters, September 10, 2014, http://www.reuters.com/article/2014/09/11/us-chile-tax-reform-idUSK BN0H523Z20140911 (accessed October 30, 2015).

44. Quoted in Holly Else, "Protest and Reform in Chile," *Times Higher Education*, May 21, 2015, https://www.insidehighered.com/news/2015/05/21/leaders-higher-education -chile-discuss-prospects-reform (accessed October 30, 2015).

45. Javiera Quiroga, "Chile Congress Passes Tax Bill to Finance Free Education," Bloomberg, September 10, 2014, http://www.bloomberg.com/news/articles/2014-09-11/chile -congress-passes-corporate-tax-rise-to-narrow-inequality (accessed October 30, 2015).

46. Bowen and McPherson, *Lesson Plan*, 75–76, 87–91, 97.

on charging tuition. Whereas past policy is an important consideration, it need not determine the way forward. And tuition subsidies can be capped at a specified sum for a given period and for academic performance at a satisfactory level. Bowen and McPherson's meticulous research surely deserves more attention than I can give to it here without straying too far afield. Suffice it to say that their book would benefit from noticing not just how the United States and the UK but continental European countries and others have treated the authors' objections to offsetting high-priced tuition and fees. While each higher education system must be understood with respect to its own historical and cultural moorings, the gamut of national cases shares similar pressures and standardizing influences, as posited earlier in this volume.

In the face of market-friendly reforms, members of low-income groups, the well-to-do, and the middle classes have participated in anti-austerity resistance to hikes in tuition fees in various countries. Student unions, trade unions, and political parties have mobilized popular opposition to proposals to ratchet up costs and transfer them to students and their families. Chile, Denmark, England, France, Germany, Quebec, and South Africa have been among the scenes of Occupy movements, strikes, street demonstrations, and petitions. The 2015 events in postapartheid South Africa are particularly poignant and emblematic of a backlash against neoliberal reforms on university campuses. An announcement of a 10.6 percent increase in tuition fees was greeted by barricading entrances to campuses, burning tires, singing liberation songs, and hoisting placards. In response, the police fired stun guns and rubber bullets. Yet the explosion of student activism caused embattled university and government officials to back down and reverse their decision on the heightened cost of education for all enrollees. Despite this concession, students persisted, demanding free tuition, not a freeze on the status quo. Ostensibly about the price of education, protests by disgruntled youth bespeak frustration over the general lack of structural reform at universities. This contention proved to be a lightning rod. It fueled anger and disenchantment shared by university students, employees, and other societal groups regarding corruption, unemployment, and inequality. It spread because the grievances resonated with communities' needs. Throughout the melee, politically active students and their faculty supporters stressed that education is a major mechanism in social mobility and that an elegiac future is not a foregone conclusion.

Taking into account such triggering events, however varied from one case to another, and the underlying causes, my suggestions for corrective steps are spelled out above. But how to realize them?

Practicalities

Given the political systems and interests arrayed behind the prevailing configuration of higher learning, it may seem hard to imagine how my proposals could be adopted. Yes, converting the "ought" to the "can" presents formidable challenges. But it is not a utopian endeavor. As a practical matter, structural reform depends on shifts in the ways that the public and educators think and talk about universities. Such cultural changes happen infrequently but do occur, as with the swing to the now dominant neoliberal paradigm, if they have sufficient political support. And ultimately, the practicalities of reform are a matter of adaptation. Feasible arrangements are to be hammered out at each institution. Customizing policies to fit a particular milieu requires leadership, workshops, task forces, governance bodies, and other avenues appropriate for an institution's culture. It entails a lot of conversation, negotiation, and trade-offs.

As intimated, my proposals for rehabilitating higher education institutions have a conservative bent and critical thrust. They lean to the conservative side of the spectrum in that high priority is assigned to recapturing the quintessential values on which repurposed universities are predicated in nonauthoritarian contexts: the triumvirate of democratic training, critical inquiry, and academic freedom. My propositions are critical, for universities are expected to nurture iconoclastic thinking. Critical reasoning by itself, however, is not sufficient.[47] A climate of democratic processes and free speech is conducive to developing sharp critical proficiency. Lack of the former usually inhibits the latter. Synergy among these first principles is crucial. No one point of the triangle is most important. Reciprocity and some healthy tension among the three can spur innovation.

Turning the clock back and clinging stubbornly to the past does not address the moment at which universities are situated. Periodically, higher education systems must both strengthen their old foundations and infuse new visions into their missions. Universities cannot indulge in complacency. Their iconic purposes have lasting value but warrant modifications because of changing conditions in the societies they are meant to serve. In the 2000s, their triple missions can be refreshed in creative and imaginative ways. This is best accomplished by embracing a pluralistic conception of universities without merely piling up additive purposes absent structural reform.

Imaginative teaching and rigorous research are the university's main activities. Contra the critique by observers such as Veblen, these pursuits may be but are not ineluctably opposed to the practices and thinking of business-minded managers at universities.[48] Many talented, creative people work on both the academic and administrative sides of the university. These are not a binary into which educators fit cleanly. Faculty administrators such as

47. I am responding to the contention that the main purpose of the university is to instill critical intellect among students and engage them in contesting established verities (Jackson, email message to author, April 22, 2014).

48. Veblen, *The Higher Learning in America*. On this point, see Christopher Newfield, "What Thorstein Veblen Got Right," *Chronicle Review* 62, no. 9 (October 30, 2015): B11–13.

department chairs and deans straddle them. Barring lip service, the task for scholars and managers alike is to build trust, strive for shared ends, and progress toward common purposes.

Agency must come from above and below. To effect reforms, adept administrative leaders establish a framework and direction, as did Clark Kerr. But it would be misleading to limit discussion of enabling leadership to the senior executive level. Leaders on high are only part of a complex. Structural reforms are animated by multilevel leadership. At governmental levels, leaders establish an overall framework and process for policymaking. Faculty leaders produce new ideas and help enact them. So too leaders among the general staff provide ideas and facilitate programs. Seizing the initiative, some student leaders tread the main route while others represent social movements that seek another path.

Student movements have shaken the status quo by organizing uprisings, mobilizing for political activism, and offering moral vision. Avowedly nonleader-centric student groups of late like Black Lives Matter and #RhodesMustFall have taken varied tacks: walkouts, protests over monuments to historical figures—for example, statues of Cecil Rhodes at Oxford and the University of Cape Town—and multifaceted campaigns against other commemorative statements signifying the power to shape public history.

Consider, for instance, Yale students' objections to the values of authorities who wanted to keep the name of Calhoun College, which pays tribute to its namesake, an 1804 Yale graduate who was vice president of the United States, secretary of war, and secretary of state. He was also a prominent theorist of slavery and advocate of white supremacy. Student dissent over honors bestowed on this racist past led to a list of demands and, following negotiations with administrative leaders, the adoption of specific steps: giving prominence to the study of race, ethnicity, and other forms of identity in the curriculum; hiring new faculty members who enhance diversity; expanding support services for students; developing more financial aid for low-income persons; and mounting training programs on combating racism and other forms of discrimination in the academy. Yale also agreed to fund more cultural centers, instruct administrators on ways to rein in racism, and substitute the title "head of college" for "master" in all of its residential colleges. After a long debate, it dropped the eponym Calhoun College while naming new residential colleges after Pauli Murray, an African American civil rights activist, and Benjamin Franklin, who, late in life, turned abolitionist. The stated rationale for not renaming Calhoun College is that students should learn about Calhoun's beliefs, however offensive to some, and confront his ideas.[49] This stance drew

49. David Cole, "Race & Renaming: A Talk with Peter Salovey, President of Yale," *New York Review of Books* 63, no. 10 (June 9, 2016): 42–44. For rejoinders to Salovey, see James W. Lowen, "10 Questions for Yale's President," *Chronicle Review* 62, no. 38 (June 10, 2016):

both support and ire from various constituencies, including those to which university executives are accountable. It is a major consideration at other universities, among them, Princeton, which will keep the name of its president and a proponent of segregation, Woodrow Wilson, on the School of Public and International Affairs and a residential college.

As matters stand, few university executive officers dare risk taking a firm stand against the new utilitarianism, preferring to play it safe rather than propose a different model of higher education. In engaging trustees, funders, and government officials, university leaders rarely gamble, given daunting odds, and bet on an uncommon strategy. Without too much punditry, they could, however, invite these groups to stretch the imagination and see how creative ideas for effecting transformational reforms would matter. To stay the decay of universities, one has to be brave or foolhardy enough to take chances.

And to secure backing, executive officers can advocate for their institutions most effectively not then on primarily utilitarian grounds but on the basis of the academy's distinctive role as an incubator of new thinking and a tutor for future generations. In other words, the strongest defense lies in the nonutilitarian character of higher education. While other fields such as medicine are also vital to societal well-being, universities school and provide facilities for the personnel who work in these areas. Moreover, in augmenting efforts to shore up popular support, university leaders need to reshape the reductionist narrative about a usable education and make the case that it compromises the serious, long-range purposes of higher learning.

The challenge is to reframe public understanding of educational excellence and emphasize the intrinsic values that universities are uniquely positioned to deliver. Their worth is not an either-or proposition—a private versus public benefit. Rather, it is an investment in *the greater good*: greater in the sense of encompassing both the private and public spheres.

Educators must convince people to narrate universities in terms of universities' tripartite mission and the ways in which it is evolving. The message: know-how in the form of applied job skills is best acquired through apprenticeship programs, vocational and polytechnic institutes, and employers' training courses, not from professors whose devotion to their mentees, methodical research, and independent-mindedness promises to be infectious. The bottom line is that the university's business is to inculcate an appreciation for intellectual culture, inspire critical perceptiveness, and produce educated graduates who yearn for lifetime learning.[50]

This is not to gainsay that by connecting theory and practice, universities can and should continue to adapt to the world as it is. As the philosophy

---

B11–13; Ibram X. Kendi, "Racism Is Not a Teaching Tool," *Chronicle Review* 62, no. 38 (June 10, 2016): B13.

50. Again, Jackson's remarks, email, 2014 and 2016, triggered my reflections.

of pragmatism holds, knowledge and action are interrelated. Thought and change do not constitute a dualism. Both pay off. Although some ideas may be unusable in that they are devoid of application yet theoretically interesting, the values writ large that animate higher education ultimately precipitate action. Knowledge facilitates action, and action imparts knowledge. In this sense, knowing has real consequences and can be liberating. Knowledge can make the world a better place.

For those who have a passion for creating knowledge, its purpose is to gain a deeper understanding of whether and how ideas cohere. They chase the "why," which entails explaining relationships among seemingly disparate phenomena. Higher education provides ways to attain access to these sub-surface elements. They may be causes, symbols, or logic in fields like history, literature, philosophy, and mathematics. In this way, understanding is about finding interconnections that may not be directly observable. It also involves grasping the consequences of myriad worldviews.

This text shows how and why knowledge is increasingly produced and diffused on the world market. In today's hypercompetitive environment, the purpose of research in many domains is to turn a profit quickly and secure market share. Toward this end, the economy of scale is of great importance. Small countries in particular often encounter difficulty affording ample investment in the national economy and its university system. The case studies presented in earlier chapters demonstrate that participation in the world market risks friction between powerful global actors' priorities in higher education and academic purposes that embrace local values. This is a realm in which the knowledge-power relationship can yield practical results that bolster efforts to navigate the shoals of the global marketplace.

What then could be more practical than looking at old purposes in new ways, elucidating their meanings and conceiving scenarios that have eluded policymakers? This will happen when the dominant frame of mind is changed. If the role of the university is cast as a realization of the democratic ideals of critical thinking and free expression, including opportunities for those who have been excluded from access to knowledge production, the core purposes of the university will be reinforced and geared toward a better yet still unwritten future.

Over the next half century or so, no matter what the university scoreboard says and when you read it, the competitive game is not about to end. The competition for world-class stature marches on. Unlike in sports and the corporate world, higher education is not however for winning big time in the standings. Universities are for doing your best to strive, to create, and to discover. They are spaces for understanding your own values, why you hold them dear, and those of other people. They are crucibles where critical dispositions can lead to constructive proposals for correcting the current course. This is what makes universities joyful, educators proud, and students successful.

INDEX

Note: Page numbers followed by *t* indicate a table; those followed by *f* indicate a figure.

Stanford, A. Leland, 99

Stanford University, 54, 99; economic diversity at, 110; endowment of, 112–14; Hoover Institution at, 81; military and corporate sponsorship at, 27, 95

the state. *See* governments

Steinberg, Darrell, 28

Strange, Susan, 32n49

strategic planning, 20n16, 49, 132–33

Strategy 2020, 67–68

Strauss, Leo, 42–43

structural adjustment programs (SAPs), 66

structural reforms, 5, 12, 51–52, 220–43; basis for, 222–25; of the California Master Plan for Higher Education, 131–32; challenging austerity programs in, 234–39; commitment to cultures of creativity in, 229–32, 240–41; horizontal systems of institutions in, 229; incentives for public intellectuals in, 232–34; as investments in the greater good, 242; mission differentiation in, 227; multilevel leadership of, 241; polymorphism and, 7–8; as practical adaptations, 239–43; relinking to local and regional communities in, 227–29; student movements and, 241–42; taming the narrative of scores and ranking in, 225–27

Student Debt Campaign, 219

student financial burdens, 2, 18, 26, 93, 96, 235–39; in Finland, 137, 160–63, 181, 208; government grants and, 110, 118; "Pay It Forward, Pay It Back" financing of, 133; in Uganda, 174, 178–82, 185, 187, 190, 208; in the United States, 110–11, 125–26, 133, 136, 181, 208, 219

students: activism of, 185, 241–42; as consumers, 45; cross-border programs for, 56–57, 129–31, 159–60; educational globalization and, 24–25, 56–57, 129–31; mobility of, 30–31, 64, 68, 75, 78, 101, 129–32, 159; in Uganda, 177, 179t, 182; at world-class institutions, 133–35. *See also* mission of the university; student financial burdens

Studley, Jamienne S., 75

study-abroad programs, 3, 53–56, 63, 69, 74, 130; of African educators, 172, 231; in Finland, 137, 160; international

students and, 24–25, 56–57, 129–31; reverse brain drain and, 95

subregional development banks, 65n11

Sullivan, Teresa, 114–15

Supercell, 145

Sustainable Development Goals, 63

Sweden, 8, 235–36

Swedish International Development Cooperation Agency, 187

Sylvan Learning Systems, Inc., 118

tacit regulation, 124, 128–29

Taiwan, 74

Tampere University of Technology (Finland), 140, 149, 157

Tanzania, 178

technology: applied training in, 127–28; innovation in, 27–28, 47, 105–8, 205–6, 226–27; as sources of revenue, 126–27; technology communities, 82–84

TED, 23

tertiary education (as term), xvii

Texas A&M University, 101, 113t

Thatcher, Margaret, 93, 143

Theile, Max, 231

Theses on Feuerbach (Marx), 58

think tanks, 79–82. *See also* consultancies

Thomas, Keith, 219

Tilly, Charles, 9

Times Higher Education Supplement's World University Rankings (THES), 72

Tobin, Eugene M., 119–20

Tobin, James, 235n30

trade: education as commodity in, 130–31, 144, 175; global governance organizations and, 63–70; Trade-Related Aspects of Intellectual Property Rights agreement, 64; UN Conference on Trade and Development, 165n82; World Trade Organization (WTO), 63–65, 165, 175, 197. *See also* cross-border programs; educational globalization; neoliberalism

transdisciplinarity, 101, 215

transnational programs. *See* cross-border programs

Truman, Harry, 125

trust, 2, 55, 105, 135, 207; manageralism and, 37; Nordic social accountability and, 5, 152, 163–66; in postconflict

A NOTE ON THE TYPE

THIS BOOK has been composed in Miller, a Scotch Roman typeface designed by Matthew Carter and first released by Font Bureau in 1997. It resembles Monticello, the typeface developed for The Papers of Thomas Jefferson in the 1940s by C. H. Griffith and P. J. Conkwright and reinterpreted in digital form by Carter in 2003.

Pleasant Jefferson ("P. J.") Conkwright (1905–1986) was Typographer at Princeton University Press from 1939 to 1970. He was an acclaimed book designer and AIGA Medalist.

The ornament used throughout this book was designed by Pierre Simon Fournier (1712–1768) and was a favorite of Conkwright's, used in his design of the *Princeton University Library Chronicle.*